THE SENTIMENTAL NOVEL IN THE EIGHTEENTH CENTURY

As a literary movement, the sentimental novel reached the height of its vogue in the 1770s and 1780s and was still popular as the eighteenth century drew to a close. This volume presents a comprehensive exploration of the sentimental novel in the eighteenth century beginning with its origins in the so-called amatory fiction of the late seventeenth and early eighteenth centuries. Chapters from leading scholars combine the various aspects and contexts of the genre: from politics, slavery, women writers and the gothic to the sentimental novel in America, France and Germany, with historically informed close readings of novels by writers including Samuel Richardson (1689–1761), Laurence Sterne (1713–68) and Jane Austen (1775–1817). This volume demonstrates that the sentimental novel continues to engage readers and critics and that, far from being obsolete or only of antiquary interest, the sentimental novel remains a vibrant and exciting area of study.

Albert J. Rivero, Professor of English at Marquette University, has published widely on British literature of the long eighteenth century. He has edited critical editions of *Gulliver's Travels* (2002), *Moll Flanders* (2004), Samuel Richardson's *Pamela: or, Virtue Rewarded* (Cambridge, 2011), and *Pamela in Her Exalted Condition* (Cambridge, 2012).

THE SENTIMENTAL NOVEL IN THE EIGHTEENTH CENTURY

EDITED BY

ALBERT J. RIVERO

CAMBRIDGE
UNIVERSITY PRESS

CAMBRIDGE
UNIVERSITY PRESS

University Printing House, Cambridge CB2 8BS, United Kingdom

One Liberty Plaza, 20th Floor, New York, NY 10006, USA

477 Williamstown Road, Port Melbourne, VIC 3207, Australia

314–321, 3rd Floor, Plot 3, Splendor Forum, Jasola District Centre, New Delhi – 110025, India

79 Anson Road, #06–04/06, Singapore 079906

Cambridge University Press is part of the University of Cambridge.

It furthers the University's mission by disseminating knowledge in the pursuit of education, learning, and research at the highest international levels of excellence.

www.cambridge.org
Information on this title: www.cambridge.org/9781108418928
DOI: 10.1017/9781108292375

First published 2019

Printed and bound in Great Britain by Clays Ltd, Elcograf S.p.A.

A catalogue record for this publication is available from the British Library.

Library of Congress Cataloging-in-Publication Data
NAMES: Rivero, Albert J., 1953– editor.
TITLE: The sentimental novel in the eighteenth century / edited by Albert J Rivero, Marquette University, Wisconsin.
DESCRIPTION: Cambridge, United Kingdom ; New York, NY : Cambridge University Press, 2019. | Includes bibliographical references and index.
IDENTIFIERS: LCCN 2018048298 | ISBN 9781108418928
SUBJECTS: LCSH: English fiction – 18th century – History and criticism. | Sentimentalism in literature.
CLASSIFICATION: LCC PR858.S45 S46 2019 | DDC 823/.509353–dc23
LC record available at https://lccn.loc.gov/2018048298

ISBN 978-1-108-41892-8 Hardback

Contents

Notes on Contributors

ROS BALLASTER is Professor of Eighteenth-Century Studies in the Faculty of English, Oxford University. She has published widely in the field of eighteenth-century literature and has particular research interests in women's writing, oriental fiction, and the interaction of prose fiction and the theatre. She is the editor of Delarivier Manley's *The New Atalantis* (1993) and Jane Austen's *Sense and Sensibility* (2004), and author of *Seductive Forms: Women's Amatory Fiction, 1684–1740* (1992) and *Fabulous Orients: Fictions of the East in England, 1662–1785* (2005).

JOSEPH F. BARTOLOMEO is Professor of English and Associate Dean of the College of Humanities and Fine Arts at the University of Massachusetts, Amherst. Along with several articles and book chapters, he is the author of *A New Species of Criticism: Eighteenth-Century Discourse on the Novel* (1994) and *Matched Pairs: Gender and Intertextual Dialogue in Eighteenth-Century Fiction* (2002), and the editor of Susanna Rowson's *Reuben and Rachel* (2009).

BARBARA M. BENEDICT holds the Charles A. Dana Chair of English at Trinity College, Hartford, Connecticut. She has published *Framing Feeling: Sentiment and Style in English Prose Fiction, 1745–1800* (1994), *Making the Modern Reader: Cultural Mediation in Early-Modern Literary Anthologies* (1996) and *Curiosity: a Cultural History of Early Modern Inquiry* (2001). She has also edited *Eighteenth-Century British Erotica*, vol. IV: *Wilkes and the Late Eighteenth Century* (2002) and, with Deirdre Le Faye, *Northanger Abbey* (Cambridge, 2006). She is currently writing on collecting in the early modern literary imagination.

BRYCCHAN CAREY is Professor of English at Northumbria University. He is the author of *From Peace to Freedom: Quaker Rhetoric and the Birth of American Antislavery, 1658–1761* (2012) and *British Abolitionism and the Rhetoric of Sensibility: Writing, Sentiment, and Slavery, 1760–1807* (2005), as well as numerous articles and several editions and edited collections, most recently, an edition of Olaudah Equiano's *Interesting Narrative* (2018).

GILLIAN DOW is Associate Professor in English at the University of Southampton, working closely with the library at Chawton House (as its Executive Director from 2014 to 2019). In 2019, she will take up a twelve-month Leverhulme Research Fellowship to complete work on her current monograph project. This project focuses on women writers and the commissioning, marketing and reception of British and French novels from 1780 to 1830, and examines the role played by translations of women's writing and female translators in the novel of the Romantic period.

MAUREEN HARKIN is Professor of English and Humanities at Reed College, Portland, Oregon. She has published essays on Adam Smith and Henry Mackenzie, the sentimental novel and memoir, and eighteenth-century debates on aesthetics, and edited Mackenzie's *The Man of Feeling* (2005). She is currently at work on a study of Adam Smith and eighteenth-century British literature.

HANNAH DOHERTY HUDSON is Assistant Professor of English at Suffolk University, Boston. Her research on eighteenth-century and Romantic popular print culture, periodicals and the Minerva Press novel has appeared in publications including *The Eighteenth-Century Novel*, *European Romantic Review* and *Women's Periodicals and Print Culture in Britain, 1690–1820s*, ed. Jennie Batchelor and Manushag N. Powell (2018).

GARY KELLY is Distinguished University Professor at the University of Alberta, Canada. He has published more than twenty volumes of research and numerous essays on women's writing, on the novel and on popular print culture, mainly of the Romantic period in Britain. He is general editor of the multi-volume Oxford History of Popular Print Culture and director of the Streetprint media-object archiving and exhibiting application, about to launch version 5.0. Current projects include a history of modern fun, a manual of British Romantic fiction, and a topography of sixpenny print, pleasures and politics in the late eighteenth century.

JONATHAN LAMB is the Andrew W. Mellon Professor of the Humanities at Vanderbilt University, Nashville. His most recent book is *Scurvy: the*

Disease of Discovery (2017) where he explores the curious stimulation of the senses in the latter stages of that disease, leading to intense reactions to textures, smells, colours and sounds. He has followed that line of inquiry in the chapter appearing in this volume in order to exhibit the contrast between Sterne's two heroes, Tristram, the advocate of the eye, and Yorick, who is learning not so much to look at things as to handle them. He would like to write a book called *A Short History of Colour*.

BONNIE LATIMER is Associate Professor of Restoration and Eighteenth-Century Literature at the University of Plymouth. She has published *Making Gender, Culture, and the Self in the Fiction of Samuel Richardson* (2013) as well as essays on Richardson, Pope, Wollstonecraft and other subjects of eighteenth-century interest. She is co-editor of the Routledge series New Textual Studies.

ALBERT J. RIVERO is Professor of English at Marquette University, Wisconsin, where he teaches courses on Shakespeare, Austen and British literature of the long eighteenth century. He has published several books and articles, and edited *Gulliver's Travels* (2002) and *Moll Flanders* (2004) as well as *Pamela: or, Virtue Rewarded* (2011) and *Pamela in Her Exalted Condition* (2012) for the Cambridge Edition of the Works of Samuel Richardson.

MELISSA SODEMAN is Associate Professor of English at Coe College, Cedar Rapids, Iowa. She has published essays on Jane Austen and other women novelists, as well as *Sentimental Memorials: Women and the Novel in Literary History* (2015).

Acknowledgements

I am grateful to Linda Bree for suggesting that I undertake this project and for her expert guidance and efforts to make it happen. I thank Bethany Thomas and her staff at Cambridge University Press for excellent advice and support. The inevitable difficulties of editing a collection were eased by the good humour, patience and professionalism of my contributors. Closer to home, I am indebted to my colleagues in the English Department at Marquette University for their personal and professional kindness, especially my chairs, Angela Sorby and Sarah Wadsworth, and to Rick Holz, dean of the Klingler College of Arts and Sciences, for his sustained support of my scholarship. I offer my special thanks to the Committee on Research at Marquette University and its chair, Jeanne Hossenlopp, for awarding me a summer faculty fellowship and a Way Klingler Humanities Fellowship, and to the late Helen Way Klingler and the Klingler family for their generosity in funding my research as well as other faculty initiatives at Marquette. As always, I owe my deepest felt gratitude to my wife, Lisa (who, a professional indexer, assembled the index), and to my son, Albert Harley, and daughter-in-law, Jamie, for their love and encouragement.

Introduction

Albert J. Rivero

This volume aims to present an authoritative and suggestive exploration of the sentimental novel in the eighteenth century. Sentimental novels reached the height of their vogue in the 1770s and 1780s and were still popular in the 1790s. Their origins may be traced to the so-called amatory fiction published in France and Britain in the late seventeenth and early eighteenth century.[1] Samuel Richardson's spectacularly popular reworking of amatory fictional tropes, *Pamela: or, Virtue Rewarded* (1740), with its emphasis on feeling, sympathy and moral instruction, served as a catalyst for this literary movement. *Clarissa* (1747–8), Richardson's second novel, is often cited as the first fully sentimental novel in English. By century's end, sentimental novels were omnipresent in the British book market, some of them proclaiming themselves as such on their title-pages: for example, *Louisa. A Sentimental Novel* (1771); *Emma; or, the unfortunate attachment. A Sentimental Novel* (1773); *Harcourt; a sentimental novel* (1780); *Anna: A Sentimental Novel* (1782); and *Edward and Harriet, or the happy recovery; a sentimental novel* (1788).[2]

The Sentimental Novel in the Eighteenth Century

According to *The Sentimental Magazine* (March 1773), a sentimental story 'at the same Time that it forces the Tears of Sensibility from the Eye, shall inspire the Heart with the Love of Virtue'.[3] As David Hume and Adam Smith declared, sympathy with the sorrows of others defines our moral being. Thus, in his 'Eulogy of Richardson' (1762), Denis Diderot describes a friend 'of sensibility' reading the account of Clarissa's death: 'I watched him: soon I perceived tears dropping from his eyes; he paused, he sobbed; on a sudden he started up, hurried backward and forward, cried out like a man in agony.'[4] But, as Henry Mackenzie, author of *The Man of Feeling* (1771), one of the century's most celebrated sentimental novels, warned, such displays of sensibility called for sceptical review: 'In the enthusiasm of sentiment there is much the same danger as in the enthusiasm of religion, of substituting certain impulses and feelings of what may be called a visionary kind, in the place of real practical duties'.[5] Reading sentimentally can become an end in itself, not a summons to moral action. In *Camilla* (1796), which Austen praises in *Northanger Abbey* (1818), Frances Burney cautions against 'wayward Sensibility – that delicate, but irregular power, which now impels to all that is most disinterested for others, now forgets all mankind, to watch the pulsations of its own fancies'.[6] Adam Smith, however, asserted that sympathy 'cannot, in any sense, be regarded as a selfish principle'.[7]

This double orientation of sensibility, towards our fellow human beings and away from them, from sociability to solipsism, troubled eighteenth-century thinkers. It also provided the deep structure of such sentimental novels as Sterne's *A Sentimental Journey* (1768), in which Parson Yorick, its exquisitely sensitive protagonist, oscillates between fellow-feeling and self-love. The cohabitation of sensibility and irony in Sterne's works reveals – and attempts to repair – the fault lines threatening to fracture sentimental novels. We must also recall the Christian, communitarian emphasis of such sentimental novels as Henry Brooke's *The Fool of Quality* (1766) – abridged in 1781 by John Wesley, one of the founders of Methodism – and the role they played in the anti-slavery movement as well as the creation of philanthropic schemes.[8] As R. S. Crane argued long ago in 'Suggestions toward a Genealogy of the "Man of Feeling"', the origins of the sentimental movement may be traced to the humanitarian theology of such Latitudinarian divines as Joseph Glanvill (1636–80) and Isaac Barrow (1630–77), who stressed essential human goodness to counter Puritan claims of human depravity.[9] Latitudinarian doctrine became a significant strain of Anglicanism in the eighteenth century, influencing such novelists as Henry Fielding and Laurence Sterne. Jane Austen's father, a clergyman, was also heir to this tradition.

As James Raven has noted, 'the clear fashion-leader' in the British fiction market for the period 1770–99 'was the sentimental novel'.[10] Most of these novels, as Raven's figures show, were written by women. Sentimental novels were the product of what G. J. Barker-Benfield has called 'the culture of sensibility' emerging in eighteenth-century Britain.[11] Indeed, the adjective 'sentimental' became a pervasive cultural marker, prompting Lady Bradshaigh, Richardson's correspondent, to ask in November 1749 for his 'interpretation of it'; sadly, his answer to this specific query has not survived.[12] Sentiment was also a major feature of later Restoration drama and the Georgian stage, informing such plays as Thomas Otway's

The Orphan (1680), Thomas Southerne's *The Fatal Marriage* (1694), Nicholas Rowe's *The Fair Penitent* (1703), Colley Cibber's *The Careless Husband* (1704), with its famously affecting 'Steinkirk scene', and Sir Richard Steele's *The Conscious Lovers* (1722), in which, according to Henry Fielding's Parson Adams, 'there are some things almost solemn enough for a Sermon'.[13] Sermons, devotional manuals, hymns, poems, paintings, popular songs were all permeated with the sentimental ether.

Whatever their cultural genealogy and affiliations, sentimental novels are best understood and studied as constituting a *literary* movement, as speaking a common language and style, as machines explicitly and self-consciously manufactured to feel with. Simply put, sentimental novels reflect, represent and appeal to sensibility. If the culture of sensibility encouraged men to shed tears like women, it rendered women potentially weaker because presumably more prone to falling prey to their overheated imaginations. Thus, the heroine of Elizabeth Sophia Tomlins's *The Victim of Fancy* (1787), deluded by her uncontrolled 'Werteromania', attributes her early death to her failure to 'regulate the passions'.[14] Failure to exercise self-control also afflicted men. Young Werther is destroyed by his excessive jealousy and sensibility, as is, for example, the Werther-like Delamere in Charlotte Smith's *Emmeline, the Orphan of the Castle* (1788). But women had more at stake. As Mary Wollstonecraft argues in *A Vindication of the Rights of Woman* (1792), because women were denied access to formal education and political power, sensibility was particularly enervating for them, undermining their ability to act as free agents and rational creatures. In her review of *Emmeline* in *The Analytical Review* (July 1788), she warns against novels 'whose preposterous sentiments our young females imbibe with such avidity' and refuses to describe a scene 'of violent emotions and attitudes' because she fears that 'the description will catch the attention of many romantic girls, and carry their imaginations still further from nature and reason'.[15] In *The Heroine, or Adventures of a Fair Romance Reader* (1813) – 'a delightful burlesque, particularly on the Radcliffe style',[16] as Austen writes to her sister Cassandra – Eaton Stannard Barrett, claiming kinship with Sterne, makes light-hearted fun of his heroine's female quixotism. The following year, in Maria Edgeworth's *Patronage* (1814), Mrs Percy recalls Wollstonecraft's polemic against sentimental novels when she asserts that 'both in novels and in real life, young ladies generally like and encourage men of feeling, in contradistinction to men of principle, and too often men of gallantry in preference to men of correct morals'.[17] For female authors, as Melissa Sodeman has recently reminded us, sentimental novels, identified primarily with women by the closing decades of the eighteenth century, were not so easily dismissed.[18] Austen's first published novel, *Sense and Sensibility* (1811), early drafts of which were written in the 1790s, grapples with the mixed legacy of sentimental novels for women authors.

A survey of scholarship on the sentimental novel must begin with R. F. Brissenden's magisterial and still influential *Virtue in Distress: Studies in the Novel of Sentiment from Richardson to Sade* (1974). For Brissenden, 'the distinguishing feature of the sentimental novel is that it takes for its theme the impact of the world on sensibilities delicate enough to perceive the finest moral distinctions'.[19] But, as the eighteenth century wore on, Brissenden argues, the finely calibrated 'novel of sentiment' of Richardson and Sterne gave way to the increasingly mawkish, clichéd 'novel of sensibility' popular from the 1770s onward. This tale of decline holds some explanatory power – as the supply grew, quality suffered – but a consequence of Brissenden's approach is that many important and popular sentimental novels published in the last three decades of the century, most of them written by women, are left out of his narrative. Burney and Radcliffe are briefly noted but Edgeworth, Lee and Smith are not mentioned at all. Because feminist scholars have recovered – and continue to recover – once-forgotten or neglected novels by women novelists and given us a better sense of their social, political and literary significance, Brissenden's exclusionary account of sentimental novels no longer persuades.

Sentimental novels, and the culture of sensibility that produced them, have attracted much scholarly interest in the past few decades. Important studies have shed valuable light on various aspects and contexts of this complex subject, such as gender and politics,[20] language and style,[21] culture and society,[22] race and slavery,[23] ethics and religion,[24] sympathy,[25] emotion and affect,[26] empire,[27] French connections.[28] Todd [29] offers an excellent introduction to the topic (as well as a corrective to Brissenden) and Rawson[30] analyses how satire and sentiment play off against each other in the long eighteenth century. Finally, to close this brief survey, Chandler[31] has shown how the 'sentimental mode' informs not only literature beyond the eighteenth century, as in novels by Charles Dickens, but also films, thus illustrating that the culture of sensibility is still very much with us.

We risk critical incoherence and imprecision, however, in extending a study of the sentimental novel beyond its specific manifestation in the eighteenth century and the opening decades of the nineteenth. This volume focuses on a moment in literary history when the protocols of the emerging English novel were being established and contested. The sentimental novel played a crucial role in that process. Because of new digital tools, scholars with institutional access to such databases as ECCO and EEBO are able to explore a wide archive of original sources with relative ease and convenience. There are also new and exciting ways of doing things with literary texts nowadays, from object and thing theory to animal studies to speculative capitalism, which may be deployed in the study of the sentimental novel. But the literary critic or, in my case, editor of a volume of critical essays, must choose from many, sometimes competing interests and possibilities. Henry James's words on the choices artists must make also apply to critics and scholars: 'Really, universally, relations stop nowhere, and the exquisite problem of the artist is eternally but to draw, by a geometry of his own, the circle within which they shall happily *appear* to do so.'[32] I hope that I have judiciously wielded my power of selection.

Although *The Sentimental Novel in the Eighteenth Century* focuses primarily on sentimental novels in the British Isles, the volume also looks at sentimental novels in France, Germany and North America. The chapters address general theoretical and practical issues, some focusing on topics, others on specific authors and works. They are arranged to tell a coherent, roughly chronological story, using Richardson and Sterne as anchoring points, and ending with Austen, not because she delivers the final death blow to the sentimental novel, but because she redefines and repurposes the sentimental novel as it moves forward into the nineteenth century and down to our own day. Without compromising overall coherence, I have not attempted to suppress differences of opinion or critical methodology. Generally speaking, the chapters approach their topics from historically inflected perspectives.

Summaries of Chapters

The volume opens with Gary Kelly's 'The Sentimental Novel and Politics'. As Kelly advances, the sentimental novel was fundamentally political. It offered its authors and readers a space for imagining, representing, promoting and contesting different versions of modernity. It was thus concerned with modernity's preoccupations with self-reflexive personal identity as well as relationships of intimacy, domesticity, conjugality, community and nation. Kelly's wide-ranging account combines various critical approaches, from integrational linguistics, effective semiotics, ethnomethodology and conceptual history to book history and social theories of modernity, as well as social, cultural and political history. Kelly shows how producers and users of the sentimental novel adapted the novel form to the politics of modernity, generally and in specific moments of political crisis and conflict.

In 'Sensible Readers: Experiments in Feeling in Early Prose Fiction by Women', Ros Ballaster argues that, in the amatory fictions by women of the late seventeenth and early eighteenth century, close attention to the modulation of feeling in the protagonist sits alongside self-conscious reference to the anticipated response of the reader. Eliza Haywood, for example, defends the warmth of her amatory representations in her preface to *Lasselia* (1723) by declaring that otherwise the reader would not be 'sensible how far it touches him' and hence forewarned against the sway of passion. Both intradiegetic and extradiegetic narrators consistently seek to imagine and anticipate their effect in the mind of the reader. While the feeling character is most often represented as female, the receptive mind is most often ungendered. Reading is thus conceived as a virtual mechanics of affect. In these early prose fiction experiments, as Ballaster shows, we can see the novel anticipating its own future grip on the feelings of the reading public. The chapter addresses the importance of 'variety' of plot and feeling, on the part of both characters and readers, in amatory collections by (in chronological order) Delarivier Manley, Eliza Haywood, Elizabeth Rowe and Penelope Aubin. These collections provide their authors with the opportunity to explore the variety and variation of sentimental response.

Bonnie Latimer's 'Reading for the Sentiment: Richardson's Novels' challenges assessments of Richardson's sentimentalism as a largely affective mode. The chapter explores the nature of Richardsonian 'sentiment' and how it shapes the role of the reader. Examining 'sentiment' as a moral proposition and rhetorical unit, Latimer re-evaluates its role in Richardson's works, contending that sententiousness is a critically underplayed dimension of his fiction. In Richardson, 'sentiment' refers not only to displayed emotions which elicit responses from readers both intradiegetic and extradiegetic, but also to 'moral sentiments', pithy distillations of key moral tenets, abstracted from the original narratives. To read for the sentiment is to read both *for* and *beyond* the story, to become immersed in, but also to transcend, the fiction. This complex reading activity requires a reader who is not merely feeling, but also critical. The chapter places Richardson's use of moral sentiments in the context of popular compendia of moral sayings and enchiridions from the period, and concludes that a focus on the neglected quality of sententiousness allows us to appreciate how Richardson's fiction in fact imagines a vital, active and morally effective form of reading, which Latimer calls purposeful reading.

In 'The Virtuous in Distress: *David Simple, Amelia, Memoirs of Miss Sidney Bidulph*', Barbara M. Benedict examines the moral ambiguity surrounding the heroes of Sarah Fielding's *The Adventures of David Simple* (1744), Henry Fielding's *Amelia* (1751) and Frances Sheridan's *Memoirs of Miss Sidney Bidulph* (1761). In these narratives, the sensitive and upright titular protagonists are not only entangled in complex intrigues perpetrated by fools and villains, but also betrayed by the their own naïveté, honesty, fidelity, and an excessive sensibility that leads them to misjudge other people. However, whereas Henry Fielding portrays a married heroine whose endurance of her profligate but sentimental husband appears as Christian humility in a wicked world, the two women writers reveal the comic absurdity of a high-flown virtue that persists in the face of experience. Nonetheless, all three novels employ a narrative irony that shows how idealistic sentimentalism entails an unwitting complicity in the vices of the mercenary, duplicitous and weak-willed, and how these virtuous heroes and heroines contribute to their own distress.

Gillian Dow's 'Sentiment from Abroad: French Novels after 1748' examines cross-Channel sentimental exchange in the fiction of the latter half of the long eighteenth century. Depicted as torn between appropriate Christian reading and the reading of *Clarissa*, Laclos's sentimental heroine in *Les Liaisons Dangereuses* (1782), Madame de Tourvel – at a critical moment in her own seduction narrative – accurately embodies the extraordinary vogue for Richardson's novels in France. France experienced an extended period of Anglomania in the latter half of the eighteenth century. Decades after their first appearance in print, both Pamela and Clarissa remained living heroines for the French reader. Richardson himself elicited 'éloges' from writers as diverse as Denis Diderot and Stéphanie-Félicité de Genlis, and was widely emulated in French fiction. But where it might be tempting to view the French sentimental novels that found a market and readership in Britain after 1748 as inspired, largely, by Richardsonian fiction (notably *Clarissa*), cultural exchange is more complex. Dow's chapter examines the French sentimental novel after the publication of Richardson's *Pamela*, focusing not only on Rousseau's influential *Julie* (1761) but on a range of sentimental fictions, including the now largely neglected novels published in the 1750s by Marie-Jeanne Riccoboni, in the 1780s by Isabelle de Montolieu, and in the early 1800s by Sophie Cottin and Benjamin Constant. Adopting a cross-Channel approach, Dow complicates arguments that examining national traditions is the best way to interrogate the literature of the eighteenth and early nineteenth century.

'I laugh 'till I cry', Laurence Sterne wrote to David Garrick from Paris in April 1762, 'and in the same tender moments, *cry 'till I laugh*'.[33] In a similar vein, Sterne promised a prospective female reader of *A Sentimental Journey* that any scene she wept over would hold strict proportion with the mirth it had provoked in him while writing it – 'or I'll give up the Business of sentimental writing'.[34] As Jonathan Lamb demonstrates in 'Sterne's Sentimental Empiricism', this emotional ambidexterity might not be altogether true because the comedy of *Tristram Shandy* (1759–67) and the pathos of *A Sentimental Journey* are substantially at odds. The reason lies in Sterne's retreat from the materialist-empiricist account of sensation and cognition that organized his first novel, and the more attenuated refinement of sensibility that seems to be the aim of the second. The early encounter between Yorick and a nameless lady in Calais provides the important prologue to this theme. Left standing in front of a blank locked door, holding the hand of a lady he does not know, he has no resources (he believes) but inner ones, so he makes an awkward allusion to the unscheduled intimacy of the scene. Since it was one that was at least mutually tolerable, if not mildly exciting, the lady asks, 'Who but an English philosopher would have sent notices of it to the brain to reverse the judgment?'[35] This tendency to translate the sensations of a situation into ideas persists throughout Yorick's travels, hindering if not blocking the reciprocal action of impressions and ideas that David Hume, for instance, regards as crucial to the counter-translation of ideas into impressions. Lamb's chapter moves to resolve why this should be and why Yorick appears incapable of learning from his experience, relying instead on ideas which, like balloons, rise into rarefied and non-situational spheres of thought.

As Maureen Harkin illustrates in 'Virtue Not Rewarded: *The Man of Feeling* and *The Sorrows of Young Werther*', Mackenzie and Goethe hold the distinction of creating the two most self-destructive male protagonists in the history of sentimental fiction. Werther (1774) is the most famous eighteenth-century literary character driven to suicide by thwarted love and an inability to tolerate the hypocrisies of bourgeois society. However, in Mackenzie's slightly earlier *The Man of Feeling* (1771), Harley shares many of the same features: an exquisite sensibility, disappointment in love and a profound inability to negotiate successfully the hierarchies, duplicities and scheming of modern social life. Though Harley is baffled, rather than embattled like Werther, both characters recoil from the compromises demanded of them. Their deaths – violent suicide, mysterious decline – might be seen as offering a form of inchoate political critique of their societies, despite both novels' habitual representations of emotions that do not affect behaviour and critiques that result in no action. Harkin's chapter tracks the nature and force of their resistance, a resistance that is complicated by the way in which both Werther and Harley often undermine their positions with their own words and actions – a fact which produces a peculiar and strikingly similar atmosphere of futility and squandered energies in both texts.

Although its contribution was barely recognized two decades ago, the sentimental novel is now understood to have played a prominent role in turning public opinion against the slave trade in the 1770s and 1780s. Recent studies by Ellis, Carey, Festa, Boulukos, Swaminathan and Ahern[36] have confirmed that sentimental novels frequently focused attention on the suffering of enslaved Africans, sometimes merely drawing a tear, but often encouraging an 'active sensibility' that prompted political engagement in the abolitionist movement. Drawing on these six major studies, and revisiting several of the texts they discuss, including novels by Laurence Sterne, Henry Mackenzie and Sarah Scott, Brycchan Carey's 'Slavery and the Novel of Sentiment' reasserts the importance of the novel of sensibility to the debate over the slave trade, as well as demonstrating its shifting and unreliable nature as a political tool. The chapter starts off by examining the role of the sentimental novel in the pre-abolitionist debate about the amelioration of slavery and concludes with an extended reading of 'Shandean anti-slavery writing' in Sterne, Ignatius Sancho, Susanna Rowson and the anonymous *Memoirs and Opinions of Mr Blenfield* (1790). The last of these contains a portrait of Shirna Cambo, an African man of sensibility loosely modelled on Ignatius Sancho, who 'for every decent merriment had a smile, for every sorrow had a tear'. The chapter concludes that Cambo represents both a type of the sentimental hero and a central trope of British literary abolitionism.

Hannah Doherty Hudson's 'Sentiment and the Gothic: Failures of Emotion in the Novels of Mrs Radcliffe and the Minerva Press' asks whether the gothic novel is sentimental. Hudson reads Ann Radcliffe's *Mysteries of Udolpho* (1794) alongside six gothic novels published by the Minerva Press in the first half of the 1790s. She argues that early gothic novels share many traits with their sentimental predecessors, but ultimately display a fundamental distrust of sentiment. Even though such novels as Anna Maria Mackenzie's *Danish Massacre* (1791), Eliza Parsons's *Castle of Wolfenbach* (1793) or Richard Warner's *Netley Abbey* (1795) feature sensitive, tearful protagonists who praise benevolence and practise forgiveness, their inexorable gothic plots cynically refigure and undermine older sentimental models, casting the useful and admirable functions of sentiment into doubt.

As Joseph F. Bartolomeo shows in 'The Sentimental Novel in America: *The History of Emily Montague, Charlotte Temple, The Power of Sympathy, The Coquette*', eighteenth-century sentimental novels set in America are directed at different audiences and offer divergent representations of the nature and significance of sensibility. *The History of Emily Montague* (1769) and *Charlotte Temple* (1791), originally published in England, emphasize sentimental longing to return home. The former novel confines sensibility almost exclusively to British characters, while the latter magnifies the isolation of the heroine by exiling her in a foreign land. The novels directed explicitly to American readers offer complex and often contradictory messages about the importance of feeling, its relationship to reason, and its connection to communities of class and gender. *The Power of Sympathy* (1789) undercuts its stated moral purpose by representing sympathy as both dangerous and admirable, and renders an equivocal verdict on the levelling of class distinctions enabled by sympathy. The title character of *The Coquette* (1797) is admonished to prefer reason over fancy, but this advice is compromised by emotional male suitors and unsympathetic female mentors.

In the early nineteenth century, two grand dames of the eighteenth-century novel published belated works that were widely dismissed as old-fashioned and passé. In 'Novel Anachronisms: Sophia Lee's *The Life of a Lover* and Frances Burney's *The Wanderer*', Melissa Sodeman argues that these two novels may be read as works of temporal and aesthetic rupture that testify to the declining status of sentimental fiction in the early nineteenth century. However, when read together, they speak to a shared effort to hold on to sentimental fiction for its ability to incorporate what more sedate literary forms tended to leave out – not only the gendered forms of experience Burney called 'female difficulties', but the ugly feelings those difficulties inevitably induced. Self-consciously aware of their startling violations of literary chronology, Lee and Burney's final works push back against the decline of sentimental fiction even as they suggest what might be gained by hazarding anachronism in our own literary histories.

The volume closes with my chapter on Jane Austen's complex relation to the sentimental novel. Austen both critiqued and embraced the sentimental novel. Like Henry Fielding, who began his novelistic career by parodying *Pamela* in *Shamela* (1741), Austen started hers by satirizing sentimental novels in a series of miscellaneous pieces she wrote as a young girl. She ended it with the unfinished *Sanditon*, the novel she was writing during her last illness, a satirical anatomy of projectors and patrons of seaside resorts, which, in its uncompromising anti-sentimentality, recalls the author of the juvenilia. In it, we meet the would-be Lovelace, Sir Edward Denham, who 'had read more sentimental novels than agreed with him. His fancy had been early caught by all the impassioned and most exceptionable parts of Richardson's.'[37] Austen's first published novel, *Sense and Sensibility* (1811), analyses sentimentalism in an almost schematic fashion. Her last completed novel, *Persuasion* (1818), presents a creative synthesis of good and bad sentimental impulses. Like Sterne, Austen understood that irony and satire are not inimical to the sentimental but integral to it. All of Austen's novels are sentimental and end in marriage – a satisfyingly sentimental payoff for readers then and now. Austen encourages her readers to read her novels sentimentally, with feeling and judgement, to be moved but not to be stupefied by sensibility.

The Aims of the Volume

Building on previous scholarship, *The Sentimental Novel in the Eighteenth Century* brings together, in one book, various aspects and contexts for thinking about the genre. One advantage a collection of essays has over a single-author book is that it can present a multiplicity of critical viewpoints. It is the hope of both the editor and contributors that our collective efforts will suggest possible areas of future exploration. What the following chapters certainly demonstrate is that the sentimental novel continues to engage readers and critics. Far from being obsolete or only of antiquary interest, the sentimental novel remains a vibrant and exciting area of study.

Notes

1. See Ros Ballaster, *Seductive Forms: Women's Amatory Fiction from 1684–1740* (Oxford: Clarendon Press, 1992). I am grateful to Gillian Dow and Bethany Thomas for their comments and suggestions.
2. For more on this marketing strategy, see 24–6 below.
3. Advertisement, *The Sentimental Magazine: Or, General Assemblage of Science, Taste, and Entertainment*, 1 (London, 1773), 3.
4. 'Eulogy of Richardson', in *The Works of Samuel Richardson*, ed. Edward Mangin, 19 vols. (London, 1811), 1: xxiv.
5. *The Lounger*, 20 (Edinburgh, 1785–6), 79.

6. Frances Burney, *Camilla or A Picture of Youth*, ed. Edward A. Bloom and Lillian D. Bloom (Oxford University Press, 2009), 680.
7. Adam Smith, *The Theory of Moral Sentiments* (London, 1759), 496.
8. See Thomas Keymer, 'Sentimental Fiction: Ethics, Social Critique and Philanthropy', in *The Cambridge History of English Literature, 1660–1780*, ed. John Richetti (Cambridge University Press, 2005), 572–601.
9. R. S. Crane, 'Suggestions toward a Genealogy of the "Man of Feeling"', *ELH* 1 (1934): 205–30. For a dissenting view, see Donald Greene, 'Latitudinarianism and Sensibility: the Genealogy of the "Man of Feeling" Reconsidered', *Modern Philology* 75 (1977): 159–83.
10. Peter Garside, James Raven and Rainer Schöwerling, eds., *The English Novel, 1770–1829: a Bibliographical Survey of Prose Fiction Published in the British Isles*, 2 vols. (Oxford University Press, 2000), 1: 31.
11. G. J. Barker-Benfield, *The Culture of Sensibility: Sex and Society in Eighteenth-Century Britain* (University of Chicago Press, 1992). See also Paul Langford, 'The Birth of Sensibility', in *A Polite and Commercial People* (Oxford University Press, 1989), 461–518.
12. Lady Bradshaigh to Richardson (<Early November?> 1749), in *Correspondence with Lady Bradshaigh and Lady Echlin, Volume I: 1748–1753*, ed. Peter Sabor (Cambridge University Press, 2016), 80: 'Pray, Sir, give me leave to ask you . . . what, in your opinion, is the meaning of the word *sentimental*, so much in vogue amongst the polite, both in town and country? In letters and common conversation, I have asked several who make use of it, and have generally received for answer, it is – it is – *sentimental*. Every thing clever and agreeable is comprehended in that word . . . I am frequently astonished to hear such a one is a *sentimental* man; we were a *sentimental* party; I have been taking a *sentimental* walk . . . I should be glad to know your interpretation of it.' As Sabor notes, this passage is cited in the *OED* as the first illustrative example of the word. For a similar list, see 25 below. For a still useful account of the word and its history, see Erik Erämetsä, *A Study of the Word 'Sentimental' and of Other Linguistic Characteristics of Eighteenth Century Sentimentalism in England* (Helsinki: Helsingin Liikekirjapaino Oy, 1951).
13. Henry Fielding, *Joseph Andrews*, ed. Martin C. Battestin (Middletown, CT: Wesleyan University Press, 1967), 267. On this topic, see Frank H. Ellis, *Sentimental Comedy: Theory and Practice* (Cambridge University Press, 1991) and Lisa A. Freeman, *Character's Theatre: Genre and Identity on the Eighteenth-Century English Stage* (Philadelphia: University of Pennsylvania Press, 2002), esp. chapter 5, 'Sentimental Comedy: Or, The Comedy of Good Breeding', 193–234. Sentimental drama remained popular into the next century. *First Impressions, A Sentimental Comedy, in Five Acts* (1811) is an early nineteenth-century example of this dramatic type.
14. Eliza Sophia Tomlins, *The Victim of Fancy*, ed. Daniel Cook (London: Pickering and Chatto, 2009), 107.
15. *The Analytical Review, or History of Literature, Domestic and Foreign*, vol. 1 (London, 1788), 333, 331.

16. To Cassandra Austen (2–3 March 1814), in *Jane Austen's Letters*, 4th edition, ed. Deirdre Le Faye (Oxford University Press, 2014), 267.
17. Maria Edgeworth, *Patronage*, 4 vols. (London: Printed for J. Johnson and Co., 1814), 1: 363.
18. Melissa Sodeman, *Sentimental Memorials: Women and the Novel in Literary History* (Stanford University Press, 2015).
19. R. F. Brissenden, *Virtue in Distress: Studies in the Novel of Sentiment from Richardson to Sade* (London: Macmillan, 1974), 119.
20. Rita Goldberg, *Sex and Enlightenment: Women in Richardson and Diderot* (Cambridge University Press, 1984); Gary Kelly, *Women, Writing, and Revolution, 1790–1827* (Oxford: Clarendon Press, 1993); Claudia L. Johnson, *Equivocal Beings: Politics, Gender, and Sentimentality in the 1790s: Wollstonecraft, Radcliffe, Burney, Austen* (University of Chicago Press, 1995).
21. Barbara M. Benedict, *Framing Feeling: Sentiment and Style in English Prose Fiction, 1745–1800* (New York: AMS Press, 1994).
22. John Mullan, *Sentiment and Sociability: the Language of Feeling in the Eighteenth Century* (Oxford: Clarendon Press, 1988); G. J., Barker-Benfield, *The Culture of Sensibility: Sex and Society in Eighteenth-Century Britain* (University of Chicago Press, 1992).
23. Markman Ellis, *The Politics of Sensibility: Race, Gender and Commerce in the Sentimental Novel* (Cambridge University Press, 1996); Brycchan Carey, *British Abolitionism and the Rhetoric of Sensibility: Writing, Sentiment, and Slavery, 1760–1807* (Basingstoke: Palgrave Macmillan, 2005).
24. Isabel Rivers, *Reason, Grace, and Sentiment: a Study of the Language of Religion and Ethics in England, 1660–1780*, 2 vols. (Cambridge University Press, 1991–2000).
25. Jonathan Lamb, *The Evolution of Sympathy in the Long Eighteenth Century* (London: Pickering and Chatto, 2009).
26. Ann Jessie Van Sant, *Eighteenth-Century Sensibility and the Novel: the Senses in Social Context* (Cambridge University Press, 1993); Adela Pinch, *Strange Fits of Passion: Epistemologies of Emotion, Hume to Austen* (Stanford University Press, 1996); Julie Ellison, *Cato's Tears and the Making of Anglo-American Emotion* (Chicago University Press, 1999).
27. Lynn Festa, *Sentimental Figures of Empire in Eighteenth-Century Britain and France* (Baltimore: Johns Hopkins University Press, 2006).
28. Ann Lewis, *Sensibility, Reading and Illustration: Spectacles and Signs in Graffigny, Marivaux and Rousseau* (Oxford: Legenda, 2009).
29. Janet Todd, *Sensibility: an Introduction* (London: Methuen, 1986).
30. Claude Rawson, *Satire and Sentiment, 1660–1830* (Cambridge University Press, 1994).
31. James Chandler, *An Archaeology of Sympathy: the Sentimental Mode in Literature and Cinema* (University of Chicago Press, 2013).
32. Henry James, Preface to *Roderick Hudson*, in *The Art of the Novel: Critical Prefaces by Henry James*, with introduction by R. P. Blackmur and new foreword by Colm Tóibín (University of Chicago Press, 2011), 5.

33. *Letters of Laurence Sterne*, ed. Lewis Perry Curtis (1935; Oxford: Clarendon Press, 1965), 163.
34. To Hannah, [Coxwold, 15 Nov. 1767], in *Letters*, 401.
35. Laurence Sterne, *A Sentimental Journey through France and Italy*, ed. Melvyn New and W. G. Day (Gainesville: University Press of Florida, 2002), 24.
36. Ellis, *The Politics of Sensibility*; Carey, *British Abolitionism and the Rhetoric of Sensibility*; Festa, *Sentimental Figures*; George Boulukos, *The Grateful Slave: the Emergence of Race in Eighteenth-Century British and American Culture* (Cambridge University Press, 2008); Srividhya Swaminathan, *Debating the Slave Trade: Rhetoric of British National Identity, 1759–1815* (Farnham: Ashgate, 2009); Stephen Ahern, *Affect and Abolition in the Anglo-Atlantic, 1770–1830* (Farnham: Ashgate, 2013).
37. Jane Austen, *Later Manuscripts*, ed. Janet Todd and Linda Bree (Cambridge University Press, 2008), 183.

CHAPTER 1

The Sentimental Novel and Politics

Gary Kelly

What political uses did different people in Great Britain and Ireland likely make of so-called or so-considered sentimental novels in the eighteenth century?[1] Answering this question for the present requires converging modern expert knowledges of integrational linguistics, effective semiotics, ethnomethodology, book history, conceptual history, social theory of modernity, and social, cultural and political history. Integrational linguistics argues that meaning does not inhere once and for all in words or other communication media, but is created by someone from such words or objects in and for a unique instance from all that person knows and from all elements of the communicational situation.[2] Effective semiotics argues similarly that meaning is always meaning in use.[3] Reading in classrooms is different from and does not trump reading in and for everyday life. Ethnomethodology argues that society is not an abstract system that operates on individuals and groups, but rather is created in particular moments by social actors for their own purposes.[4] Book history investigates the production, distribution, circulation and reception – or, better, use – of print objects verbal and graphic over time and place. Conceptual history ostensibly historicizes terms, concepts and discourses that are otherwise widely used as if transhistorical in social, cultural, political and other modern expert knowledges.[5] Social theory of modernity outlines the distinctive attributes of 'modernity' as ostensibly historicized discourse. Social, cultural and political historiography cannot represent the past but only provide a certain kind of more or less convincing academically validated historification.[6] Nevertheless, such historiography alone must be used in a venue such as this for imagining the supposed lived worlds and actions that were contexts for reading the sentimental novel or anything else in the 'past'.[7] Converging these methodologies and matters enables speculation, grounded according to conventions of modern expert (academic) knowledges, about the relation between the sentimental novel and politics and how the sentimental novel may have been used politically or assignified by users as political or engaged in politics in some way or other within or as part of the historically particular discourse of modernity.[8]

Modernity is regarded here as a discourse or way of communicating about a lived world but cannot be a description or account of that world. This discourse was developed in the eighteenth century to present, imagine, promote, manage and dominate the complex and accelerating social, cultural, political and economic transformation called modernization. The term 'modernize' in the sense of 'making something modern' appeared in the print record precisely in this period (1770; *OED*), just as 'modern' was losing its predominant use for simply distinguishing present and recent times from antiquity and as 'modernity' was shifting sense from mere newness or presentdayness to an entire 'reality' and condition. The discourse of modernity was modernity-speak, ways self-conscious modernizers talked and wrote when they were distinguishing, imagining and promoting the world they thought they were making from its ostensible others. Modernity-speakers were distinguishing modernity not just from the past or antiquity but from what they now represented as dialectically 'unmodern' (in a sense also emerging in this period), whether past or present, far or near. The sentimental novel may be regarded as one form of modernity-speak, part of the history of discourse rather than the history of ideas.[9] Modernity-speak, however, was not monolithic but multiple and contested – a field of struggle between different interests, continuing in today's 'late' or 'postmodernity'. In this sense, modernity and its contending versions were and are inherently political. Appropriately, by the time the discourse of modernity was being formed as a field of contest, 'politics' had expanded from referring exclusively to government, administration and the public sphere to signifying the (contested) 'acquisition or exercise of power, status, or authority' (*OED*) more generally, including in private and social life. This was the sense in which politics were commonly presented in the sentimental novel and probably used by readers.

This plural and contested discourse of modernity centred on the topic of self-reflexive personal identity as the basis for 'pure' or disinterested yet more intensely interested relations of intimacy, conjugality, domesticity, sociability, community, ethnicity, nationality, citizenship, humanity, nature and spirituality.[10] The modern subject formed, nurtured and healed in such relations was supposedly better able to manage modernization's major complexes, as modernity's major topics. There was accelerating and broadening change. There were more critical relations of risk and trust. The period, for example, saw the birth of modern commercial insurance and actuarial science. There were larger and remoter abstract systems such as modern knowledges and institutions. There were ever-changing chronotopes or representations and formations of time-space, from subjective interiority and 'home' through locale and nation and empire to globe and cosmos. There was need to dis-embed from one habitus or lived world and re-embed in a more or properly modern one. This scheme or myth of modernity was represented repeatedly in what soon was known as the 'modern novel' and its major kind, the sentimental novel, for readers eager to be properly modern, if not all in the same way.

Print was indispensable for circulating differing versions of modernity. Because the novel had relatively wide circulation among middle and upper ranks, those with most at stake in the onset of modernity, it was a highly useful form of print for imagining, promoting and contesting versions of modernity in their interests, along with and often incorporating its symbiotic forms – newspapers, magazines and popularized modern knowledges. Because of this usefulness, the novel became increasingly modern in the sense of produced as an advertisably modern (commercial) object and as culturally assignifiable in ever more modernized processes of fashionable or distinction-asserting consumption. Accordingly, the kinds of novel that became commonplace by mid-century were increasingly referred to as the 'modern novel' to distinguish them from kinds that were not just earlier but supposedly unmodern, while earlier fiction that was republished or still accessible could be read in a 'modern' way. The novel was modernized in the sense of refashioned to comprise central topics of modernity, in the following ways. Characterization showed the formation and experience of self-reflexive personal identity and the pure social relations enabled thereby. Relations of risk and trust and engagement with abstract systems and new chronotopes were narrativized in incident and plot. Descriptive techniques were elaborated for representing chronotopes moving the modern subject. Dis-embedding from one habitus and re-embedding in a properly modern one were emplotted. 'Modern novel' began to appear in the print record[11] about the time when the culture of Sensibility became prominent, suggesting that a readership eager to learn that culture as a certain way of being modern found a manual in the sentimental version of the modern novel.[12]

From Richardson and Fielding to Austen and Scott, an important way in which the modern novel narrativized modernity's thematics in relation to politics in the emerging sense of contested inequities of power was through what can be called the identity-mystery romance. Here a protagonist is ejected from 'home' out of error, malice, mischance, or family or state politics and deprived of proper or rightful social or moral identity. Thereby left relatively powerless, this protagonist is precipitated on a journey, actual or subjective, or in the sentimental novel often both, through social terrain dominated by unmodernity or false modernity wielding greater power. During this journey the protagonist's identity as self-reflexive sovereign subject is formed and/or tested in a series of encounters with unfamiliar abstract systems and chronotopes typically dominated by the more powerful, and by challenges of risk and trust in the face of such inequity. After a variable number of similar vicissitudes the protagonist is usually rewarded by re-embedding in a modern habitus and home, and restoration of original social status and property or bestowal of better ones, often by a *deus ex machina*. Here was a political myth or story explaining and protesting inequities of power felt in everyday life, for a readership that, judging by the cost of buying or borrowing modern novels, mainly comprised the middling sort, who were largely excluded from politics in the older sense of governing structures, institutions and social networks.

Such people would obtain most of their novels from commercial circulating libraries. These libraries' catalogues from the 1760s through the rest of the century list numerous sentimental novels, whether so labelled or not, alongside earlier amatory and scandal fiction and comic, humorous, adventure and satirical novels past and contemporary, indicating the breadth of borrowers' interests and producers' and suppliers' relentless market-probing. In this populous field modern novels could be identified or assignified as sentimental in different ways for various reasons. 'Sentimental novel' occurred rarely in the period's print record. At a time when title-pages were advertisements, the term 'sentimental' or 'sensibility' appeared in a few novels' titles, in some fiction marketing, and in titles of a wide variety of other kinds of print. This is identification by producers. There were numerous eighteenth-century novels not titled or marketed as sentimental but that seem to have been assignifiable as more or less sentimental. This is assignification by private users on one hand and public cultural mediators and gatekeepers on the other, each pursuing different, usually conflicting interests. Such assignification would be by genre, a word that came into English in this period within an expanding lexicon of interpretation and evaluation, or assignification and use. Rather than a set of elements inhering once and for all in a 'text' belonging to a set with similar traits, genre-in-use was a provisional sense of ostensible formal and thematic traits knowledge of which was circulated by cultural discourse and learned through social interaction and experience, and applied in particular acts of assignification, in the cultural politics of competing modernities. As illustrated at the end of this chapter, by late in the period popularizers of modern expert knowledges could use such genre politically to promote a certain kind of modernity by literary canon-formation including certain forms of the sentimental novel in the interests of people like themselves.

For such genre-work, readers needed knowledge and experience to use the sentimental novel's formal and thematic traits in their own ways and interests. The most prominent formal technique serving sentimental modernity's myth of subjectivity would be narrative focalization, either in first- or third-person narration, and later a fusion of both, on the subjectivity of the protagonist, the narrator and sometimes other characters. The protagonist's sentiments and sensibility were typically related to the lived body, or 'sensibility' as treated alternatively in the modernized expert knowledges of physiology, medicine and philosophy.[13] The famous example was Sterne's *A Sentimental Journey* (see Chapter 6). Sensibility as both subjective and embodied would be narrated in relation to setting, or the circumambient social, natural, humanly made and transcendental worlds. The 'confessional' mode was often used to narrativize the modern subject's distressing encounters with unmodern or falsely modern practices and institutions, as in Brooke's *Fool of Quality* and Hays's *Victim of Prejudice*, or occasionally sublime experiences of self-conscious free subjectivity despite such distresses, as in *A Sentimental Journey*, Rousseau's *Julie* or Wollstonecraft's *Wrongs of Woman*. Such narration was also politically modern in the non-comic prominence it could give to socially marginal or abject characters, often in inset narratives such as George Primrose's in *The Vicar of Wakefield*, Jemima's in Wollstonecraft's novel or the shepherd's in Hannah More's *Shepherd of Salisbury Plain*. Disruption or disregard of plot could foreground representation of the protagonist's subjective vicissitudes, as indicated in Samuel Johnson's famous remark on reading Richardson: 'you must read him for the sentiment, and consider the story as only giving occasion to the sentiment'.[14] But such plot disruption could also formalize the protagonist's confusion by, and alienation in, chronotopes and abstract systems of unmodernity and false modernity, as in Mackenzie's *Man of Feeling* or Radcliffe's gothic romances. Setting typically served to stimulate the subjectivity of the protagonist while also representing the mysterious architecture of unmodernity and the soothing or inspiring landscape of the natural. This device was especially notable in the gothic, historical and 'national tale' versions of the sentimental novel by writers such as Radcliffe, Jane Porter and Sydney Owenson. Manipulation of typography, especially proliferation of exclamation points and dashes, could be assignified as representing visually an expressive mode, while also seeming excitingly modern in its unconventionality, as in *A Sentimental Journey.* Syntax was shaped to similar effect, with devices such as incomplete sentences and paratactic discourse to signify immediacy of utterance, and frequent use of rhetorical devices such as anacoluthon, hyperbole, exclamatio and polysyndeton to the same end, as in Brooke's *Fool of Quality.*

Thematically, sentimental novels could be assignified as such by users as typically incorporating topics related to subjective experience and pure relationships narrativized as characters, incidents and settings liable to move or affect the protagonist. Here the ubiquitous political crisis of sensibility was modernized love that is opposed by superior social and financial power. As in literature going back to classical antiquity, love was treated as a subjective absolute, not a merely social desire, or amenable to power of wealth or status or the politics of corporate family dynastic interests. Sentimental modern love differed, however, in its elaborated language of affect and emphatic correlation with subjective merit. Other, often related themes functioned similarly in occasioning modern affect. There was humanitarian sympathy for the poor, oppressed, incarcerated, unfortunate, wronged and the like. There was feeling for beautiful, sublime and picturesque chronotopes from waterfalls through ruins to domestic interiors. There was personal religious devotionalism. This prompted John Wesley to adapt *The Fool of Quality* for Methodists. There was self-sympathy arising from negative encounters with the unmodern or falsely modern. In many instances these and similar topics were given an expressly political relevance regarding unmodernity or false modernity. Some of these topics were assignifiable in different sentimental novels and all in Brooke's *Fool of Quality*, the novelistic encyclopaedia of sentimental modernity. Readers being what we are would assignify certain print objects as having these formal and thematic traits, do so in their own ways, focus on certain ones more than others, skip passages or pages, lose attention, attend more to this or that character, focus on a particular feature, and so on, pursuing their own changing interests.

In these ways the sentimental novel was fashioned and marketed and could be assignified for its role in modernity as a field of contesting interests. Variation in these novelistic formalities was likely driven less by artistic ambition or political mission than by demands from the novel market for (advertisable) signs of the diversity-in-similarity, novelty-in-familiarity characteristic of the fashionable consumption whereby people practised and exhibited their modernity. Nevertheless, political import could be assignified to the sentimental novel in general and particular ways.

In general, this would typically be through depiction of 'politics' in the emerging sense of acquisition, exercise and inequities of power from the public-political to and especially in the private-local sphere. Such politics were correlated with differences of class, gender and other social ascriptions of identity, in turn correlated with characters' sensibility. Gender politics were a major topic for several reasons.[15] There was woman's relation to and role in modernity as supposed vessel of sensibility and potential presiding and guiding sensibility of 'pure' relations in home, community and nation. The character and value of woman was commonly taken as index of a family's, community's and nation's unmodernity, proper modernity, or false modernity. Man's relation to modernity similarly correlated sensibility and masculinity, as sentimental novels offered versions of the properly modern man.[16]

There were several ongoing general concerns regarding the political import of the sentimental novel in contested modernity. A prominent concern was over sentimental literature's supposed threat to the established order in culture, society and politics through its purportedly glamorized representation of emotional, behavioural, sexual, social or any transgression or almost-transgression. There was concern that the sentimental novel was used by readers to undergo merely sensationalist experiences destabilizing their subjective identity and self-regulation and thereby undermining their ascribed, conventional and useful roles in society and nation. This concern seemed sensationally confirmed by the Europe-wide moral panic over what was much later called the 'Werther effect', or supposed emulation by numerous readers of the protagonist's suicide in Goethe's *Sorrows of Werter*. There was concern that the sentimental novel encouraged self-absorption displacing social engagement (see Introduction and Chapter 7). A similar claim was that the sentimental novel glamorized an excessive and disruptive sensibility in depicting modern love. In 1780, for example, a writer in the London *Lloyd's Evening Post* deplored 'those seductive engines of female dishonour, "Sentimental Novels"'.[17] There was the claim that the sentimental novel typically depicted characters superior in station to most readers, arousing socially destabilizing emulative desire in readers. So a writer to the *St James's Chronicle* could complain humorously in November 1794 that as part of wider and corrupting emulation, 'our good old English' names were being displaced by alien-sounding ones found in the high society of the sentimental novel.[18] One way of reading prominent sentimental novels is as producers' complex formal and stylistic negotiations with such real or imagined concerns by users.[19]

Related concerns were that sentimental sympathy for the unfortunate and oppressed could be feigned and was treated as an end in itself rather than a spur to positive modernizing social or political action (see Chapter 8).[20] Another concern was the commerciality of the sentimental novel, supposedly symptomatic of unmodern courtly decadence or falsely modern fashionable consumption, in either case undermining the social distinction maintaining economic and political order. The greatest concern, however, was that Sensibility and the sentimental novel were part of French cultural and hence political subversion, for all the above reasons, at a time when Britain and France were engaged in intermittently bellic contest for global domination.[21] As 'Epictetus' declared in 1777 in a jeremiad addressed to the editor of the London *Morning Post*, knowledge of French as well as 'a thorough knowledge of the Sentimental Novels, this happy age has produced' were thought necessary by young British practitioners of a certain (false) modernity.[22] Some, however, asserted that Sensibility and the sentimental novel imbued with properly British values would support an Anglified Sensibility surpassing both the unmodern and 'enlightened' falsely modern absolutism. In February 1771, a reviewer or puffer in the London *St James's Chronicle* urged readers to prefer the 'chaste' (and British) *Louisa. A Sentimental Novel* to 'some of the pernicious Bagatelles lately imported into this Country, and to others of a less delicate Cast, fabricated here by a Native of France'.[23]

In terms of particular politics, the sentimental novel could often be assignified in reference to information of political conditions circulated in one of its symbiotic forms, newspapers, coinciding with a novel's publication or not. Here important contributions were made by and seem to explain frequent republication of translated works such as Marmontel's *Belisarius*, Rousseau's *Julie*, Goethe's *Sorrows of Werter* and St Pierre's *Paul and Virginia*. All had explicit and broad political reference and were republished often enough to become part of the literary and hence political culture of the novel-buying and novel-borrowing public. But political analogies assignifiable to such works would be different for readers in Britain and those reading in original languages, places and times of publication, and would also be different over time. For example, Marmontel's *Bélisaire* (1767), ostensibly representing corruption and decline in the sixth-century Byzantine Empire, would for French readers have applied to France when the book was published. This was immediately after France's defeat in the Seven Years War, blamed on unmodernized government and associated social inequality and cultural decadence, while Britain was celebrating victory in that war when the English translation was published in 1767. Significantly, however, frequency in reprint of the English *Belisarius* surged when it became assignifiable as applying to Britain during and after the American War of Independence and again during the French Revolutionary and Napoleonic wars, after which republication quickly dropped away.

In particular, too, sentimental novels could be assignified as having political import from pointed passages. Chapter 19 of *The Vicar of Wakefield* (1766) contains the hero's discourse on the British constitution. This presents the by-then familiar Tory political theory that the royal prerogative had to be sustained so that the monarch could protect 'the people' (the middling sort) from aggrandizement by the landed class and financial interests inciting the 'rabble' in the name of a false liberty. The topic had particular relevance because of George III's controversial attempts to reassert royal prerogative following his accession in 1760. The Primroses, like the flourishing Tory nation envisaged by the vicar, are a model Tory-modern family based on pure relationships guided by benevolent patriarchal authority. Like the kingdom, however, they have been victimized and almost destroyed by a decadent, falsely modern representative of the landed class. Primrose's political discourse is emplotted, and also reinforced by the sympathy of other characters (and presumably readers) that the Primroses have earned. Toryism was often portrayed as unmodern by their Whig opponents, who represented themselves as the modernizers. By defending Toryism through the sympathetic, Abraham-like yet Job-like figure of Primrose, Goldsmith deployed the modern discourse of sentimentalism with familiar biblical archetypes to promote a Tory modernity and discredit a Whig false modernity, represented by the Primroses' persecutors.

The political import of the sentimental novel may be illustrated from a different perspective here by a brief history of its thematic, formal and commercial development through interaction of users, producers and contesting modernities of domestic politics and the ongoing Franco-British contest. In 1754, during a brief interval in the wars of this contest, Scottish man of letters William Guthrie complained about sentimental novels in the bullyingly learned Preface to his avowedly sentimental novel *The Friends: A Sentimental History*. Guthrie declared that 'this Manner of Writing has become much more frequent of late in *England* than any other', singling out 'those *French* Novels, which are every Day translated or disguised into our Language'.[24] Guthrie also deplored the stale form and matter of sentimental novels and claimed his own exercise of the form was more original, natural and authentically sentimental and hence more morally improving for the reader (and thus the nation) than 'those *French* Novels'. Guthrie's move here would become common as producers competed for sales by staging contests within the field of the sentimental novel. There were, for example, translations aiming to 'English' French Sensibility and sentimental fiction culturally and morally as well as linguistically. 'Chaste' French novels could be chosen, as with *Agreeable Ugliness* (1754), translated anonymously from Pierre Antoine de la Place by Sarah Scott, soon author of the feminist utopian novel *Millenium Hall* (1762) and sister of Elizabeth Montagu, leader of the 'Bluestocking' circle that aimed to modernize elites' social practice with women's culture. Another was *Select Moral Tales, Translated from the French, by a Lady* (1763), which 'selected' several highly moral tales from Marmontel's often titillating *Contes moraux. Select Moral Tales* was dedicated to Montagu and possibly by someone connected to both her and Richardson's circles.[25] Meanwhile, the sentimental novel maintained dialogue with another of its symbiotic forms, popularization of modern knowledges, as accounts of theories of aesthetic and moral affect, social sympathy, civil society and similar topics published from the 1750s by Francis Hutcheson, David Hume, Adam Smith and their successors.

Despite Guthrie's claim that sentimental novels had 'become much more frequent of late', and though the term 'sentimental' appeared in the print record and titles of works in various genres from the 1750s, the phrase 'sentimental novel' only appeared in the print record in the late 1760s and early 1770s. This was as a subtitle on English works such as *Margaretta, Countess of Rainsford: A Sentimental Novel* (anon., 1769), Treyssac de Vergy's *Henrietta, Countess of Osenvor: A Sentimental Novel* (1770; not a translation), *Louisa. A Sentimental Novel* (anon., 1771), *Emma; or, the unfortunate attachment. A Sentimental Novel* (anon., 1773; attrib. Georgiana, Duchess of Devonshire), *The Assignation: A Sentimental Novel* (anon., 1774), and more. 'Sensibility' began to appear in fiction titles by the early 1770s, with the English translation *The Tears of Sensibility: Novels* (1773), from François d'Arnaud's French. Titles were advertisements and these suggest that authors and publishers in the late 1760s and early 1770s, perhaps responding to the success of Sterne's *Sentimental Journey* (1768), thought readers wanted novels styled 'sentimental' to offer gynocentricity and conflicted modern love amid fashionable society with an occasional Continental touch. Further, the sudden appearance of 'sentimental' in novel titles when it had been circulating in culture and print for a while suggests an already existing common understanding between producers and readers about its meanings and formation of a novelistic vogue from readers' interest or from instigation by producers, or both.

While eighteenth-century producers nervously issued ever novel versions of the sentimental novel, Sterne's *A Sentimental Journey*, manifestly engaging in the ongoing contest of modernities with France, conducted war by other, cultural means. It caused a sensation on publication, imprints appeared once a year or more, and excerpts were widely reprinted in magazines and anthologies, suggesting that it became a manual for Sensibility-speak and assignifying sentimental anything. So by 1774 the burlesque *Sentimental Exhibition; or, Portraits and Sketches of the Times*, by Edward Long, could complain that the sentimental had become ubiquitous and commercialized: 'this is the Age of *Sentimentality*. We have Sentimental Comedies, Operas, Sermons, Farces, and Puppet Shows; Sentimental Novels, Histories, Journies, and Voyages; Sentimental Toasts; Sentimental Gingerbread; Sentimental Tobacco-boxes; Sentimental Handkerchiefs; Sentimental Pictures . . . ' (iii–iv). The writer could have added 'sentimental' songs, as the term frequently appeared in titles of cheap songsters, or song anthologies, along with other song types, indicating that the term had a certain circulation and positive signification downmarket. Publication history of the sentimental novel through the 1750s to mid-1770s, then, suggests emergence of an important and inevitably controversial commercialized medium for communicating the contested discourse of modernity.

Through the later 1770s and the 1780s 'sentimental' continued to be a common enough generic and marketing label on novels and quasi-novels, as in John Bew's *Memoirs of a Clergyman . . . A Sentimental History founded upon Facts* (1774), Alexander Bicknell's *Isabella; or, The Rewards of Good-nature: A Sentimental Novel* (1776), *Harcourt; a sentimental novel* (1780; spuriously attributed to Frances Burney), James Thistlethwaite's *The Man of Experience: A Sentimental History* (1781), the anonymous *Anna: A Sentimental Novel* (1782), the anonymous *Sentimental Memoirs, by a Lady* (1785), T. Potter's *Novellettes Moral and Sentimental* (1785), and the anonymous *The Mental Triumph: A Sentimental Novel* (1789). Such titles may suggest producers thought readers' desire was waning for sentimental novels of French or 'not British' origin or association that perhaps enabled them to 'feel' their selves as deliciously other, but was waxing for those properly (or defensively?) 'English' or 'British' in content, substance, culture, morality and values. From 1773 to 1777 *The Sentimental Magazine*, initially published by George Kearsley, assiduous purveyor of modern culture and knowledges mid- and downmarket, signalled a broader dialogue between the sentimental novel and one of its major symbiotic media, proliferating amateur-authored commercial miscellany magazines.[26] From 1771 Mackenzie's avant-garde *The Man of Feeling* had moved behind Sterne's *A Sentimental Journey* as a frequently reissued and excerpted, context-providing modern classic.[27] At the same time other kinds of works were also marketed in titles as 'sentimental', including an acting manual, poems, a magazine, a songster, literary anthologies, a pedagogical work for youngsters, familiar essays, several stage comedies, and travel journals and narratives. These indicate that the sentimental was now a familiar and Anglicized if shifting, contested and in some quarters controversial cultural-political category.

In the late 1770s and 1780s, as disparagement of certain kinds of sentimental novel increased and probably taste for these kinds decreased, producers of the sentimental novel responded successfully to political events and their market by variegating, diversifying and developing the form. In the public sphere the American crisis increased doubts of the ruling order's ability to modernize effectively, boosting existing reform movements, prompting new ones, expanding public political literature and inspiring representation in the belles-lettres as crisis in subjective identity, pure relationships and chronotopes of power. The 'sentimental citizen' was being formulated in literature and political activism as basis of, and necessary identity for, participation in a modernized political nation, while unmodern politics were supposed to exclude sentimental modern subjects from citizenship and require and produce people of damaged, corrupted or no sensibility, as illustrated particularly in 'philosophical romances' such as John Moore's *Zeluco* (1789).[28] Sentimental novels were often gynocentric in form to sharpen political import, centring on a conventional figure of disempowerment, but now that import was heightened by devices of gothic fiction in representing contested legitimacy, inheritance and property as analogues to the national and imperial crisis.[29] Cuing on *Clarissa*, kept contemporary by recurring imprints, such novels could be assignified as analogizing the unmodernized monarchic state operating through patriarchy, paternalism and patronage. These could be represented novelistically in the landed family as corporate identity and interest persisting over time and its oppressive power to restrict modern individualism and suppress modern love perceived as threatening its hegemony. This power was represented legally in, and fictionally by, the power to control women as necessary to the unlitigable transfer of property and power from one generation of men to the next. Examples were Reeve's *Old English Baron*, Sophia Lee's *The Recess* and novels by Charlotte Smith, Frances Burney and Mary Robinson, and later by Radcliffe, Wollstonecraft, Edgeworth and Austen.

To heighten representation of such politics of everyday life, some of these authors elaborated the language of affective description. This more complex subjectivity was emplotted as protagonists' struggle to self-discipline a sensibility provoked to extremes by powers and terrors, actual and illusory, of unmodernity or false modernity (see Chapter 9). Increasingly, sentimental affect was framed in the new technique of third-person narration with free indirect discourse, or filtered representation of characters' inner speech and thoughts. Emerging in the late 1780s, this technique seems designed to meet criticism of sentimental 'excesses' by converging supposedly more sensational and reader-engaging first-person narration and supposedly more controlled and authoritative third-person narration, and could be seen to resolve a conflict in politics of form and affect going back to the debate over Richardsonian reader engagement against Fieldingesque detachment. Again, readers who were aspiring men of modern feeling but little or no property or patronage could assignify common interests with heroines estranged in the architecture and operation of the landed estate as analogue to the national-imperial state and its ruling order.

At the end of the 1780s, however, the context for assignifying sentimental novels and similar literature politically was altered by the notorious 'Della Cruscan' verse exchange in *The World* magazine.[30] The periodical was one of numerous similar venues, one of the sentimental novel's principal symbiotic forms, for practice of fashionable amateur belletrism by aspirational men and women of the middle and would-be-genteel ranks. In literature, the sense of crisis caused by political dysfunction and middle ranks' political grievances could be thematized as crisis in personal identity and pure relations and formalized in unconventional or transgressive language and style. 'Della Crusca' (Robert Merry), and his similarly pseudonymous, predominantly female respondents, effectively did so in an exchange played out serially in the magazine, causing a sensation, imitation and reaction traceable into early Romanticism.[31] Almost immediately, the outbreak of the French Revolution prompted intense political debate and culture wars in Britain and Ireland. Some commentators ramped up existing critique of Sensibility to assign it a political purpose that was sinister and specific rather than indirect and general. They could cite Merry's prominent celebration of the Revolution in verse and actions, or outspoken support for the Revolution by the prominent sentimental poet and novelist turned Revolutionary political tourist, Helen Maria Williams. Della Cruscanism particularly and Sensibility generally were seen to represent a dangerously disruptive and seditious politicized cultural modernity expressed through excessive and delusively modern literary themes and forms. Some claimed that the potential of Sensibility as ground for cultural, social and political transgressiveness and 'excess' was exemplified in the 'excesses' of the French Revolution, leaders of which claimed leading French writers of Sensibility as inspiration and used the language of sensibility in political discourse.[32]

Sentimental literature was attacked as false modernity in verse burlesques such as Gifford's *Baviad* (1791) and *Maeviad* (1796) and Mathias's *Pursuits of Literature* (1794) and prose-fiction burlesques such as Beckford's *Modern Novel Writing; or, The Elegant Enthusiast* (1796). In a 1797 sermon of thanks for defeat of the French invasion of Ireland, the Revd Richard Graves condemned sentimental novels along with philosophical treatises and polemical pamphlets as instruments for undermining religion preparatory to revolution.[33]Certain market-alert writers and publishers provided a relatively short-lived wave of novels, much later termed 'Anti-Jacobin', indicting novelists Thomas Holcroft, William Godwin, Mary Wollstonecraft, Mary Hays and others for basing their expressly revolutionary versions of modernity on 'Jacobin' or radical French Revolutionary formulations of Sensibility.[34] Henceforth 'sentimental' may have gone almost unused in titles and advertisements, but the sentimental-modern topoi were incorporated in novels with other generic and marketing labels. There were attempts to distinguish 'false' and 'true', feigned and 'real' sensibilities: the 1797 imprint of Sarah Scott's 1766 humanitarian novel *The History of Sir George Ellison* was retitled *The Man of Real Sensibility; or, The History of Sir George Ellison*. This effort included Austen's 1811 *Sense and Sensibility*, after which, again, the term was rarely used in titles.

A year earlier, however, there was a prescient attempt to resolve this conflicted politics of theme and form. A large conger of London and provincial booksellers published a multi-volume set of *The British Novelists*. It belonged to a wave of similar publishers' projects originating in the 1770s. These were designed less to form a canon of the 'national' literature than to meet demand for authoritative, displayable, modern-looking, status-affirming sets of approved literary works affordable by the socio-culturally aspirational middle ranks. At the crisis of Britain's struggle for national survival against Revolutionary and Napoleonic modernity, *British Novelists* addressed patriotic sentiment by selecting English modern novels, and especially sentimental novels, that would supposedly enable eventual triumph over the historic national rival by forming individuals, families and communities for a superior, British modernity. The fifty-volume *British Novelists; with an Essay; and Prefaces, Biographical and Critical* by Anna Laetitia Barbauld was published in 1810 and republished in 1820. Price, format, quality, publishers, mode of distribution, editorial apparatus and especially novelists selected indicated that the set was designed for a niche market of self-conscious practitioners of the discourse of a certain modernity, what social history would suggest was an emergent professional, commercial, cultural and administrative elite, or people like Barbauld herself.

Barbauld was a prominent and respected daughter of the English provincial and Dissenting Enlightenment that had been leading British modernization in all spheres for more than half a century.[35] She was a respected poet of the politics of both public and domestic spheres, innovative writer for children and their subject-formation for modernity, (anonymous) political reform polemicist during the 1790s French Revolution debate, editor of Richardson's letters asserting his continuing relevance for British modernity, and supposed author of a pioneering and influential gothic 'fragment' emphasizing the protagonist's sensibility *in extremis*, published in 1773. Her *British Novelists* had competition in similar sets from publishers such as Harrison and Cooke, but it was purposely distinguished in particular ways, notably by its emphasis on sentimental novels. Competing sets of 'British Novelists' were typically marketed as both 'elegant' and 'cheap'. They were sold in sixpenny or shilling weekly numbers (or parts) to reach a wide market. They were designed when complete as sets for binding and display in the modern home. Advertisements emphasized illustrations, modernness of typography and quality of paper. They included some sentimental novels and much English humorous, adventure and satirical fiction of popular and down-market appeal and translations of similar kinds. Such collections seldom had named editors.

Like its competitors, Barbauld's selection was designed to be displayed as furniture books in the home. Unlike its competitors, however, it seems to have been sold only in complete sets requiring significant one-time outlay affordable by the middle and upper ranks – twelve guineas at a time when a labourer might earn half a guinea a week. It thereby distanced itself from the sixpenny- and shilling-number market. It was published by a large conger of respected and energetic mid-market firms and was advertised as suitable for commercial circulating libraries of the kind frequented by people like Barbauld. In her, it had a named editor who was a widely respected female intellectual, educator, literary innovator, and representative of a reformist but respectable modernity that would become identified in the nineteenth and twentieth centuries with a large portion of the middle classes. The major difference between Barbauld's *British Novelists* and others', however, was in content. Barbauld's set excluded non-British authors. It diminished broad humour, satire and earlier fiction, making itself less 'popular' and unmodern. By including a substantial proportion of novels published since the 1760s, it affirmed the worth of the 'modern novel' in supposedly forming its reader-subjects for modernity. Barbauld's set included eight sentimental novels from the 1760s on by women.[36] Her introductory 'essay' and the novels selected offered a genealogy of the modern novel as the novel for a specific modernity. Her introduction's contrast of the modern novel with chivalric romance prioritized sentimental modernity's core themes of subject formation and pure relationships of domesticity and sociability. Barbauld attributed the origin of such modern fiction to Richardson, widely seen then as originator of the sentimental novel in Britain and Continental Europe, thereby implicitly rejecting British Sensibility's supposed indebtedness to France.

Barbauld's *British Novelists* was republished in 1820 and heralded a succession of multi-volume sets and series of modern 'standard' and 'classic' novels, most elaborating the sentimental novel's formulation of modernity, priced at five or six shillings per volume for a mid-market readership many of whose adult males would, after intense struggle, be enfranchised nationally by the 1832 Reform Act and increasingly dominate local and municipal politics in the decades following. Meanwhile, technological innovation would enable the sentimental novel in sixpenny numbers to become the sentimental novel as sixpenny volume, priced for a downmarket readership many of whose adult male members would, after intense struggle, be enfranchised by the 1867 Reform Act. By then, however, the sixpenny-volume sentimental novel was more often deplored by the kind of people who read five-shilling sentimental novels for being as dangerously 'sensational' in its readers' politics. The political career of the sentimental novel continued in this way to the present, but that is another story.

The story here has used particular theories, methods and matters to essay a reader- or user-centred understanding of its title topic. It proposes that eighteenth-century producers' identification of a novel as sentimental was political in locating (marketing) that artefact within the field of what those producers speculated was knowledge of contested modernity desired by users. Correspondingly, assignification by such users of a novel as sentimental, regardless of how producers or others identified it, was likely political in each user's creation of meanings related to 'acquisition or exercise of power, status or authority' within a contested discourse of modernity, of which the sentimental was part and in which they had an interest. The same things happen today.

Notes

1. For the sentimental novel in North America, see Chapter 10.
2. See Roy Harris, *Introduction to Integrational Linguistics* (Kidlington: Pergamon, 1998).
3. See Alec McHoul, *Semiotic Investigations: Towards an Effective Semiotics* (Lincoln, NE: University of Nebraska Press, 2006).
4. See Harold Garfinkel, 'Evidence for Locally Produced, Naturally Accountable Phenomena of Order, Logic, Reason, Meaning, Method, etc. In and as of the Essential Quiddity of Immortal Ordinary Society (I of IV): an Announcement of Studies', *Sociological Theory* 6 (1988): 103–9.
5. See Reinhart Koselleck, *The Practice of Conceptual History: Timing History, Spacing Concepts*, trans. Todd Samuel Presner et al. (Stanford University Press, 2002), chapter 10, 'The Eighteenth Century as the Beginning of Modernity', 154–69.
6. See Roy Harris, *The Linguistics of History* (Edinburgh University Press, 2004). Harris denies that historiography can depict 'the past' and treats it as only one of a number of different kinds of historification such as historical fiction, heritage industries, monuments, state ceremonies and so on that may be credited by users as 'historical' to varying degrees.
7. Among the histories I have found useful are John Rule, *Albion's People: English Society, 1714–1815* (London: Longman, 1992); Geoffrey Holmes and Daniel Szechi, *The Age of Oligarchy: Pre-industrial Britain, 1722–1783* (London: Longman, 1993); John Brewer, *The Pleasures of the Imagination: English Culture in the Eighteenth Century* (University of Chicago Press, 1997).
8. The term 'assignify', a neologism as used here, indicates the process of assigning meaning, or of meaning-making.
9. For Sensibility in the history of ideas, see Markman Ellis, *The Politics of Sensibility: Race, Gender and Commerce in the Sentimental Novel* (Cambridge University Press, 1996).
10. The account of modernity here is adapted and historified from Anthony Giddens, *The Consequences of Modernity* (Stanford University Press, 1990); *Modernity and Self-identity: Self and Society in the Late Modern Age* (Stanford University Press, 1991); and *The Transformation of Intimacy: Sexuality, Love and Eroticism in Modern Societies* (Stanford University Press, 1992).
11. The print record used here includes online library-subscription versions of the Burney newspapers, British Library newspapers, Eighteenth Century

Collections Online, oclc Worldcat, English Poetry database and English Fiction database.

12. I use Sensibility for the eighteenth-century cultural movement and sensibility for the putative physico-subjective experience or condition.
13. See Ann Jessie Van Sant, *Eighteenth-Century Sensibility and the Novel: the Senses in Social Context* (Cambridge University Press, 1993).
14. James Boswell, *Life of Johnson* (1791), ed. R. W. Chapman (Oxford University Press, 1998), 480. See Chapter 3.
15. See R. F. Brissenden, *Virtue in Distress: Studies in the Novel of Sentiment from Richardson to Sade* (London: Macmillan, 1974).
16. See John Mullan, 'Sentimental Novels', in *The Cambridge Companion to the Eighteenth-Century Novel*, ed. John Richetti (Cambridge University Press, 1996), 243–4; Bonnie Latimer, *Making Gender, Culture, and the Self in the Fiction of Samuel Richardson* (Farnham: Ashgate, 2013).
17. 'Theatrical Intelligence', *Lloyd's Evening Post*, 7–9 Aug. 1780, n. p.
18. 'Names', *St James's Chronicle*, 15–18 Nov. 1794, n. p.
19. See Barbara M. Benedict, *Framing Feeling: Sentiment and Style in English Prose Fiction, 1745–1800* (New York: AMS Press, 1994).
20. See Thomas Keymer, 'Sentimental Fiction: Ethics, Social Critique and Philanthropy', in *The Cambridge History of English Literature, 1660–1780*, ed. John Richetti (Cambridge University Press, 2005), 587–91.
21. See Josephine Grieder, *Translations of French Sentimental Prose Fiction in late Eighteenth-Century England: the History of a Literary Vogue* (Durham, NC: Duke University Press, 1975).
22. 'Epictetus', 'For the Morning Post', *Morning Post*, Tues. 25 Mar. 1777, n. p.
23. '*Louisa, A Sentimental Novel*', *St James's Chronicle*, 19–21 Feb. 1771, n. p.
24. William Guthrie, *The Friends: a Sentimental History*, 2 vols. (London: T. Waller, 1754), 1, n. p.
25. The book was published at Gloucester, suggesting that it may have been by Sarah Chapone, who lived nearby and was mother-in-law of Hester Chapone, member of both Richardson's and Montagu's circles.
26. See Robert D. Mayo, *The English Novel in the Magazines, 1740–1815* (Evanston: Northwestern University Press, 1962).
27. See chapter 5, 'Polite Reading: Sentimental Fiction and the Performance of Response', in Paul Goring, *The Rhetoric of Sensibility in Eighteenth-Century Culture* (Cambridge University Press, 2005), 142–81.
28. See George E. Marcus, *The Sentimental Citizen: Emotion in Democratic Politics* (University Park: Pennsylvania State University Press, 2002).
29. See Melissa Sodeman, *Sentimental Memorials: Women and the Novel in Literary History* (Stanford University Press, 2015).
30. See W. N. Hargreaves-Mawdsley, *The English Della Cruscans and their Time, 1783–1828* (The Hague: Martinus Nijhoff, 1967).
31. See Jerome McGann, *The Poetics of Sensibility: a Revolution in Literary Style* (Oxford: Clarendon Press, 1996), chapter 9, 'The Literal World of the English Della Cruscans', 74–93.

32. See David J. Denby, *Sentimental Narrative and the Social Order in France, 1760–1820* (Cambridge University Press, 1994), chapter 4, 'Sentimentalism in the Rhetoric of the Revolution', 139–65.
33. Richard Graves, *A Sermon on the Deliverance of the Kingdom of Ireland from the Invasion lately Attempted by the French* (Dublin: W. Watson and Son, 1797), 22.
34. See C. B. Jones, *Radical Sensibility: Literature and Ideas in the 1790s* (Abingdon: Routledge, 2016).
35. See William McCarthy, *Anna Letitia Barbauld: Voice of the Enlightenment* (Baltimore: Johns Hopkins University Press, 2008).
36. These were: Frances Brooke, *History of Lady Julia Mandeville* (1760); Frances Burney, *Evelina* (1778) and *Cecilia* (1782); Elizabeth Inchbald, *A Simple Story* (1791); Charlotte Smith, *The Old Manor House* (1794); Ann Radcliffe, *The Romance of the Forest* (1791) and *The Mysteries of Udolpho* (1794); Maria Edgeworth, *Belinda* (1801).

CHAPTER 2

Sensible Readers: Experiments in Feeling in Early Prose Fiction by Women

Ros Ballaster

In amatory fiction by women of the early eighteenth century, narrators play close and unusual attention to the modulation of feeling in both protagonist and reader. Eliza Haywood defends the warmth of her amatory representations in her dedication to *Lasselia: or the Self-Abandoned. A Novel* (1723) by saying that 'without the Expression being invigorated in some measure proportionate to the Subject, 'twou'd be impossible for a Reader to be sensible how far it touches him, or how probable it is that he is falling into those Inadvertencies which the Examples I relate wou'd caution him to avoid'.[1] Only when we are 'sensible', she observes, are we effectively forewarned against the sway of passion. What is it to be 'sensible' how far something touches us? Haywood proposes that we pay attention to our feeling responses. Modern-day usage of the term 'sensible' suggests a lack of feeling, but in the eighteenth century it pointed to an *alertness* to feeling. What is sensible is 'That which can be perceived by the mind, intellect, or senses' or that which is perceptible through the senses.[2]

Inflaming Experiments

John Bender notes the proximity of the terms 'experiment' and 'experience' in the prose fiction of Daniel Defoe and Jonathan Swift. In the fiction of these authors' female contemporaries, it is arguable that we can observe female experiment in the experiential variations of amorous feeling.[3] Karen Bloom Gevirtz elaborates, arguing that the novel provided an environment for women to test and contest the increasingly scientific, specialized and exclusionary forms of authoritative knowing, fielded in natural philosophy and embodied in masculine institutions such as the Royal Society. Both the new form of the novel and the new technologies of science (the microscope and the air pump) distance and detach us from the bodily senses that are the ground of our perception in order to correct inevitable error. Emergent structures of 'omniscient' narration, Gevirtz suggests, are experimented with in fiction by Aphra Behn, Jane Barker, Eliza Haywood and Mary Davys.[4]

Narrative is a laboratory in which readers can test different kinds of response and predict outcomes. And the 'sensible' was often in the eighteenth century concatenated with 'experiment': not only in terms of a testing of observed phenomena but also testing the sensitivity of the *instrument* used for such observation. In describing experiments with heat and an iron tube and the force of the air expelled in relation to the angle at which it is heated over a fire, a short pamphlet on *Fires Improv'd* notes, 'If such a Tube be bent, the Experiment will be much more sensible.'[5]

Returning to Haywood's defence of her fanning of amatory flames in *Lasselia*, and newly alert to the language of experimentation, we should also recognize the presence of an element of calculation in that same defence. We read, Haywood argues, in order to protect ourselves from falling victim to a powerful external force – passion – by learning to manage our response. There is no question that passion will touch us. It is for the reader to judge *how far* the warmth of a representation touches him – not whether it does or not. It is the job of the amatory fiction writer to take readers to just the right point, a point where readers can both feel and observe themselves feeling. Because, after all, the job of amatory fiction is to provide its readers with a surrogate experience of being moved to feel by an external object so that they can accurately calculate how – in real life – to defend themselves from it. The second-hand or surrogate experience of fiction is not so much a spatial substitute as a temporal one: it prepares a reader. It provides a cognitive affordance for future understanding.

Amatory fiction is the privileged mode of representation of the early eighteenth century to explore the power of minds to feel with and alongside others. Both intradiegetic and extradiegetic narrators consistently seek to imagine and anticipate their effect in the mind of their reader. The feeling character with whom we sympathize in these fictions is explicitly gendered. Male and female characters feel differently, although both genders feel intensely. As Kate Williams helpfully summarizes, 'Haywood distinguished between masculine and feminine ardour: her virtuous heroines dream, sigh, faint, and totter while men are intent on sexual content.'[6] However, the receptive mind – the mind of the imagined reader – is most often conceived as *un*gendered. Reading is conceived as a virtual mechanics of affect. In these early experiments we can also see the novel anticipating its own future grip on the feelings of the reading public.

See, for example, a telling moment in Penelope Aubin's *The Noble Slaves*. Here, the Spaniard Lopez conceals his love for and marriage to Teresa in order to play along with Venetian Eleonora's sudden passion for him. He and his companion, the more refined Frenchman Hautville, are lodged as prisoners of the Algerian governor with Eleonora, the governor's cast-off slave, as their jailer. Eleonora promises to aid the European men's escape if they will take her with them. Readers are aware that there is a more delicate approach to the situation than Lopez's duplicity: Hautville, loyal to his beloved Emilia, is shocked at Lopez's hypocrisy. Nonetheless, the extradiegetic narrator breaks off to offer a mitigation of Lopez's behaviour:

> Life is sweet, and I hope my Reader will not condemn him for what his own Sex must applaud in Justification of themselves: For what brave, handsome young Gentleman would refuse a beautiful Lady, who loved him, a Favour?[7]

The narrator's 'I hope' is ambiguous. We are not only uncertain whether the narrator does indeed 'hope' that readers will see this is excusable in a young, lustful man, or rather have arrived at more refined forms of judgement in the course of seeing heroic and sensible virtue displayed in its many varieties in this complex transnational tale of multiple couplings, separations and sexual danger. We are also uncertain as to which 'sex' is assumed to be reading the passage. Is it the Reader who should refer to his 'own Sex' or are we referred to Lopez's 'own Sex' (as opposed to our own as readers, assumed to be female) for this, admittedly weak, justification? Narrator and reader are either ungendered or have the facility to identify across both masculine and feminine genders in their reading. But characters' sensations and behaviours tend to be strongly gender-marked in terms of the ethical licence they are afforded in the fiction. In other words, male characters are apparently afforded more freedom of action and feeling than female characters; however, the narrator's diegetic stance is often, as in the case of *The Noble Slaves*, shaded with an irony that invites the reader to scrutinize the justification for taking such freedoms.

Variety and Uniformity

Recent work by critics such as Earla Wilputte, Aleksondra Hultquist and Rebecca Tierney-Hynes has invited us to look more carefully at the rhetoric of feeling in fiction of the later seventeenth and early eighteenth century.[8] Wilputte identifies with clarity the tension originating in eighteenth-century empiricist theory of the mind between the specificity of the individual case and the universality of the general response. 'Poets, authors, and painters', she contends, 'struggled to find the appropriate mode for communicating an individual's passions and ideas so that people could share in and understand the feelings of others'.[9] One way to address this tension in amatory fiction was to package stories in collections that illustrate variety. Sensitivity to feeling could then be cultivated as well as disciplined in a reader through the experience of variants within a shared field (that of the passions). So too, on the individual level, we must pass through a variety of passions in order to differentiate them and arrive at an ethical evaluation of their respective worth. In amatory fiction, 'variety' is explicitly understood as a necessary presence at the level of plot for working out what we might see as a set of experiments in narrative affect which would come to provide the (later silenced) ground for the sentimental novel.

As William Warner outlines, the rise to cultural legitimacy of the novel in the mid-eighteenth century is predicated on the suppression of the shaping force of earlier, immersive (absorptive) fictions.[10] Warner characterizes the 'novel' as a mid-eighteenth century media event, the product of a media industry's attempts to respond to and shape the pleasures of (new kinds of) the reader. Its entertainment values are licensed (made respectable as well as liberated) by the claim to overcome the 'absorptive' pleasures of reading fostered by popular fictional entertainments of the early eighteenth century by encouraging a counterforce of 'critical' reading.

Aubin was, as Warner identifies, the poster girl for the ethical turn of amatory fiction towards the licensed novel. The 'Preface' to her 1739 *Collection of Entertaining Histories and Novels* understands variety to be a necessary vehicle of virtuous instruction, in terms of not only a variety of incident but also a variety of tone: from the energetic narration of incident to the assertion of general truths.

> Her Relations are interspersed with a very entertaining Variety of Incidents, which flow naturally from her Subjects, and keep the Mind attentive and delighted; so that the longest of them cannot tire: And she mingles every where, as Occasions offer, very instructive Observations and Reflections, all tending to that one uniform End which was the Principal Scope of her Writings; the mending of the Hearts of her Readers; the Encouragement of Religion and Virtue; and the discountenancing of Impiety and Vice. And so well has she observed the Rules above set down for constituting a good Novel, that her Heroes and Heroines are generally made successful or unsuccessful, happy or unhappy, according to their Merit. [11]

It was Aubin's contemporary, Haywood, who illustrated the counterexample. Albert J. Rivero summarizes the compelling evidence that Samuel

Richardson was the author of the anonymous preface to this 1739 Aubin collection (Aubin had died in 1730), evidence that supports the argument that Richardson identified himself with what he saw as Aubin's moralized fiction by contrast to Haywood's libertinism. Richardson had printed the first and fourth volumes of the third edition of Eliza Haywood's *Secret Histories, Novels, and Poems* in 1732, but appears to be targeting Haywood when he complains on the title-page of *Pamela* that 'too many Pieces ... tend to *inflame* the Minds they should *instruct*'.[12] Haywood was characterized as a writer who – by the terms of her own argument for the virtue of romantic fiction – took her reader *too* far. As the theory of sentiment goes, *over*-stimulation (too much touching) makes readers *in*sensible to feeling, unable to observe themselves responding. And the theory of sentiment requires not only that we feel ourselves feeling, but that the stimulation and our response lead to the production of *virtue* rather than imitative vice.

Other critics have paid attention to the rise of the novella sequence in this period and its special attraction to women: most notably Josephine Donovan in her *Women and the Rise of the Novel, 1405–1726*.[13] Donovan does not set her examples, however, in the context of theory of mind and the phenomenology of reception. Her interest is in juridical models, casuistry and the exceptional case as the proof of rule.

If we look at the longer history of sentimental fiction, we come to realize that the forensic observation of the mechanics of feeling – which was later to become an impediment to moving plot forward in the increasingly fragmented form of sentimental fiction such as Laurence Sterne's *A Sentimental Journey* (1768) and Henry Mackenzie's *The Man of Feeling* (1771) – was integral to *plot* and acts of *plotting* in the earlier works. To put it more simply, plots must proliferate for the rich variety of feeling to unfold and be subjected to the reflective consideration of the narrator on behalf of, or in anticipation of, the judgement of readers. While plots vary, it is assumed that readers are consistent: at least in their desire for the stimulation of feeling.

Acts of plotting are, of course, also frequently associated with forms of political intrigue. And literary historical accounts of seduction or amatory fiction have long recognized that the anxious oscillation between resistance and complicity, in the depiction of the female protagonist who is the object of predatory male sexual attention, serves as a means to explore urgent debates about the nature of political authority and the extent and limits of political obedience to it.[14] Toni Bowers argues that the political energies that generated the seduction fictions of Behn, Manley and Haywood resulted in a new kind of fiction 'where inner motivation and conflict could be represented in detail, in ordinary language, by non-elite writers (including women), and in something approaching, or at least mimicking, real time'.[15]

However, the part played by variety and the sequential performance of story in amatory fiction is not adequately explained by the proposition that they test different ways of playing out scenarios of political probability. Indeed, the complex and contradictory impulses of mind and sense staged in these works risk being reduced to representation of political ambivalence in which sentiment is little more than an analogue of political loyalty. Casting a light backward from the later developments in sentimental fiction of formal narrative techniques of fragmentation, and narratological distantiation from character – rather than forward from partisan models (Whig and Tory) of contractual power relations – invites a rather different analysis: one that proposes amatory fictions as forms of thought-experiment.

At the heart of these thought-experiments lies an apparent paradox: that a shared and single model of sentimental mind (among readers) is premised on 'variety' (the serial and sequential plotting of story). Only through an exploration of the variety and variation of romantic story does the 'sensible' reader come to participate in a sociable community and recognize the sameness of the structure of mind. Not only should a collection display variety, but within each story variety is also a necessary stimulus to keep a reader interested. See, for example, the conclusion to a story entitled 'Fortune Favours the Bold: or, the Happy Milaneze', which is inset into Aubin's *The Life and Amorous Adventures of Lucinda*. A well-read sailor named Jonathan has entertained on a long sea journey a group of travellers, including Lucinda, now happily reunited with her long-lost first love Charles. He draws to a close and the narrator observes: 'Here the Mariner finished his Story, which by the Variety of Accidents very much pleased the Company.'[16]

Stories require variety of accident and incident, but early experiments in fiction also mix genre – letter, poetry and prose narrative – in a conscious promotion of variety. When short novellas are published separately, they are often brought together into collections in which readers are invited to test out the variation across cases (as in Aubin's *Collection*). As later in the period, sententious moralism is not so much opposed to sentimental stimulus as an integral part of its effect and affect. Amatory fictional works by women writers of this type include Delarivier Manley's *The Power of Love* (1720), Eliza Haywood's *Love in Its Variety: Being a Collection of Select Novels* (1727) and Penelope Aubin's *A Collection of*

Entertaining Histories and Novels, Designed to Promote the Cause of Virtue and Honour (1739).

Stories in these collections originated in and were translated from other European sources. Our interest here does not lie in variation from source material but rather in the attention that the authors – as translators, as narrators – pay to the temporal anticipation of 'sensible' reading, the effect of the external object (plot) on the mind of their readers. The nature of the plots told is not arbitrary and unmotivated in this dynamic. We might characterize this as a process whereby the passions become an 'object' of attention and analysis. The passions are understood to drive the person towards or away from another object – we are either attracted or repulsed by that object which we seek to possess or evade. But we can see that passion is constructed in this process as a force *external* to the person: it is a force open to enquiry by the mind but still not capable of full integration *into* the self.

Reflecting on Various Effects

Eliza Haywood explicitly theorizes the role of variety in understanding love in precisely these terms in her *Reflections upon the Various Effects of Love* (1726). The extradiegetic narrator early asserts that we have over-invested love with a power over us:

> Let us take away a little of that almighty Power which we ascribe to *Love* and allow something more to *Nature* and those Inclinations born with us, and we shall immediately reconcile the seeming Impossibility. *Love*, like the Grape's potent Juice, but heightens *Nature*, and makes the conceal'd Sparks of Good, or Ill, blaze out, and show themselves to the wond'ring World! It gives an Energy to our Wishes, a Vigour to our Understanding, and *adds* to the *Violence* of our Desires, but *alters* not the *Bent* of them.[17]

The direct address to the reader mirrors the argument made. The argument is that Love is something *outside* of individual character which only exacerbates its natural tendencies. So too, the first-person plural 'we' (the 'wond'ring World') are positioned outside this dynamic to watch how the encounter with the passion makes visible the 'true' character of those on which it impacts. By extension, the act of observing the interaction of passion and person will also reveal the 'true nature' of the reader. However, where the effects are various at the level of plot, the proposition of the speculating author is that they are consistent in the 'shared' mind of the reader. Indeed, the narrator shapes the notion of 'sentiment' as a reflective response to the feeling of others, which can be generalized and is common to all thinking beings.

Exactly the same sentiment was explained in an earlier work that Haywood was clearly conversant with: Delarivier Manley's *The Power of Love in Seven Novels* (1720). Manley's collection took five of its stories from William Painter's *Palace of Pleasure* (1566), which Painter had taken from stories by Matteo Bandello and Marguerite de Navarre. In *Love in Its Variety: Being a Collection of Select Novels* (1727), all the stories in which came from Matteo Bandello, Haywood included a variation on one of the tales in *The Power of Love*. Haywood's 'The Female Revenge; or, the Happy Exchange' reworks Manley's 'The Wife's Resentment', a tale in which a genteel woman violently dispatches the aristocratic man who persuaded her into a secret marriage, on discovering that he has married another woman of his own class.

Although both Manley's and Haywood's tales have their source in the Italian original of Matteo Bandello, it is evident that Haywood is ringing the changes on Manley's bloodthirsty rendering. In Haywood's version the first wife's attempts at revenge fail, her own infidelity is revealed and she dies of poison, leaving the husband to marry a virtuous woman of his own class. Penelope Aubin also reworked this same story in 1722 in her *Life and Amorous Adventures of Lucinda*; the inset story, 'Conjugal Duty rewarded; or, The Rake reform'd', has the first wife, Panthea, prove her virtue to her unfaithful husband, Sebastian, by saving him from assassination by her vengeful brothers; she eventually wins him back after the death of his second wife.[18]

Resemblance lay in more than a shared spine of a plot. Another tale in Manley's collection entitled 'The Fair Hypocrite' concerns a virtuous duchess whose decision not to act on her passion for the young man she fell in love with when she was the young bride of an elderly man is rewarded by marriage to her beloved on her husband's death. The narrator describes the villainy of the old duke's counsellor, Sigisbert, who is himself enamoured of the duchess and the cause of her many trials and tribulations:

> I have often thought, that the Passions of Love, or Anger, are more or less violent according to the Temper of the Person who is seized by them. We esteem such a One very wrathful, or very amorous; call his Rage dreadful, his love extream, an implacable Enemy, or a raging Lover; without considering, that this proceeds purely from the Nature of the Man.[19]

The narrators in Manley's and Haywood's collections arrive at the same conclusion having reviewed their familiarity with a variety of tales. This they express as a general sentiment proved by a range of particular and various incidents: ergo, the passion of love exacerbates the natural tendency of the soul rather than inventing it. So, too, sentimental fiction will have an impact on the mind of the reader to stimulate its natural character. Early sentimental fictions are designed to train the natural tendency of the reader's passions, to harness those passions to virtue. In so doing, they mix a variety of genres and styles and sentiments within a general explicit framework: tutelage combined with sensation.

Reflections works this way, mixing contemporary narratives, past historical and classical precedents, extracts from poetry familiar and ascribed to Haywood's circle – all with an eye to anticipating and framing how a reader should 'sense' them. Readers both sense/feel the tale *and* make sense of it. The narratives that are embedded in *Reflections* illustrate the point: that diverse example (variety) generates general sentiment. *Reflections* opens by listing a series of historical and classical examples. First listed are examples of those with a reputation for wisdom who reveal their vulnerability in love and the terrible violence that ensues: Ninus's passion for Semiramis; Philip I of France and the Countess of Anjou; Crispus's incestuous desire for his father Constantine's wife; the passion of the Countess of Castile for the Moor Abdellraiser; the loss of Troy for love of Helen; Antony and Cleopatra. 'How frequently do we see', the narrator asks us to recall, examples in everyday life of those brought low by love? 'He that woul'd go about to decide the Contest in favour of either opposite, wou'd find his Judgment extremely at a Loss, and at last be oblig'd to leave that Question undetermin'd.' However, an equal number of counterexamples swiftly follow: Artemisa, whose love for her husband Mausolus continued beyond death; Paulina's attempted suicide to die with her husband, Seneca; Sulpitia's fine writings prompted by her love for her future husband; the authors Sappho and Ovid, Aphra Behn, Sidney and Sedley who are all inspired by the 'melting God'.[20]

The last half of *Reflections* concerns two extended narratives designed to demonstrate a number of sentiments. The story of Sophiana demonstrates the extremity to which love can drive a violent spirit as well as the fact that second love can be as strong as first: Sophiana's obsessive passion for the lover Aranthus, who has lost interest in her, leads her to be taken for a madwoman. However, she is saved by Martius who courts her; her passion for him proves equally strong. That of Hibonia of Norbania demonstrates the strangeness of male taste: the nobleman's passion for his prostitute mistress, Putania, remains strong despite evidence of her infidelity and decline in attractiveness. Both examples evidence consistency in that the main protagonists remain true to their ruling passions (if not their love object) despite variety of incident. Throughout, the extradiegetic narrator deploys *occupatio*, the apparent denial of a rhetorical purpose, in order to prove her point. Thus, when Aranthus sends Sophiana a dismissive letter, the narrator turns to her reader for judgement:

> With what Emotions the Breast of this unhappy Lady was agitated at reading Admonitions so insolent in him who gave them, I need not inform any who will give themselves the Trouble to consider Nature even in the meanest person, much more how it must operate in a Woman of *Sophiana's* Birth and Quality and who had been accustom'd to receive only Admiration.[21]

The reader is invited to occupy the responses of the female protagonist by an imaginative projection which the narrator does not need to spell out. When Sophiana falls for Martius, the narrator intervenes again to defend her from possible opprobrium by her readers: 'I appeal to those most fix'd in their Devoirs, if they have not felt some of the Waverings I speak of, and imagin'd themselves in Love many times before they became so in earnest.'[22]

So too is the case of Hibonio. After ten years of happiness with his lovely well-born wife, Harmonia, who gives him ten children, he falls into bad company. Ensnared by a woman of pleasure, he falls passionately in love, sets her up as his mistress and is corrupted by her into many other vices. On his return to his family, he moves his mistress with him. Putania, the mistress, demonstrates the dangerous outcomes of 'variety' – 'having been accustomed to subsist by Variety of Embraces',[23] she cannot help taking other lovers and even the realization of her infidelity does not cause Hibonio to reject her. She elopes with one of her sparks but returns to him for money. The narrator confirms that she continues to entertain lovers: 'Impossible, one would imagine, it must be, that after this repeated proof of the highest Baseness, she could be thought on by *Hibonio* but with the utmost Detestation, yet so prevailing to him were the Endearments of her Embraces, that rather than not partake of them at all, he could be contented to share them with others.'[24] In this final tale, Haywood resorts to another ploy in her sentimental arsenal: the 'impossibility' of feeling with a protagonist hardened to absolute vice, or so immersed in sense that he or she cannot demonstrate the kind of sense the reader learns – that necessary critical distance – through the act of reading and exposure to the variety of the stories encountered.

Expanding on Variety

Story collections by women of the first decades of the eighteenth century provided a larger canvas to experiment with the same effect Haywood's *Reflections* achieve: they exploit 'variety' to render sentimental connection for characters and their readers alike. They provide a bridge between the abstracted allegorized treatments of the passions found in earlier romances and the particularized depictions of the mechanics of feeling in the novel of the later eighteenth century. While they draw on the short novellas popular in Spain, Italy and France for their sources, they often relocate them to England. For example, Haywood's version of the Bandello story provides it with an exiled cavalier hero who travels from Portsmouth to Cadiz to evade capture by the Cromwellian forces. And – amid the familiar patterns of violent revenge and state intrigue – the collections also provide moments that have the limpid lachrymosity of later works. The hero of Manley's first tale in *The Power of Love*, the Count of Mendoza, melts into tears at the earliest opportunity rather than seizing his chance to seduce Reginia, Duchess of Savoy, with whom he shares a violent mutual attraction. As he delivered the story of his faithful love, 'he sigh'd a thousand times whilst he continued his mournful Tale, his Colour often changed, his fine Eyes stood full of Tears, which sometimes in large Drops roul'd down his lovely Face'.[25] They admit their mutual feelings but nobly lay them aside and she returns to her husband.

The first story in Haywood's six-story collection, *Love in Its Variety*, [26] is entitled 'The Distress'd Beauty; or, Love at a Venture' and has a number of resemblances to Richardson's *Pamela.* A Spanish grandee, Don Basilio, walking in his estates, comes across a young woman breast-feeding her child and she falls before his feet. She says she has been deserted by her husband, and has begged for assistance but been turned away; his heart was 'so much affected with it [her story], that he could not restrain his Tears'.[27] He ensconces the woman Letitia with her child under the protection of the gardener's family, but Basilio finds himself falling in love with her despite the fact he is already married. Letitia undertakes sewing for his wife and becomes part of the family but, when Basilio's wife dies suddenly, rejects his advances. Furious, he casts her out to return to her destitute state, but has a change of heart when he overhears her melancholy conversation with her child at the gates of the estate, in which she robustly defends the preciousness of her virtue. Proclaiming her the 'Wonder of thy Sex',[28] Basilio reforms and accepts her back into his household, discovering soon after that she is in fact the well-born wife of his own son who returns suddenly to the family home after unavoidable delays in Italy.

Aubin's story collections include acts of resistant violence by women of more frequency and extremity than those found in either Manley or Haywood. These cohabit with more overtly sententious interventions by a narrator keen to extol the values and virtues of a militant Christian heroism often contrasted with oriental despotism and proving God's merciful providentialism. Her heroes and heroines travel across and between Islamic Africa, Turkey and Christian Europe accumulating companions, confidantes and antagonists in equal measure. Scenes of sentimental reunion are of equal force to those of violent resistance. Eleonora in *The Noble Slaves* illustrates the agential violence Aubin invests in her heroines when she tells the sea captain who has abducted her, 'my Tongue shall never call you Husband; I would sooner suffer hot Pincers to rend it from the Root than speak those Words, or answer to such a Question'.[29] But equally, in *The Noble Slaves*, Charlot is providentially reunited with the man who seduced and abandoned her when he is shipwrecked on the Algerine shore and brought to her house to recover. On recognizing her:

> He fell at her Feet transported, all he said was confused, he embraced her Knees, gazed on her Face, and at length fainted falling down on his Face. Her Tenderness for him revived; she strove to raise him, but through Weakness and Surprize swooned falling by him. This Sight was extremely moving.[30]

It was Elizabeth Rowe who was, however, to turn the physiological drama of the passions into the kind of spiritual elevation that suffused later sentimental works. Her 1728 *Friendship in Death* provides twenty letters from deceased persons to those for whom they had earthly attachments. Rowe's correspondents admit their continuing attachment to those they loved in life (a two-year-old to his mother, a devoted wife to her rakish husband) and they leave their epistles in closets or make visitations in order to console or reform their correspondents. Heaven is not somewhere free of sensation but rather a place where divine love brings sense into full alignment with the higher order of reason and understanding. Hence, a young man who has died writes to the dependent girl with whom he grew up in a privileged household: 'I remember no Engagement to the World, but my Affection for you nor has Death effac'd the tender Impression, but what was then a natural Sympathy, is now a rational Esteem.'[31] Indeed, earthly sensation, he argues, is a form of training in preparation for the afterlife: 'This gentle Passion was the Stamp of Heaven on my Soul, the first soft Impression it receiv'd, and it gains new Energy in these happy Regions, of pure Beneficence and Love.'[32]

Rowe takes the erotic dynamics of the amatory fiction sequence and repurposes them to express metaphysical sentiments. Peter Walmsley observes that Rowe was shaping a Whiggish view of reformed religion, building on the insights of Joseph Addison's *Spectator* papers and Isaac Watts's *Death and Heaven* (1722).[33] For both, sense is not suddenly removed in death but rather liberated into virtue. Watts insists that heaven will be a place of not 'dull Uniformity', but 'delightful Variety'.[34]

Sceptical Conclusions

The proto-sentimental explorations we have identified in the amatory fictions of the first decades of the eighteenth century share with the later developments of sentiment an abiding paradox. Dealing in the currency of the heart appears to challenge the checks and balances of market forces. It asserts a transcendent value beyond calculation. And yet, counting the variety of ways and measuring the cost of feeling only reconfirms the categorial dominance of the language of trade. Instances of feeling arouse sympathetic responses in readers of equal and equivalent force. Gillian Skinner and Markman Ellis have forcefully impressed on modern readers the coincidence of economies of feeling and finance in later eighteenth-century fiction.[35] So too in the early sentimental experiments under discussion here, community of feeling might be seen as a market ploy. The very assertion and assertiveness of sentiments about the power of variety to produce cognitive community invites our suspicion. This dynamic is, of course, radically *un*stable and could be seen as an attempt to conceal the fear that in fact the *reader's* responses might be various and the *characters* repetitive and formulaic. The imagining of virtuous community as the product of a depiction of individualistic passion may be a necessary strategy for writers struggling to create an audience for a new medium.

In the new ecology of the novel, by contrast with the dominant popular vehicle for story before its arrival – the theatre – there is an inevitable nervousness about the unknown nature of an audience not physically present at the point of production. The novelist/narrator responds by trying to imagine reception in the mind of an absent reader. Haywood's *Reflections* again provides a telling illustration: in January 1727 a second part of *Reflections on the Various Effects of Love* was advertised as part of a new edition with 'a Key to the whole'.[36] Sadly no copies survive.[37] The proposal to publish a key may have been a repurposing of a text for the market (a way of generating variety in the mode of reception). Or it might be taken as an admission that there were different responses and ways of reading works despite the vision of a single cognitive pattern of response. Some readers may have recognized 'real' persons in the text. They certainly should have done. One of Haywood's examples in *Reflections* of the various ways in which love takes a person, depending on the character of her soul, is a poetic contest between two women over a lost lover entitled 'Celia and Evandra'. [38] This is certainly a secret historical rendering of the competition between female authors Martha Fowke Sansom (known as 'Clio') and Eliza ('Evandra') Haywood for the affections of Aaron Hill.[39] Evandra, unsurprisingly, proves her finer nature in being generous and nobly reconciled to the rival who has displaced both women, where Celia is selfishly indulging her sensible distraction at the loss.

The promise of a published key affords this 'secret' kind of reading to a wider public. Equally, it tends to militate against the 'general' sentiments that such narratives are apparently designed to afford their reader. The sensational pleasure promised in the secret history, of identifying the historical and contemporary figures behind the pastoral aliases, is very different from the pleasure of extrapolating universal understanding of the passions from individual cases. However, as we have seen, variety harnessed to virtue is the motivating force of these early experiments.

Later sentimental fiction may have learned from these earlier examples, even as authors like Samuel Richardson sought to distance themselves from some of the more obviously stimulating, absorptive effects in the works of Haywood especially. Inconsistency, the constant variation of feeling, sudden shifts from the very particular to the apparently universal, did not hinder the aesthetic experience of readers. It was what they came to expect: the probabilistic pleasure they learned to anticipate through reading amatory fiction.

Notes

1. 'To the Right Honourable the Earl of Suffolk and Bindon', *Lasselia; or, the Self-Abandoned. A Novel* (London: D. Browne and S. Chapman, 1724), vi–vii
2. 'Sensible, adj., n., and adv.' OED Online. June 2017. Oxford University Press.

3. John Bender, 'Novel Knowledge: Judgment, Experience, Experiment', in *This Is Enlightenment*, ed. Clifford Siskin and William Warner (University of Chicago Press, 2010), 284–300.
4. Karen Bloom Gevirtz, *Women, the Novel, and Natural Philosophy*, 1660–1727 (Basingstoke: Palgrave Macmillan, 2014).
5. Nicolas Gauger, *Fires improv'd: being a new method of building chimneys, so as to prevent their smoaking: in which A Small Fire, shall warm a Room better than a much Larger made the Common Way. With the manner of altering such Chimneys as are already Built, so that they shall perform the same Effects. Illustrated with Cuts. Written in French, by Monsieur Gauger: made English and improved, by J. T. Desaguliers, M. A. F. R. S. By whom is added, the manner of making coal-fires, as useful this new-way, as the wood-fires propos'd by the French author, Explain'd by an Additional Plate. The whole being suited to the Capacity of the meanest Work-Man* (London: J. Senex, and E. Curll, 1715), 22.
6. Kate Williams, 'Women Writers and the Rise of the Novel', in *The History of British Women's Writing, 1690–1750*, ed. Ros Ballaster, vol. iv of *The History of British Women's Writing*, general eds. Jennie Batchelor and Cora Kaplan (Basingstoke: Palgrave Macmillan, 2010), 113–26, 115.
7. Penelope Aubin, *A Collection of Entertaining Histories and Novels, Designed To Promote the Cause of Virtue and Honour. Principally founded on FACTS, and Interspersed with a Variety of beautiful and instructive Incidents. By Mrs PENELOPE AUBIN. And now first collected IN THREE VOLUMES*, 3 vols. (London: D. Midwinter, A Bettesworth and C. Hitch, J and J Pemberton, R. Ware, C. Rivington, A. Ward, J. and P. Knapton, T. Longman, R. Hett, S. Austen and J. Wood, 1739), 1: 45–6.
8. Earla Wilputte, *Passion and Language in Eighteenth-Century Literature: the Aesthetic Sublime in the Work of Eliza Haywood, Aaron Hill, and Martha Fowke* (New York: Palgrave Macmillan, 2014); Aleksondra Hultquist *Equal Ardor: Female Desire, Amatory Fiction, and the Recasting of the Novel*, 1680–1760 (Charleston, SC: Proquest UMI Dissertation Publication, 2011); Rebecca Tierney-Hynes, *Novel Minds: Philosophers and Romance Readers, 1680–1740* (Basingstoke: Palgrave Macmillan, 2012).
9. Wilputte, *Passion and Language in Eighteenth-Century Literature*, 5.
10. William B. Warner, *Licensing Entertainment: the Elevation of Novel Reading in Britain*, 1684–1750 (Berkeley: University of California Press, 1998).
11. Aubin, *A Collection of Entertaining Histories and Novels*, n.p.
12. Albert J. Rivero, 'General Introduction', *Pamela: Or, Virtue Rewarded*, vol. II of *The Cambridge Edition of the Works of Samuel Richardson* (Cambridge University Press, 2011), xxxvi–xxxvii.
13. Josephine Donovan, *Women and the Rise of the Novel, 1405–1726* (Basingstoke: Palgrave Macmillan, 1999).
14. See in particular, Toni Bowers, *Force or Fraud: British Seduction Stories and the Problem of Resistance*, 1660–1760 (Oxford University Press, 2011);

Ros Ballaster, *Seductive Forms: Women's Amatory Fiction from 1684 to 1740* (Oxford: Clarendon Press, 1992).

15. Bowers, *Force or Fraud*, xv.
16. Penelope Aubin, 'Fortune Favours the Bold', in *A Collection of Entertaining Histories and Novels*, II: 277.
17. Eliza Haywood, *Reflections on the Various Effects of Love* (1726), in *Fantomina and Other Works*, ed. Alexander Pettit, Margaret Case Croskery and Anna C. Patchias (Peterborough, ON: Broadview Press, 2004), 107–60, 114.
18. See Donovan, *Women and the Rise of the Novel*, 96-7; Debbie Welham, 'The Political Afterlife of Resentment in Penelope Aubin's *The Life and Amorous Adventures of Lucinda* (1721)', *Women's Writing* 20 (2013): 49–63.
19. Delarivier Manley, *The Power of Love in Seven Novels*, ed. Rachel Carnell, in *The Selected Works of Delarivier Manley*, ed. Rachel Carnell and Ruth Herman, 5 vols. (London: Pickering and Chatto, 2005), IV: 70.
20. Haywood, *Reflections on the Various Effects of Love*, III, 113.
21. Ibid., 141.
22. Ibid., 152.
23. Ibid., 158.
24. Ibid., 159.
25. Manley, *The Power of Love in Seven Novels*, 96.
26. Eliza Haywood, *Love in Its Variety: Being a Collection of Select Novels; Written in Spanish by Signior Michael Bandello. Made English By Mrs ELIZA HAYWOOD* (London: W. Feales and J. Jackson, 1727).
27. Ibid., 7.
28. Ibid., 39.
29. Aubin, 'The Noble Slaves', in *A Collection of Entertaining Histories and Novels*, I: 52–3.
30. Ibid., 135.
31. Elizabeth Rowe, *Friendship in Death. In Twenty Letters from the Dead to the Living. To Which are added, Thoughts on Death. Translated from the Moral Essays of the Messieurs du Port Royal* (London: T. Worrall, 1728), 51.
32. Ibid., 52.
33. Issac Watts, *Death and Heaven: or the Last Enemy Conquer'd, and Separate Spirits made Perfect* (London: J. Clark et al., 1722).
34. Peter Walmsley, 'Whigs in Heaven: Elizabeth Rowe's "Friendship in Death"', *Eighteenth-Century Studies* 44 (2011): 315–30. See also Paula R. Backscheider's compelling case, *Elizabeth Singer Rowe and the Development of the English Novel* (Baltimore: Johns Hopkins University Press, 2013).
35. Gillian Skinner, *Sensibility and Economics in the Novel, 1740–1800: the Price of a Tear* (London: Macmillan, 1999); Markman Ellis, *The Politics of Sensibility: Race, Gender and Commerce in the Sentimental Novel* (Cambridge University Press, 1996).
36. Alexander Pettit, Margaret Case Croskery and Anna C. Patchias, 'Introduction' in Haywood, *Reflections on the Various Effects of Love* (1726), in *Fantomina and Other Works*, 28.

37. In February 1727 the second part with a 'Key to the Whole' was advertised as 'just published' and Haywood's bibliographer concludes that 'there seems little doubt it was actually published'. See Patrick Spedding, *A Bibliography of Eliza Haywood* (London: Pickering and Chatto, 2004), 247.
38. Haywood, *Reflections on the Various Effects of Love,* 117–19.
39. On the rivalry between Haywood and Samson for the literary, if not sexual, patronage of Aaron Hill, see Kathryn King, *A Political Biography of Eliza Haywood* (London: Pickering and Chatto, 2012), 30–3; and Christine Gerrard, *Aaron Hill: the Muses' Projector, 1685–1750* (Oxford University Press, 2003), 94–5.

CHAPTER 3

Reading for the Sentiment: Richardson's Novels

Bonnie Latimer

> 'Why, Sir, if you were to read Richardson for the story, your impatience would be so much fretted that you would hang yourself. But you must read him for the sentiment, and consider the story as only giving occasion to the sentiment.'[1]
>
> '*Reading* is indeed very excellent and useful ... but Thinking is *necessary*.'[2]

Johnson's dictum, made in conversation with the Honourable Thomas Erskine, is one of the most famous pronouncements on Richardson – and the most ambivalent. Overtly, Johnson refers to Richardson's sentimentalism, which produced literature 'written more to the heart than the head': earlier, Johnson had asserted that 'there is more knowledge of the heart in one letter of Richardson's, than in all *Tom Jones*'.[3] Critics certainly use Johnson to frame Richardson as a novelist of feeling: Charlotte Sussman glosses him as referring to the 'high feeling' and 'intense reactions' that Richardson's fiction provoked.[4] Similarly, Hina Nazar argues that Johnson means that 'the interest of the narrative is given by sentiment', equating to 'the language of the heart' and 'the feelings of spectators'.[5]

Such assertions will surprise no one: there is a long tradition of Richardson's novels eliciting emotion. From the first readings of *Pamela* (1740), we have the seven-year-old Harry Campbell secreting himself in Aaron Hill's parlour, discoverable by his 'heart-heaving Sobs' as he listened.[6] Jane Austen caricatured such reactions in Sir Edward Denham, who reads 'more sentimental novels than agreed with him', particularly 'the most exceptionable parts of Richardson's', and was 'very full of some feelings or other'.[7] In *The Rise of the Novel* (1957), Ian Watt allied Richardson to 'sentimentalism', his fictions evoking 'emotional enthusiasm'.[8] John Mullan and Janet Todd see Richardson as 'sentimental' in his featuring of 'responsive feminine sensibility', and as 'the most important figure in early sentimental fiction'.[9] Barbara Benedict's important study views 'the privileging in sentimental literature of feeling and nature over rationalism' as typified in 'Samuel Richardson as the progenitor of sentimental fiction'.[10] Recent critics see Richardson as participating in 'the politeness–sensibility paradigm', as a pioneer of 'sentimental fiction', or as a sentimentalist interested in 'social love'.[11] The tradition that Richardson's fiction is invested primarily in feeling is so strong that, as John Dussinger points out, his biographers emend his nonce-word 'sentimentizing' to 'sentimentalizing', assuming that this is what he meant.[12]

And yet, neither Johnson nor Richardson had a strictly affective *sentimentalism* in mind. The term 'sentiment' as opposed to 'sentimental' referred, in the period's argot, to 'thought, notion, opinion' or 'a striking sentence in a composition'.[13] In *Clarissa* (1747–8), when Anna Howe lists Clarissa's sentiments, she means it in this sense.[14] Thomas Keymer contends that we *must* read Johnson thus: 'in Richardsonian usage, a sentiment is a statement of opinion or truth ... To be sentimental is to be sententious.'[15] In fact, classic accounts which locate Richardson as a novelist of feeling rather hedge their bets. Ian Watt admits that the term 'sentimentalism' is 'somewhat misleading' when applied to Richardson.[16] R. F. Brissenden's *Virtue in Distress* (1974) remarks that 'it might be both more accurate and more useful to call *Clarissa* not a sentimental novel but a novel of sentiment'.[17] Considering that Richardson is often positioned as a father to the novel of sensibility, many important studies of this literature feature no extended discussion of his novels, including Barbara Benedict's study, as well as Adela Pinch's *Strange Fits of Passion: Epistemologies of Emotion, Hume to Austen* (1996), Julie Ellison's *Cato's Tears and the Making of Anglo-American Emotion* (1999), Jonathan Lamb's *The Evolution of Sympathy in the Long Eighteenth Century* (2009) and Ildiko Csengei's *Sympathy, Sensibility, and the Literature of Feeling in the Eighteenth Century* (2012). This is no criticism of those valuable scholarly works: instead, it encourages caution about the neat fit of Richardson's fiction within that tradition.

I suggest that a focus on Richardson as a novelist of *affective* sentiment, to the practical exclusion of *moral* sentiment or sententiousness, results in distorted readings of his work. There are two critical trends to isolate here. One sees Richardson's fictions, particularly *Clarissa*, as textual prompts to feeling, in which the author elicits a sympathetic response from the reader – sometimes against that reader's better judgement. Perhaps the most notorious of such arguments is William Warner's *Reading* Clarissa (1979), which saw Richardson 'lur[ing] the reader into the coils of the fiction', making them 'swerve' towards 'virtue' through the affecting 'story of romantic love [told so as] to engage reader identification' and disable judgement.[18] Later correctives to this reading – which nonetheless replicate some of its premises – include Scott Paul Gordon's essay, which sees the novel 'deploying pathos' to engage readers on the heroine's side, and Heather Zias's argument that Richardson 'employ[s] pathos and evok[es] tears . . . causing readers to *feel* the injustice of Clarissa's situation . . . in a way that bypasses . . . critique'.[19]

The other tendency is a resistance to Richardson's Editor and his moral sentences. Mark Kinkead-Weekes's seminal essay saw Richardson's editorial interventions in *Clarissa* as 'deplorable', lacking in 'literary tact', and designed to coerce the reader into one interpretation of the Clarissa *v.* Lovelace struggle by 'hardening' and 'converting' the picture his narrative presented.[20] Such an account presents the moral sentiments as clogs on the reader's exegetical powers, which a robustly intelligent reader can and should resist. Terry Eagleton and Terry Castle have both made similar points.[21] One way or another, all these classic accounts frame Richardson's ideal reader as passive. As Peter Sabor points out, 'hostile criticism from modern critics' sees the Editor as cudgelling readers into submitting to his interpretations, 'distrust[ing]' their 'distinguishing powers', 'prod[ding]' them into a 'correct interpretation', or even 'propagandizing'.[22] In this chapter, I suggest that such interpretations arise when we de-prioritize the importance of moral sentiment to Richardson's work, and that to do so is to half-read him.

There are exceptions to the trends outlined above. I position my argument in relation to Thomas Keymer's *Richardson's* Clarissa *and the Eighteenth-Century Reader* (1992), which sees Richardson's project not as the imposition of a single moral meaning, but as engaging the reader in a difficult process of recalibrating their own opinions. I draw throughout on Glen Johnson's essay on Richardson's Editor, and on John Dussinger's and Ann Jessie Van Sant's work on the *Moral and Instructive Sentiments* (1755).[23] This chapter suggests that 'reading for the sentiment' in Richardson entails a process of judging, understanding, reflecting and applying, and that Richardson's investment in *moral* sentiment leads him to propose an active, morally productive reading. Attending to that 'Pith and Marrow' of Richardson's novels, the moral sentiment – or, to adopt Geoffrey Bennington's term, the sententious proposition – allows us to envision a type of reading in which the reader does more than weep and less than resist the monitory Editor, who becomes a guiding voice rather than a querulous nuisance.[24] In so doing, this argument re-thinks what 'sentiment' means in relation to

Richardson's work, and to his culture. This chapter focuses on *Clarissa* and its intertexts, such as the *Moral and Instructive Sentiments* (1755) and *Letters and Passages Restored* (1751), while also suggesting applications for the wider *oeuvre*.

Purposeful Reading

Lois Chaber expresses bafflement at the *Moral and Instructive Sentiments*, whose 'varied tenor would have enfeebled it as a work of practical moral guidance for [Richardson's] contemporary audience'.[25] In this, Chaber aligns with others who see Richardson's didacticism as ineffective because of the formal and epistemological instability of his chosen genres: Terry Castle, too, argues that 'the shifting of authority to the reader makes the classic epistolary novel marvelously unfit, obviously, for didacticism of any kind'.[26] Such readings depend on the idea that sententious propositions must be swallowed wholesale – and that Richardson did not notice, or tried to suppress, the contradictions between his works' moral propositions. In fact, however, these inconsistencies are crucial to making moral meaning.

Richardson's sententious propositions are not consistent – between the different novels, between each novel and its intertexts, or within given novels. As Van Sant remarks, sententious propositions in Richardson's work have a 'contextual, situational nature' rather than enjoying absolute 'authority'; it is not possible to 'buil[d] . . . a single case' from them.[27] This is evident in the *Moral and Instructive Sentiments*, derived from the novels. Its opening extracts, from *Pamela*, concern a virtuous woman's ability to modify the behaviour of sexual assailants: 'it is in a Woman's power, effectually to over-awe an audacious predator', for example.[28] *Pamela* itself is rather more ambiguous: in fact, Mrs Jervis's intervention interrupts the manservant Harry in '[taking] hold' of Pamela.[29] Equally, the quotations from *Pamela* contradict those from *Grandison*: the *Pamela* 'sentiments' opine that there are 'things [which] disgrace not men' but which 'ruin Women', whereas the *Grandison* portion asks 'how that crime can be pardoned in a man, which renders a woman infamous?'[30]

Within the fictions, the weight and meaning of sententious propositions vary. Sometimes, as when Clarissa and Lovelace discuss the reprehensibility of 'public loves', they express similar opinions – but mean very different things (703). Lovelace begins a compilation of moral thoughts, 'encourag[ing] and collect[ing] everything of this sort I had ever had . . . to bring [Clarissa] into good humour with me' – and it is Elias Brand who imagines extracting the '*sentiments* and *aphorisms*' from his own letters to 'work . . . up into a *methodical Discourse*' (447).[31] This should alert us to the need to read any collection of moral sentiments critically, as should the use of unexceptionable sententious propositions as rhetorical and argumentative weapons. Characters such as Lovelace and 'Captain Tomlinson' use sententious propositions this way, but so too do the Harlowes. Arabella carps at her sister that 'I *hid not my light under a bushel*, she would say that for me', while Uncle Antony's letters to his niece rain pithy moral pronouncements like so many blows (196). Clarissa is not exempt from this tendency; when she wishes to shame Lovelace for swearing at Will, she remarks, with seeming innocence, on the shamefulness of bad language: 'Well do they make it a proverb – *like a trooper*!' (396). Elsewhere, Clarissa discusses generosity as a general moral quality: 'Generosity, sir, will not surely permit a worthy mind to doubt of its honourable and beneficent intentions' (594). Of course, this abstract conversation has the very practical purpose of eliciting a declaration from Lovelace. Within the novel's own terms, sententious propositions are legible as mere argumentative counters: *all* sententious propositions can be made to serve this combative function, unmoored from sincere moral meaning. This effect is increased when we consider how the novel's arch-villain, Lovelace, parrots formulations we are encouraged to read as straight elsewhere in the canon, as indicated in Table 3.1.

Thus, *no* sententious proposition is a freestanding verity. As Richardson put it, 'many of ye Sentiments are Characteristical [and] wou'd have sounded strange . . . propos'd for general Imitation, as from a moral Writer'.[32] This may seem, as Chaber hints, to defeat the didacticism of the *Moral and Instructive Sentiments* – and of all Richardson's work – because its moral propositions cannot be taken as 'true'.

This relies, however, on a one-dimensional understanding of sententious propositions. Geoffrey Bennington argues that sententious propositions are different from other novelistic sentences. They enjoy a distinctive freedom from the novel's universe, because they are applicable outside it: 'Whereas sentences belonging to the narrative-descriptive complex tend to generate or present a *diegesis* or "universe" with a certain spatio-temporal coherence . . . the sententious proposition enjoys a freedom with respect to the "co-ordinates" of that

Table 3.1 *A Comparison of Lovelace's Sententious Propositions with Similar Formulations in Richardson's Works*

Lovelace	Compare
'I reflected, with a sigh, *that tame spirits must always be imposed upon.*' (810)	'The person who will bear much shall have much to bear all the world through: 'tis your own [Clarissa's] sentiment . . . ' Anna and Clarissa (69)
'*Ill-jesting . . . with edge-tools . . .* ' (676)	'But is there not more danger from a sharp tool, than from a blunt one?' Mrs Howe (*LAPR*, 16)
'For, are we [men and women] not devils to each other? They tempt us: We tempt them.' (*LAPR*, 59)	'Men and women are devils to one another.' Sir Charles Grandison (*Grandison*, II: 439)[a]
'Shall I give you another fine sentence of his . . . "D – n him if he would marry . . . the finest princess on earth, if he but thought she balanced a minute in her choice of him . . ."' (467)	'he would not marry the greatest princess on earth, if he were not assured, that she loved him above all the men in it' Sir Charles Grandison (*Grandison*, II: 423)
'girls who are disengaged seldom hate, though they may not love' (801)	'Women . . . do not, with earnestness, reject a man . . . if they are absolutely unprejudiced in another's favour.' Sir Charles Grandison (*Grandison*, II: 400)
'happiness consists in being pleased with what we do' (1098)	'The happiness of human Life, my dears . . . is at best but comparative. The utmost we should hope for here, is such a situation as, with a self-approving mind, will carry us best through this present scene . . . ' Mrs Shirley (*Grandison*, VII: 396)
'[Familiar letter-writing] was writing from the heart . . . the *soul* was in it. Nothing of body, when friend writes to friend . . . ' (*LAPR*, 109)	'correspondence is, indeed, the cement of friendship: it is friendship avowed under hand and seal: friendship . . . more pure, yet more ardent, and less broken in upon, than personal conversation can be . . . The pen . . . makes distance, presence . . . which makes even presence but body, while absence becomes the soul . . . ' Richardson[b]
'I laid down two rules to myself. The first, whenever I went into company to hear every one of them speak before I gave myself liberty to prate . . . ' (1147)	'A young Man should rather *hear* than *speak*, and a *close Mouth* is generally the Sign of a *wise Head.*' Richardson[c]

Notes:

[a] Richardson, *Sir Charles Grandison* (1753–4), ed. Jocelyn Harris (Oxford University Press, 1986). Hereafter cited as *Grandison.*

[b] SR to Sarah Wescomb, 27 August 1746, in Richardson, *Correspondence with Sarah Wescomb, Frances Grainger and Laetitia Pilkington*, ed. John A. Dussinger (Cambridge University Press, 2015), 6–7.

[c] Samuel Richardson, *The Apprentice's Vade Mecum* (London, 1734), 31.

universe.' He sees them as a discrete genre intruding into the novel.[33] This sense of their mobility is one I want to keep alive: Richardsonian sententious propositions are unique because they initially occur in a fictional text, and they are allegedly that fiction's *raison d'être*: Richardson writes 'more for the Sake of the Instruction, than the Story!'[34] They then, however, regroup and reform outside that originary fiction in such intertexts as the *Letters and Passages Restored* (1751), the *Meditations Collected from the Sacred Books* (1750), and especially the *Moral and Instructive Sentiments*. They have a kinesis, an agility, which the other sentences that comprise the novels lack – and their applicability outside the novel entails a different type of readerly engagement. The disparities between Richardsonian sententious propositions (most visible when ranged alongside one another in the *Moral and Instructive Sentiments*) provoke comparison and reflection. I term such reading *purposeful reading*; it involves reading *for* the sentiment. The *Moral and Instructive Sentiments* teaches the reader how to read the novels because it forces readers to confront the fluctuating value of sententious propositions, and the moral ideas they encapsulate.

Richardson writes his sententious propositions within a well-worn tradition that includes not only 'classical' wisdom literature (such as Plutarch) or esteemed collections of maxims (La Rochefoucauld), but a popular Anglican devotional tradition that prizes moral extracts.[35] This heritage is embodied in the demotic enchiridion, which differs from the *Enchiridion* of Epictetus (a concise system of moral guidance).[36] By contrast, the demotic enchiridion is a ragbag of an instructional genre which encompassed 'high' and 'low' culture authors and practices, ranging from Sir John Fielding to William Penn to Edmund Curll's ravagings of Addison.[37] Richardson was deeply familiar with such texts. As Keith Maslen notes, he printed collections of moral formulae such as Atterbury's *Maxims* (1723), Joshua Smith's *A Select Manual of Divine Meditations and Prayers* (1733, 1734 and 1750), and James Mauclerc's *The Christian's Magazine* (1750).[38] Clarissa and Belford read such literature: her library contains 'divinity and miscellany classes', and he envisages the Widow Lowick 'writ[ing] *for* me, out of books, passages she shall recommend' (411, 1435). Anna and Clarissa swap John Norris's *A Collection of Miscellanies* (1687). The *Moral and Instructive Sentiments* itself follows common generic tropes, from alphabetical organization of sentiments to professions of retirement and reluctant publication. This was a popular genre that did not prize originality: as the compiler of one collection noted, 'to many of these *Maxims* it would be difficult to assign any particular author; for meeting with the same sense differently expressed by different writers, I have often taken the liberty to gather from each what I liked best, and form them into one'.[39] One finds the same ideas and the same language repeated:

> 'Does any thing shine so bright as Vertue, and that even in the Eyes of those who are void of it?'
>
> 'Virtue hath such Charms, that even the Vicious inwardly reverence it.'
>
> 'What a praise it is to Honesty, that every man pretends to it, even at the instant that he knows he means to be a knave.'[40]

Richardson shares formulae with such collections, from his novels' ideas on pity to deathbed repentance. An example is a common reflection in Clarissa's correspondence, the theme of adversity as ultimate benefit. Anna Howe opines that 'ADVERSITY IS YOUR SHINING-TIME' and Clarissa repeats that she was 'taught by my good Mrs Norton that the best of schools is *that of affliction*' and on her deathbed, she utters, '*It is good for me that I was afflicted!*' (579, 359, 1362). This formulation recurs in the *Moral and Instructive Sentiments*, and in the *Meditations*, where Clarissa writes that as 'gold is tried in the fire', so are 'acceptable men in the furnace of adversity'.[41] Stemming from Psalm 119:71, this formula occurs in many enchiridions:

> The Best of us need Afflictions for the Trial of our Virtue: How can we exercise the Grace of Contentment, if all Things succeed well? Or that of Forgiveness, if we have no Enemies?
>
> The best need affliction for trial of their virtues; what would patience be good for, without sufferings to exercise it?
>
> Adversity is the best school of virtue.[42]

Not only the *Moral and Instructive Sentiments*, then, but Richardson's fictions engage with the popular enchiridion or moral extract tradition – and this tradition assumes an active mode of reading.

David Allan concludes that Georgian commonplace books required a personally 'transformational' style of reading, involving reflection and self-application.[43] Collections of sententious propositions frame a comparable practice, in which readers consume books for moral improvement, achieved through exercising judgement. The pseudonymous 'Bob Short' is explicit:

> the reader . . ., like a man in a good way of business, should take care to mind what he is about and get as much profit from [this collection] as he can . . . to

> inform his *judgment*, and regulate his *actions* . . . Too much eating does not make a man healthy, and too much reading does not make a man wise. *Reflection* and *practice* are the soul of study, as mastication and digestion are the quintessence of eating.[44]

The Counsels of Wisdom comparably warns that 'These Maxims were not . . . set here to be read, but to be Meditated on'; the reader should 'Discourse with himself . . . to Discover by his own thoughts what he has a desire to know'.[45] Or, as John Norris puts it, '*Reading* is indeed very excellent and useful . . . but *Thinking* is necessary.'[46] This is a mode of reading important to mainstream contemporary Anglicanism; Archbishop Tillotson noted that 'reading and hearing, and meditation' were the way to 'improve . . . in real goodness'.[47] This hardly resembles the absorptive, feeling engagement sometimes posited of novel-reading; reading for moral ends is labour-intensive. Pursued further, this mode of reading has implications for how we understand Richardson's deployment of sententious propositions.

The Sententious Novel

The full title of the *Moral and Instructive Sentiments* evinces its generic complexity: *A Collection of the Moral and Instructive Sentiments, Maxims, Cautions, and Reflexions, Contained in the Histories of Pamela, Clarissa, and Sir Charles Grandison*. 'Sentiment' does not capture all these types of utterance. Instead, as an overarching term, I prefer Bennington's 'sententious proposition', which he theorizes in relation to the eighteenth-century French novel: the 'sentiment' is one sort of sententious proposition. Although it is unhelpful to draw schematic distinctions between the genres of sententious proposition, three stand out as important to Richardson's fiction: the proverb, the maxim and the sentiment proper.[48]

Within *Clarissa*, different characters employ different types of sententious proposition, reflecting how they understand experience. Many characters use proverbs – in Bennington's terms, 'anonymous quotation[s] from the culture at large'.[49] Arabella cites an 'old saw' that '*it is good to be related to an estate*' and Solmes opines that 'coy maids make fond wives' (81, 238). Anna frequently invokes the proverbial: '*so in for the lamb*, as the saying is, *in for the sheep*', '*Talk of the devil* is an old saying', 'as the old phrase has it, to take a thorn out of one's friend's foot, to put it in our own', '*far fetched and dear bought*, you know, is a proverb' (70, 75, 355, 631). Such pronouncements root Anna's letters in a demotic culture, but they are not reliable: when she tells Clarissa on 25 April that 'when things are at worse they must mend' and 'Good often comes when evil is expected', she is clearly wrong (511). The problem is proverbs' generic nature: they purport to derive from experience, but this is not individual experience. Rather, it is a greater heritage, so broad that it risks falling into insignificant cliché. Proverbs, instead of explaining or predicting experience, serve in *Clarissa* as rhetorical counters with little moral value. This is most visible in Lord M, Lovelace's uncle, whose letters employ proverbs to a comical degree. In fact, M, despite his ridiculousness, is often right. His letter of 15 May is peppered with proverbs, but they accurately express his relationship with Lovelace: 'He thought, I suppose, that *I could not cover him with my wings without pecking at him with my bill*'. 'I could wish the young lady [Clarissa] were apprised that *delays are dangerous*': so indeed they prove (606–7). M, however, cannot see 'the notorious fact that any proverb can be matched with another', as Clarissa proves when she 'caps' proverbs with Betty Barnes (263).[50] He does not understand them as counters, and his subscription to the wisdom of ages is undermined when the reader discovers his delight in Lovelace's antics, as Elaine McGirr points out (1023).[51] Proverbs emerge as a sterile system, in which any proposition can be batted away with another, and in which the proverbialist need not reflect on the relation of his utterances to his practice.

Lovelace scorns his uncle's proverbs, but they are no more arbitrary than his own maxims. Maxims in *Clarissa* are a male mode – the Harlowe brothers characteristically deploy this form, as when Clarissa notes that '*No conditioning with a Father!* is a maxim with my Father, and with my Uncles' or when she is told that '*Too ready forgiveness does but encourage offences*: that's your good father's maxim' (156).[52] Maxims represent rigid rules, a code to be imposed upon human interactions rather than derived from them, and their lack of moral responsiveness is a crucial theme in *Clarissa*. John Dussinger distinguishes between maxims and sentiments in Richardson's work by noting that, generally, maxims are 'axioms or self-evident propositions' – or, as Johnson defines it, 'An axiom, a general principle . . . '[53] The novel's chief purveyor of maxims is Lovelace and they are his undoing, as he appreciates too late their inapplicability to his experience.

Lovelace's letters and conversation are structured through maxims or 'rules': '*Always be careful of back doors* is a maxim with me in all my exploits', 'This, thou knowest, was always my rule – *Once any other man's*, and *I* know it, and *never more mine*' (448, 674). Even his virtues are expressed so: 'it was a maxim with his family, from which he would by no means depart, never to rack-rent old tenants' (79).

In fact, rakishness itself emerges as a 'code' or 'creed', a coherent web of maxims:

> Has it not been a constant maxim with us that the greater the *merit* on the woman's side, the nobler the victory on the man's?
>
> ... that part of the libertine's creed, that once subdued, is always subdued ...
>
> Many and many a pretty soul would yield, were she not afraid that the man she favoured would think the worse of her for it. This is also a part of the rake's creed ...
>
> After all, what have I done more than prosecute the maxims by which thou and I and every rake are governed ...
>
> (559, 634, 703, 970)

Rakishness is a credo requiring implicit subscription. Defending himself to Belford, Lovelace warns that 'thou must be sensible, that I can answer every tittle of what thou writest, upon the foot of the *maxims we have long held and pursued*' (719): like proverbs, maxims constitute a set of truisms, which do not relate to experience. Lovelace's dreams and fantasy-plots – the Isle of Wight excursion, the twin Lovelaces fantasia, the dream of Mother H, the two subdued sister-beauties – fail to figure forth the future. They are projections which have no purchase in the world of the novel's action. Similarly, the rakish maxim is finally powerless: in some sense, the novel is about Lovelace's *failed* attempts to use his maxims to organize experience. The 'rules' which Lovelace 'laid down to myself upon my entrance into active life' are confounded during his attempts to seduce Clarissa: 'The more perverse she, the more steady I; that is my rule', he boasts. Women 'lik[e] an uncontroulable passion. They like to have every favour ravished from them ... Don't I know the Sex?'[54] In fact, his preconceived 'notions' explode in the face of experience. 'But who would have thought there had been such a woman in the world?' he laments: 'Of all the sex I have hitherto known, or heard, or read of, it was *once subdued, and always subdued*' (904). Again and again, his maxims fail to prepare him for the reality of Clarissa, who goes 'Against all my notions, against all my conceptions' and who 'gives the lie to our rakish maxims' (906, 930). Lovelace's subscription to the prefabricated rakish 'code' forces him to live through a set of inflexible libertine clichés which do not reflect the purer dictates of his 'heart' and which the novel delights in disrupting.[55]

By contrast, the moral sentiment entails a responsiveness to lived experience which separates it from the deterministic modes of the maxim and the proverb. Several characters engage in sentimentizing, but Clarissa is most associated with this form, which is 'based on personal experience', involving 'application'.[56] Sentiments are articulations of moral ideas drawn from and modifiable by experience; they thus provide a means for ethical development. The Richardsonian sentiment is not received or prefabricated; rather, it is produced through a process of *individual* observation, *private* reflection, and then a synthesizing move towards a *universal* sentiment. The general nature of the sentiment is important, because its very universality invites readers to consider and compare it with their own experience, engaging active judgement. The following examples illustrate the pattern:

> my father was soured by the cruel distemper [gout] . . . It imprisoned, as I may say, his lively spirits in himself and turned the edge of them against his own peace, his extraordinary prosperity adding but to his impatiency; for those, I believe, who want the fewest earthly blessings most regret that they want any. (55)
>
> This custom [of regularly changing linen], although a prisoner, as I may too truly say, and neither visited nor visiting, I continue. One owes to *one's self*, and to one's *sex*, you know, to be always neat; and never to be surprised in a way one should be pained to be seen in. Besides, people in adversity, which is the state of trial of every good quality, should endeavour to preserve laudable customs, that if sunshine returns they may not be losers by their trial. (282)
>
> But my injuries being recent, and my distresses having been exceeding great, *self* would crowd into my letter. When distressed, the human mind is apt to turn itself to everyone in whom it imagined or wished an interest, for pity and consolation – or, to express myself better and more concisely, in your own words, *misfortune makes people plaintive*: and to whom, if not to a friend, can the afflicted complain? (976)

In each case, Clarissa starts with a local experience: Mr Harlowe's gout, her desire to keep her linen clean, Mrs Howe's rebuttal of her distressed letter to Anna. She considers it: her father's prosperity makes his situation more unbearable; adversity is no excuse for neglecting self-care – and so forth. Then, from this consideration arises grand moral propositions presented to the reader as more general truths:

> Those who want the fewest earthly blessings most regret that they want any.
>
> People in adversity, which is the state of trial of every good quality, should endeavour to preserve laudable customs, that if sunshine returns they may not be losers by their trial.
>
> *Misfortune makes people plaintive*: and to whom, if not to a friend, can the afflicted complain?

The sentiment arises from individual experience but is not unique: instead, it relates the particular experience to the universal. Often, in fact, the sentiment is *unoriginal*, as when Clarissa feeds Mrs Howe's words back to her, or when she ponders on adversity, a staple theme of moral enchiridions. Clarissa's sententiae are no more 'original' than Lovelace's preformed 'creed', but they are more effective because they arise spontaneously from experience, and because, like a good maths solution, we can see her workings. This point is key: the reader's observation of her processes stimulates extradiegetic replication. The couching of Clarissa's sentiments as rhetorical questions, as in the final example, encourages this.[57] In this way, I suggest, we are not asked to *assent* to the 'truth' of Clarissa's propositions; instead, we are invited to *consider* them – because, as she herself notes, 'Nothing but experience can give us a strong and efficacious conviction' (246 n.) That we are asked to reflect on moral propositions, rather than subscribe to them, means that what the reader should take from Richardson's work is not an imprinted lesson, but a sharpened judgement. Crucial to the development of judgement are Richardson's editorial figures.

Conclusion: The Reader and the Editor

Being good in Richardson is rarely a brainless activity. Instead, goodness is a consistent, effortful *practice*, rather than a *state*. This leads us back to the old debate over Richardson's editorial personae. They recur in various guises, as the Editor of the third edition of *Clarissa*, but also as the figure whom John Dussinger dubs 'the Compiler' of the *Moral and Instructive Sentiments*, and perhaps even in the hand which collated, preserved or burnt the author's own correspondence. As noted above, *Clarissa*'s Editor especially has been seen as stifling, militating against any exertion of readerly judgement.

Not so, however. Richardson's novels, as much as the sententious tradition to which they refer, require an alert and sincere reader. Part of the Editor's function is to call forth such a reader. His incarnation in the *Letters and Passages Restored* censures readers who 'have not paid a due attention to the Story', accusing some of 'want of attention', and suggesting that 'A few Observations are thrown in by way of Note in the present Edition . . . to bespeak the *Attention* of hasty Readers to what lies obviously before them.'[58] As Peter Sabor remarks, Richardson is unusually demanding in envisaging a reader who *will* re-read and re-think.[59] Equally, as Glen Johnson suggests, help with assessing the manifold details of this difficult novel is a welcome function of Richardson's Editor: 'like an insistent Shakespeare scholar sitting next to one at *Hamlet* [he] is available to clarify'.[60] For example, in the Editor's notes to Letters 45 and 46, he glosses Clarissa's mention of specific moments in her voluminous correspondence, helping the reader cross-reference (206 n.). Many of the Editor's interjections are of this type. From time to time, his notes suggest passages the reader might call to mind, as in this corrective to one of Lovelace's letters: 'It may be observed further that all Clarissa's occasional lectures to Miss Howe on that young lady's treatment of Mr Hickman prove that she was herself above affectation and tyranny', citing specific examples (1482 n.). I argue that the Editor is related to that demotic enchiridion tradition that emphasizes not new lessons, but a jogging of the memory, as when the compiler of *South's Maxims* thought that the collection would lead readers back to the original with refreshed attention, or when Sir John Fielding hoped to 'revive' his readers' 'acquaintance with . . . beautiful sentiments'.[61] And if the Editor of *Clarissa* segues into the Compiler of the *Moral and Instructive Sentiments*, then this is that figure's function: to offer up moral ideas to be considered and applied by readers. The Editor, in all his manifestations, enables readerly judgement – and the ultimate object of the reader's judgement is the reader's self.

Peter Sabor emphasizes Richardson's hope that his readers become 'textual critics'.[62] I add that his fictions encourage the development of *moral* criticism, entailing humility and a willingness to self-apply. Sitting in judgement is one of the terrors of *Clarissa*, and it is no coincidence that the characters who seek to 'try' the heroine are the Harlowes and Lovelace. Clarissa's family arrogate to themselves a right of judgement, forming an 'awful bench', and organizing themselves into 'parties'.[63] Lovelace frames his abuse of Clarissa as a trial (e.g. 714). This type of trial, however, which involves estimating the behaviour and worth of others, is a shallow activity that does not lead to any deeper understanding. Lovelace uses the motif of the public trial to show how judging others in fact involves moral blindness and distraction: 'every cause has its black and its white side', and he can 'make a bad cause a good one at any time' (1031, 1287). Readers who sit in judgement upon the characters' actions and motives, stacking them up to decide who is justified, who should be punished and how, miss the point that, for the tradition in which Richardson is writing, the legitimate aim of moral judgement is *self*-judgement and *self*-application. As Hickman puts it, ''tis pity that the man who can pronounce so fine a sentence, will not square his actions accordingly' (1096).

A sign of real judgement is, rather, that 'I can give it as freely against myself as against anybody else' (479). This involves genuine self-scrutiny, not 'resolving to *acquit*, not fairly to *try* themselves' (510). Reading Richardson's work encourages the reader to ask urgent moral questions – but of themselves, rather than of the text. The question is not 'Is Clarissa above reproach – is she right or wrong?' because, as Thomas Keymer points out, this question is insoluble, even for Richardson himself.[64] Rather, encountering the novel's moral commonplaces, exemplars and dilemmas might prompt questions like, 'Why am I reacting this way? – have I understood and considered enough? Have I read my own experience correctly?' The sententious proposition represents one crucial way in which Richardson's work nudges the reader towards such self-questioning – because, in the end, reading for the sentiment is not a matter of being swept away by feeling or even of appreciating anew assorted moral clichés. Instead, it means an ongoing, fraught practice, in which one is responsible not to the text or even to the Editor, but to that ideally harder taskmaster, oneself.

Notes

1. James Boswell, *Life of Johnson* (1791), ed. R. W. Chapman (Oxford University Press, 1998), 480.
2. John Norris, *A Collection of Miscellanies: Consisting of Poems, Essays, Discourses, and Letters, Occasionally Written* (Oxford, 1687), 147.
3. Clara Reeve, Preface to *The School for Widows* (1791), quoted in Melissa Sodeman, *Sentimental Memorials: Women and the Novel in Literary History* (Stanford University Press, 2015), 4; Boswell, *Life of Johnson*, 480.
4. Charlotte Sussman, *Eighteenth-Century English Literature* (Cambridge: Polity Press, 2012), 127.
5. Hina Nazar, *Enlightened Sentiments: Judgment and Autonomy in the Age of Sensibility* (New York: Fordham University Press, 2012), 12–13.
6. Aaron Hill to SR, 29 December 1740, in *Correspondence with Aaron Hill and the Hill Family*, ed. Christine Gerrard (Cambridge University Press, 2013), 67–8.
7. Austen, *Sanditon* (1817), in *Later Manuscripts*, ed. Janet Todd and Linda Bree (Cambridge University Press, 2008), 183, 176.
8. Ian Watt, *The Rise of the Novel* (1957; London: Pimlico, 2000), 174.
9. John Mullan, *Sentiment and Sociability: the Language of Feeling in the Eighteenth Century* (Oxford: Clarendon Press, 1988), 4; Janet Todd, *Sensibility: An Introduction* (London: Methuen, 1986), 66.
10. Barbara Benedict, *Framing Feeling: Sentiment and Style in English Prose Fiction, 1745–1800* (New York: AMS Press, 1994), 4.
11. Simon Dickie, *Cruelty and Laughter: Forgotten Comic Literature and the Unsentimental Eighteenth Century* (University of Chicago Press, 2011), 2–5; Sodeman, *Sentimental Memorials*, 3; Greg Morgan, '"Give me the consideration of being the bondsman": Embarrassment and the Figure of the Bond in

the Sentimental Fiction of Samuel Richardson', *Eighteenth-Century Fiction* 28 (2016): 667–90.

12. John A. Dussinger, 'Introduction', in *A Collection of the Moral and Instructive Sentiments . . .* (1755), vol. III of *Samuel Richardson's Published Commentary on* Clarissa,*1745–1765* (London: Pickering and Chatto, 1998), xlvii n.
13. Samuel Johnson, *A Dictionary of the English Language . . .*, 2 vols. (London, 1755), 'sentiment', senses 1 and 2.
14. Samuel Richardson, *Clarissa, Or the History of a Young Lady* (1747–8), ed. Angus Ross (London: Penguin, 1985), 1466. Hereafter cited by page number in the text.
15. Thomas Keymer, 'Sentimental Fiction: Ethics, Social Critique, and Philanthropy' in *The Cambridge History of English Literature, 1660–1780*, ed. John Richetti (Cambridge University Press, 2005), 583.
16. Watt, *Rise of the Novel*, 174.
17. R. F. Brissenden, *Virtue in Distress: Studies in the Novel of Sentiment from Richardson to Sade* (London: Macmillan, 1974), 98.
18. William B. Warner, *Reading* Clarissa: *the Struggles of Interpretation* (New Haven: Yale University Press, 1979), x, 125.
19. Scott Paul Gordon, 'Disinterested Selves: *Clarissa* and the Tactics of Sentiment', *ELH* 64 (1997): 477; Heather Zias, 'Who Can Believe? Sentiment vs. Cynicism in Richardson's *Clarissa*', *Eighteenth-Century Life* 27 (2003): 100.
20. Mark Kinkead-Weekes, '*Clarissa* Restored?', *Review of English Studies* 10 (1959): 169.
21. Terry Eagleton, *The Rape of Clarissa: Writing, Sexuality, and Class Struggle in Samuel Richardson* (Minneapolis: University of Minnesota Press, 1982), 9–10; Terry Castle, *Clarissa's Ciphers: Meaning and Disruption in Richardson's* Clarissa (Ithaca: Cornell University Press, 1982), 158.
22. Peter Sabor, 'Introduction', in *Letters and Passages Restored from the Original Manuscripts of the History of* Clarissa, vol. II of *Samuel Richardson's Published Commentary on* Clarissa, 3 vols. (London: Pickering and Chatto), xiv–xv. Hereafter cited as *LAPR*.
23. Glen Johnson, 'Richardson's "Editor" in *Clarissa*', *Journal of Narrative Technique* 10 (1980): 99–114; Dussinger, 'Introduction'; Ann Jessie Van Sant, 'A Dictionary of Morality: Reading for the Sentiment', in *A Collection of the Moral and Instructive Sentiments*, vol. III, ed. Dussinger, 411–37.
24. SR to Lady Echlin, 7 July 1755, in Samuel Richardson, *Correspondence with Lady Bradshaigh and Lady Echlin*, ed. Peter Sabor, 3 vols. (Cambridge University Press, 2016), ii: 557; Geoffrey Bennington, *Sententiousness and the Novel: Laying Down the Law in Eighteenth-Century French Fiction* (Cambridge University Press, 1985).
25. Lois Chaber, 'Review Essay', *Eighteenth-Century Fiction* 12 (2000): 604.
26. Castle, *Clarissa's Ciphers*, 168.
27. Van Sant, 'Dictionary of Morality', 425–7.

28. Richardson, *A Collection of the Moral and Instructive Sentiments, Maxims, Cautions, and Reflexions, Contained in the Histories of Pamela, Clarissa, and Sir Charles Grandison* (London, 1755), 4.
29. Richardson, *Pamela: Or, Virtue Rewarded* (1740), ed. Albert J. Rivero (Cambridge University Press, 2011), 15.
30. Richardson, *Moral and Instructive Sentiments*, 4, 218–19.
31. *LAPR*, 156–7.
32. Quoted from Dussinger, 'Introduction', xlvi–xlvii n., xi.
33. Bennington, *Sententiousness and the Novel*, 4, 8–9.
34. SR to Lady Echlin, 7 July 1755, 557.
35. Mary Thomas Crane, *Framing Authority: Self, Sayings, and Society in Sixteenth-Century England* (Princeton University Press, 1993), 24–6.
36. See Epictetus, *Enchiridion in All the Works of Epictetus that Are Now Extant . . .*, trans. Elizabeth Carter (London, 1758), 435–64.
37. John Fielding, *The Universal Mentor . . .* (London, 1763); William Penn, 'Some Fruits of Solitude', in *Reflections and Maxims . . .* (London, 1693); [Charles Beckingham] *Addison's Maxims, Observations, and Reflections . . .* (London, 1719/20); cf. Paul Baines and Pat Rogers, *Edmund Curll, Bookseller* (Oxford University Press, 2007), 127.
38. Keith Maslen, *Samuel Richardson of London, Printer: A Study of his Printing Based on Ornament Use and Business Accounts* (Dunedin, NZ: University of Otago, 2001), 57, 106, 140.
39. Charles Palmer, *A Collection of Select Aphorisms and Maxims . . . Extracted from the Most Eminent Authors* (London, 1748), [A3r–v].
40. Robert South, *Maxims, Sayings, and Explications of the Scripture Phrases . . . Extracted from the Writings of the Late Reverend and Learned Dr South*, 2nd edition (London, 1719), 66; Thomas Fuller, *Gnomologia* (London, 1732), 234; Richardson, *Moral and Instructive Sentiments*, 136.
41. Richardson, *Moral and Instructive Sentiments*, 85; Richardson, *Meditations Collected from the Sacred Books* (1750; reprinted New York: Garland, 1976), 33; cf. also 30, 64.
42. *Rules and Maxims for the Conduct of Human Life* (Salisbury, 1745), 13; George Shelley, *Sentences Divine, Moral, and Historical* (London, 1712), 101; 'Bob Short', *The Sentiments of Experience . . .* (London, 1787), 13, 103.
43. David Allan, *Commonplace Books and Reading in Georgian England* (Cambridge University Press, 2010), chapter 2.
44. 'Short', *Sentiments of Experience*, x, 5.
45. *The Counsels of Wisdom, Or, a Collection of the Maxims of Solomon*, 2nd edition (London, 1735), [A6R].
46. Norris, *Miscellanies*, 147.
47. John Tillotson, *The Works*, ed. Ralph Barker, 3 vols. (London, 1752), II: 511.
48. I differ from Van Sant, who uses 'maxim' and 'sentiment' interchangeably; she argues that although maxims do represent a general truth, it is one buttressed through personal experience (see Van Sant, 'A Dictionary of Morality', 420).

49. Bennington, *Sententiousness and the Novel*, 16–17.
50. Bennington, *Sententiousness and the Novel*, 17.
51. Elaine McGirr, 'Manly Lessons: *Sir Charles Grandison*, the Rake, and the Man of Sentiment', *Studies in the Novel* 39 (2007): 271.
52. *LAPR*, 24.
53. Dussinger, 'Introduction', xii; Johnson, *Dictionary*, 'maxim'.
54. *LAPR*, 51, 70, 62.
55. For moments when Lovelace's 'heart' threatens to disrupt his scheming, see, e.g., 520, 721.
56. Dussinger, 'Introduction', xii; Van Sant, 'Dictionary of Morality', 416.
57. Many sentiments occur as rhetorical questions: 'If we suffer by an act of duty . . . is it not pleasurable upon reflection that the fault is in others, rather than in ourselves?' or 'what greatness of soul, is required in the wife, not to despise a husband who is more ignorant . . . than herself?' (105, 241).
58. *LAPR*, 19, 85, 203.
59. Sabor, 'Introduction', xvi, xxxii.
60. Johnson, 'Richardson's "Editor"', 108.
61. *South's Maxims* (1719), [A2–3]; Fielding, *Universal Mentor*, A[r].
62. Sabor, 'Introduction', xvi.
63. *LAPR*, 5, 10.
64. Thomas Keymer, *Richardson's* Clarissa *and the Eighteenth-Century Reader* (Cambridge University Press, 1992), 122.

CHAPTER 4

The Virtuous in Distress: David Simple, Amelia, Memoirs of Miss Sidney Bidulph

Barbara M. Benedict

Eighteenth-century sentimental fiction is peopled by fools and villains. However, although readers can easily identify hypocrites, misers, conmen and tyrants, sentimental heroes typically elicit mixed responses. On the one hand, they shine as exemplars of sympathy, honesty and Christian humility in a world darkened by evil; on the other, they fall – seemingly willingly – into traps of malice and duplicity evident to a reader of the meanest intelligence. Childlike, innocent to the point of stupidity, almost wantonly vulnerable, these sentimental heroes do not merely expose the flaws of a mercenary and selfish society; they also illustrate the folly of maintaining simple virtue in such a world. They experience deceit and self-delusion, and they create as well as suffer their own difficulties. Consequently their stories, whether reported by themselves or by a third-person narrator, waver between protective justification and ironic detachment. They are heroes indeed, and also they are fools.

The three novels examined here emphasize the moral ambiguity of these heroes through a structural irony that counters virtue with catastrophe, and thus undermines the authority of sentiment as a guide to life. This ambiguity primarily concerns their responses to and responsibility for the disasters that strike them. In Sarah Fielding's *David Simple* (1744, 1753), David's search for a soul-mate falters partly due to his impossibly high standards; both the eponymous heroine and her weak but well-meaning husband in Henry Fielding's *Amelia* (1751) are betrayed by their naïveté and good nature; and Frances Sheridan's heroine in her *Memoirs of Miss Sidney Bidulph* (1761) seems determined on her own unhappiness, as well as that of her lover. In each, tricked by siblings, victimized by parental prejudices, betrayed by false friends, assailed by poverty and nasty rumours, the sensitive and upright titular heroes are entangled not only in complex intrigues perpetrated by villains, but also in dilemmas brought by their own inexperience, honesty, fidelity, and an excessive sensibility that leads them to misjudge other people; their trust and love, in turn, lead them to make decisions that compromise their integrity.

David Simple and the Search for a Friend

The Adventures of David Simple, originally published in 1744, recounts the adventures of David, embittered by repeated betrayals, in his quest to find a real friend.[1] Like the protagonist of Samuel Johnson's *Rasselas* (1759), who seeks the best way to live and fails to find it, the eponymous hero meets with numerous, and predictable, disappointments. Defrauded and abused by his duplicitous brother Daniel, abandoned for a rich old man by his first love and flighty fiancée Nanny Johnson, he launches into the world to explore the varieties of humankind. However, unlike Prince Rasselas, David does discover what he seeks: both a spiritual brother, Valentine, who marries the virtuous Cynthia, and his truest friend, Valentine's sister Camilla, whom David marries. The first two volumes end with the four friends dwelling in a modest, rural utopian community, enjoying harmony and love, surrounded by children and content with themselves.

All that changes in the final instalment, subtitled *Volume the Last* (1753), which entails such a violent shift of mood that it 'shocked' contemporary readers.[2] Here, the book mutates into a bitter story illustrating how a man of deep feeling and delicate honour must endure the real and daily misfortunes of eighteenth-century life – poverty, illness, bullying by the powerful, the oppression of economic and social inequality – by means of steadfast loyalty and love, aided at the last by Christian faith. A meretricious lawsuit reduces David to destitution; relentlessly, all but one of his children die, one after another; Valentine expires from the climate in Jamaica, where he has emigrated to repair his fortunes; Camilla succumbs to a lingering malaise; and, finally, worn out by sorrows, so too does David himself, content that Camilla has gone to heaven and been spared more of the sufferings of this life. Only Cynthia survives, having rescued and provided for David's only remaining child, little Camilla.

This structure enables Fielding to counter the saccharine sentiments of the rather one-dimensional characters with the grating truths of life in an unjust society. Like most eighteenth-century prose fictions, *David Simple* weaves together elements from a number of earlier prose genres: utopian satire, allegory, quixotic romance, parable, didactic moral tale, devotional reading and picaresque.[3] It begins as a form of urban travelogue: David's determination 'To travel through the whole World, rather than not meet with a real Friend' leads to his encounters with a catalogue of Theophrastian types, each of whom acts a part to gain his ends at others' expense.[4] Most important is Mr Orgueil, the sophisticated, stoical and selfish philosopher devoted to 'the Rule of Reason', who offers an alternative to David's sentimental philosophy by maintaining that 'Man, by the Use of his own Reason alone, has a Power to prevent or heal any Misfortune' (VI, 4, 357), and the atheist who dies of drink and despair, and who is revealed in a *deus ex machina* to be David's traitorous brother Daniel (I, 3, 27). The result is a rich generic instability, as the novel simultaneously solicits from its readers laughter and pity, moral certainty and doubt about the merits of David's virtue, recognition of realistic vignettes and absorption in a fairy-tale fantasy world. Nonetheless, it ends as a harsh lesson in Christian resignation to cruelty, misfortune and injustice.

David exemplifies the sentimental hero. '[T]he sensitive, benevolent man whose feelings are too exquisite for the acquisitiveness, vulgarity and selfishness of his world', he is a version of the Christian fool whose lack of duplicity and inability to recognize it in others render him closer to divine truth than apparently wise characters.[5] He understands life on a literalistic level – he couldn't lie if he wanted to – but he also retains the simplicity of faith in clear concepts: doing good, helping others, being what you appear, empathizing. He remains extraordinary because he remains impervious to the feelings that motivate virtually every other character in the novel than the sentimental four: envy and jealousy. Mrs Orgueil, for example, is gripped by such an intense rivalry with the witty Cynthia that she goes as far as to appropriate and mistreat Cynthia's daughter. Livia, the stepmother of Valentine and Camilla, grows so jealous of their father's love for them that she spreads the rumour that her stepchildren are practising incest, thus manoeuvring their expulsion and impoverishment. Motivated by quite contrary feelings, David delights in practising what the narrator repeatedly terms his '*Darling Passion of doing good*' (IV, 8, 297). By repeating and italicizing the phrase, and by capitalizing 'Darling' and 'Passion', the narrator draws the reader's attention to the self-indulgence concealed in this altruism: David's sense of self-approval bears more in common with the vanity derided in others than at first appears.

Indeed, David is not perfect. His acute sensibilities and sentimental ideology may license him to weep in a manly way at the sufferings and joys of others, but he also experiences rather too much self-pity as he broods over his brother's and his fiancée Nanny's betrayals. Early on, the narrator remarks that, after storming out of the house he shared with his brother, he loses his way and his money, explaining that 'his Mind was so taken up, and tortured with his Brother's Brutality, that all other Thoughts quite forsook him' (I, 2, 19). Such self-absorption is dangerous in a world of thieves and hazards, but also silly in a grown man. Perhaps most significantly, his sentimental simplicity cannot accommodate the idea that other people differ from him: childishly, he assumes they feel as he does. This, in turn, blinds him to his own self-indulgence: the narrator reports his delight when he encounters a dying man with three daughters tenderly attending him 'with the utmost Duty and Care ... and at the approach of his last Moments, [shewing] such Agonies of Grief and tender Sorrow, as gave our Hero great Pleasure' (I, 7, 46). David's pleasure in others' pain stimulates in his mind a Lockean philosophical flight on education (another of the themes in the novel) as conducted through reason, love and compassion, instead of parental tyranny. However, David's single-minded appreciation of filial affection does not seem to cause him to pity the suffering daughters, and this casts the virtue of his sentimentalism in doubt. Moreover, upon the old man's death, the daughters quarrel fiercely over a carpet, preferring in the end to cut it to shreds rather than see their sisters with a better portion. This portrait of family love serves as neither a stimulus to, nor evidence of, sympathy.

In addition, David's moralism, in the first two volumes, is categorical, self-righteous and often inflexible, scarcely practical in the real world. When he meets Cynthia, locked in domestic servitude to a tyrannical relative, and begins to fall in love with her, for example, he checks his feelings by debating internally whether she is a bit too satirical to be thoroughly good, and wondering whether she is perfect enough to be his ideal friend. Since she resembles the witty narrator more than any other character does, this stern judgement serves to mark David as rather a prig. Indeed, humour largely escapes him, which, in a novel featuring Cynthia as a heroine and an ironic, learned narrator, further thins him out as a character. Again, anxious lest Camilla be not as perfect as she appears, David feels relief when she weeps at Cynthia's melancholy tale of abuse: '*David* was melted into Tenderness at the sight of [Camilla's] tears; and yet, inwardly, rejoiced at the Thoughts of her being capable of shedding them on so just an occasion' (III, 3, 173). His posture as the touchstone of just sentiment smacks of self-righteousness.

David's strong feelings interfere with his ability to act decisively. He vacillates between passions and resolutions, unable to impose on his turbulent feelings the order that reason provides, so that he magnifies his own pain: pages are dedicated to describing his internal debates, indecisiveness and irresolution: whether to leave his brother's house; what to do when he discovers he prefers Camilla to Cynthia; whether to submit to Orgueil's and Ratcliff's demands. With the cascading disasters of the third volume, David changes as experience tames his righteous convictions. He learns to fear and to flatter when he sees the opportunity of benefiting his son by permitting the selfish Mr Ratcliff to act as his sponsor. Tellingly, the narrator reports that David's affections lead to his 'Timidness of Mind' in which his responsibility for the fortunes of his children overcomes his sense of moral rectitude. 'By the help of this Timidity, both Mr *Ratcliff* and Mr *Orgueil* got an Ascendency over the Mind of *David Simple*, that no Creature on Earth could ever have obtained, had SELF alone been his Consideration' (VI, 3, 352). This timidity inveigles David into collaborating with the selfish tyranny of Mr Ratcliff. David's sentimentalism makes him ineffectual in a world where the sharp ones win.

From the novel's start, Fielding further complicates her picture of sentimental virtue by means of a narrative voice that employs literary allusion, metaphor, pragmatic asides and irony.[6] For example, early on, the narrator mocks the pretentious nattering of Lady True-wit and her companions by comparing it to 'the Cackling of Geese, or the Gobbling of Turkeys', and claiming that even 'a *Spectator*' would find it indecipherable (II, 2, 85). Often, also, the narrator breaks through the suspension of disbelief. Instead of describing her characters, for example, the narrator declares, 'Perhaps it may be expected I should give some Description of the Persons of my favourite Characters; but as the Writers of Novels and Romances have already exhausted all the Beauties of Nature to adorn their Heroes and Heroines, I shall leave it to my Readers Imagination to form them just as they like best' (IV, 9, 303). In this way, she solicits readers' empathy, and invites them to participate in the sentimental ideology of the book.[7] However, these narrative interjections also satirize the improbability of such selfless feelings as David's by invoking a rather more earthbound reality:

> And now, Reader, if you are inclined to have an adequate Idea of *David*'s Raptures on that Confession, think what Pretty Miss feels when her Parents wisely prefer her in their Applause to all her Brothers and Sisters . . . Observe her yet a little older, when she is pinning on her first manteaux and Petticoat; then follow her to the Ball, and view her Eyes sparkle, and the convulsive Tosses of her Person on the first Compliment she receives: But don't lose sight of her, till you place her in a Room full of Company, where she hears her Rival condemned for *Indiscretion*, and exults in her *Loss of*

> *Reputation* .... Imagine the Joys of an ambitious Man, who has just supplanted his Enemy, and is got into his Place ... But imagine what you will, unless you have experienced what it is to be both a sincere and successful Lover, you can never imagine any thing equal to what *David* felt. (IV, 8, 295–6)

While such imaginative opportunities enable readers to personalize the story, they also ironize David's high-flown feelings.

These appeals to the reader's imagination reflect a problem endemic to sentimental fiction: the paradox that words, the very stuff of the novel, fail to convey feelings, particularly soft feelings, accurately.[8] In order to explain why she has skimmed over David's and Camilla's emotions at the deaths of their children, the narrator explains: 'The true Reason why I dwell not on that Concern, is, that Words cannot reach it – the sympathizing Heart must imagine it – and the Heart that has no Sympathy, is not capable of receiving it' (VII, 5, 412). This distrust of language intensifies the underlying irony in a book in which the narrator dedicates long passages to describing David's feelings, even while asserting that only sensitive readers could understand such feelings, and that they already do without requiring any description. Indeed, the slightly voyeuristic aspect of imagining others' feelings further compromises the sincerity of the sentimental message: when the narrator claims, 'I have too much Regard for my Readers to make them *third Persons to Lovers*', she ironically highlights the banality of sentimental feeling, as well as the prurience of reading about it (IV, 8, 295). Like the sentimental hero himself in a selfish world, the very enterprise of the sentimental novel seems almost self-cancelling.

Amelia and the Dangers of Impulse

Like both *David Simple* and *Sidney Bidulph, Amelia*, Henry Fielding's sombre final novel, recounts a complicated plot with a large cast of characters whose stories interweave. Fielding employs more of a cause-and-effect structure than an episodic one, albeit, as with *David Simple*, episodes illustrate themes. The main narrative follows Captain Booth, an officer on half-pay, married to Amelia, who is disinherited thanks to a false will devised by her conniving sister. Not only is Booth for most of the novel confined to the verge of court, the area around the royal palace where he cannot be arrested for debt, but at the novel's start, he has been sent to Newgate for attempting to save an innocent man from beating and wrongful arrest. Worse, once there, he succumbs to the wiles of the volatile, passionate and concupiscent Miss Mathews, and falls into an adulterous affair that haunts him throughout the book, just as bailiffs hunt him for his mounting debts. His best friend, Colonel James, attempts to seduce his wife; his faithful protector, the cleric Dr Harrison, misled by malicious rumour, has him re-arrested for another, huge debt just as, from his friends' generosity, he has paid off the last one; Amelia has had to pawn their last possessions, even clothes; the family maid steals their remaining linens; and his young family is starving. The stage is set for tragedy.

However, Fielding snatches comedy from these dark circumstances by ending the novel with a *deus ex machina*. Robinson, a shady, atheistic gambler whom Booth meets in Newgate, by (improbable) chance recognizes Amelia's portrait from a miniature she is attempting to pawn, and, after receiving what seems a fatal wound and being carried to the bailiff's jailhouse where Booth is confined, reveals in a deathbed repentance that he stood as witness in the plot to defraud Amelia by means of a false will. Restored to her inheritance, fortune and mutual trust, the family retire to the country, and Booth 'hath never since been thirty miles from home'.[9] Inset autobiographical tales by subordinate characters sprout from the central trajectory of the hero's struggle to find happiness, and episodic events, accidents and digressive accounts interrupt the main story. These stories illustrate central themes in the novel, often presenting an alternative ending to stories similar to the main action. Similarly, flanking characters illustrate either aspects of the hero's personality or threats to the hero, providing occasions for misunderstanding, the hero's self-delusion or satire.

Amelia contains four versions of the sentimental hero: Amelia, her husband Booth, the naïf Atkinson and the parson Dr Harrison.[10] Each of these characters struggles with the fundamental flaws of sentimental feeling, good nature and impulse as they stumble through the murky tangles of a society entirely spun from graft, lust, malice, envy, vanity and self-interest. From good nature and weak principles, the easily persuaded Booth overspends, gambles and commits adultery; Amelia suffers from Booth's repeated tumbles into the snares of mercenary villains and her own refusal to recognize evil intentions; Atkinson endures, mainly silently, the pangs of a heart hopelessly given to Amelia; and Dr Harrison suffers seeing others suffer. On the periphery, a bevy of characters victimized by their own desires provide moral exempla of the perils of succumbing to feelings, particularly sexual feelings, unstructured by a good heart and a steady mind: the lust-driven Colonel James and rakish noble lord; the shallow, cold Mrs James; the inflammable Colonel Bath, finally dispatched in one of the unnecessary duels over honour to which he is addicted; the pimping Mrs Ellison; and the morally ambiguous Mrs Atkinson, who does not scruple to bargain with the corrupt peer who drugged and sexually assaulted her to gain her husband a promotion.

The eponymous heroine most unambiguously stands as the paradigm of long-suffering, Christian virtue and submission: tender, angelically forgiving, patient and faithful, she represents the ideal wife and mother, yet also the quintessentially desirable woman: virtually every man in the novel wants to bed her.[11] Innocent, guileless, beyond the necessary deceptions to keep herself inviolate and Booth contented, innocent, she appears perfect – barring a scar on her nose from an accident that occurs before the novel begins. The scar serves as Fielding's attempt to impose a realistic flaw, and to emphasize her internal beauty, and also Booth's moral soundness, since it was her fortitude under the pain and shame of the injury that first attracted him to her. At the same time, Amelia's passivity in the face of continual sexual harassment reveals the futility of an obstinate innocence in a two-faced world. This also leads her to self-delusion: for far too long, she persists in trusting the lustful Colonel James; she accepts unquestioningly the noble peer's extraordinary fondness for (and rich gifts to) her children. Here, indeed, Amelia falls victim to the sentimental hero's dilemma of failing to recognize otherness and, thus, others' motives, as she cannot see anything strange in an unknown, unmarried nobleman's admiration of her offspring. She exemplifies the natural faith and goodness that come from a clean heart, but also the necessity of caution and judicious deception for protection from social predators.

If Amelia stands as the clearest example of unsullied virtue, which 'exists to be assailed', Booth represents another example of the dangers of sentimental feeling.[12] Weak and wavering, amiable and impulsive, 'sweet-tempered' Captain Booth exhibits sentimental good nature undisciplined by religion or principle (8, 1, 315). For Booth, however, this self-indulgence has a darker side: it corresponds to his ill-formed philosophy, which maintains that humans cannot choose but act will-lessly according to their ruling passion. This atheistic bent points one of the problems that sentimental philosophy presented: the apparent incompatibility of acting by impulse and acting according to Christian principles. While someone naturally endowed with good nature could reconcile these, pitfalls lie ahead for those who are also naturally weak. This is Booth's dilemma. Unlike many of the other male characters in the book who pursue a rakish Restoration ethos of sexual conquest, he – like David Simple – possesses a feminized mentality: despite his career as a soldier, he shuns violence, loves his friends, adores his family, drinks alcohol only with meals, and takes people at their word. Sensitive to impressions, modest and brave, he is a hearty good fellow. His virtues, however, facilitate his vices: his sociability enables his vanity, infidelity and gambling, even when he is virtually destitute. Captain Booth also knows how to deceive and betray, but his actions result from his impulsive, self-indulgent passions rather than any deep-seated plot for personal gain. Without firm principles, he is a victim and easy dupe.

The most telling vignette in which Booth's weakness appears concerns the masquerade. As occasions of class mixing and licentious behaviour, masquerades in the eighteenth century were viewed as carnivalesque, scandalous and dangerous places in which people could act on unlicensed desires.[13] Even before Amelia learns that the tickets for the event are a gift from the noble peer who drugged and seduced – or raped – Mrs Atkinson by using a masquerade as a cover, Amelia, who prefers a domestic dinner with her family, resists. Reluctant to explain her scruples to Booth, since nothing has yet happened and she cannot betray Mrs Atkinson's secret, she tries to avoid it, but Booth becomes angry, and they experience one of several quarrels in the book, all of which occur as a result of Amelia's attempt to protect Booth from her own suspicions about their various benefactors' motives. Booth, on this and other occasions, falls back on the cliché that Amelia, like many women, is unreasonable, and angrily insists. When he discovers the peer's motives, later, he regrets his bad temper but he remains reluctant to trust his wife's judgement. This difference between the worlds, values and motives of men and women runs throughout the novel, and provides one of the main tensions in its representation of sentimental behaviour.

Christianity, indeed, provides a vital key to the virtues and flaws of the other two sentimental heroes in this novel. Less central but still important, Atkinson, Amelia's foster brother and Booth's loyal servant in the army, exemplifies the unspoiled simplicity of the pure soul: loyal, loving and self-effacing, submissive even under the tantrums of his learned wife. He exemplifies unlearned, instinctive goodness. Significantly, Atkinson propels the happy ending of the novel, snatched improbably from imminent tragedy, by providing the gold-and-diamond encrusted miniature of Amelia, which he stole as a memento of her as an eighteen-year old when she left to marry Booth. Atkinson had cherished the miniature as a representation of Amelia, but it is when Amelia uses it as a financial asset and pawns it to buy food that an acquaintance of Booth's recognizes her, and confesses that he witnessed the false will that disinherited her. Miraculously, the Booths gain a fortune, pay their debts and lose all their troubles. Valued for its representation of the inimitable heroine, it symbolizes the clash of mercenary and sentimental meaning, and the miraculous triumph of feeling.[14] Atkinson's saintly dedication to Amelia saves the day.

The crusty Dr Harrison offers a more sophisticated model of sentimental philosophy: learned, conscious, unwavering Christianity. While he stands as the moral touchstone of the novel, he too makes mistakes and exhibits flaws: he trusts the biased reports of Booth's neighbours and too quickly judges by appearances when, for example, he causes Booth's arrest for debt. Like every character in the novel, he also exhibits vanity: competing with, mocking and deploring Mrs Atkinson for her 'masculine' knowledge of Latin and Greek. Nonetheless, his animadversions against duelling and the false 'honour' men protect, and his abhorrence of adultery as the source of all domestic evil, show a practical application of Christianity to contemporary society that marks him as a model parson. This crusty, perfectionistic, exemplary clergyman, who acts as a father to the Booths, supplies a frame of righteous Christianity, a sort of moral chorus that serves as a corrective to the persuadable Booth's amiability, reminding readers that good nature and good intentions do not constitute a sound moral fundament.

Fielding's narrative voice serves occasionally to counter and contextualize the experiences of characters. This voice balances the accounts of characters who often relate long narratives from their own perspectives – particularly Booth and Miss Mathews – without the intervention of the omniscient narrator. Satirical explanations of 'great men' and, in addition, metafictional asides underscore the artificiality – or affectation – of pretended sentiment, fashionable but false feeling. When, for example, Miss Mathews in prison with Booth exclaims at his 'generosity' in declaring love to Amelia, and wonders whether he 'ever had an equal', the narrator remarks, 'Perhaps the critical reader may have the same doubt with Miss Mathews; and, lest he should, we here make a gap in our history, to give him an opportunity of accurately considering whether we have in this place maintained or deviated from that strict adherence to universal truth which we profess above all other historians' (Book 1, chap. 2, 64–5). This ironic aside alerts readers to scrutinize both characters' motives and the accuracy of their self-representations, as well as the probability of the novel. Thus, when, a little later, Booth is beginning to describe a romantic encounter with Amelia to the eager Miss Mathews, the narrator declares that he will 'place this scene in a chapter by itself', since some readers may prefer to skip it, leaving it to the judicious reader to surmise the underlying reason for Miss Mathews's interest (1, 1, 94). These narrative interjections dash some cold realism on to the heated excesses of sentimental feeling.

Miss Sidney Bidulph and Fatal Delicacy

Whereas sexual desire propels all of the interwoven plots in *Amelia*, self-conscious, unyielding sentimental honour drives the story in Frances Sheridan's *Memoirs of Miss Sidney Bidulph*. Fundamentally a conduct-novel designed to exhibit and to instil female submission, piety and duty, here sexual desire is a weakness, even a vice, the characteristic of prostitutes and undisciplined male impulse. It stands in opposition to love refined – indeed, over-refined – beyond the physical into the obsessively psychological.[15] Unlike *David Simple* and *Amelia*, the sentimental heroine of Frances Sheridan's novel largely narrates her own story to her friend Cecilia, in a series of letters and journal entries, supposedly discovered by an unnamed editor. The self-examination and unwitting self-revelation of the narrative resemble those of Clarissa Harlowe, the heroine of Samuel Richardson's popular novel (1747–8): indeed Sheridan dedicates her novel to him as *Clarissa Harlowe*'s author.[16] While Sidney seems to exemplify the 'archetypal victim' of sentimental fiction, a flawless sacrifice to duty, the narrative reveals a darker side to her self-sacrifice.[17]

The tale is terribly sad: a cascade of misunderstandings, missed opportunities and tragic events, propelled by Sidney's infuriatingly rigorous sense of justice, honour and virtue, fashioned and intensified by self-abnegating adherence to the inflexible Christian principles of her interfering mother, lies and malicious rumours.[18] Sidney, as a young, blooming, beautiful and wealthy girl, is promised by her brother Sir George as the bride of his best friend, Orlando Faulkland. A model of probity, handsome, vastly wealthy, disinterested, loyal, sensitive, passionate, honourable and good, Faulkland considers the match a commitment, although he has not met Sidney; when they do, he falls instantly in love and she, more cautiously, begins to admit her similar feelings. However, disastrously, Faulkland's brief encounter with Miss Burchell, which leaves her pregnant with his child, emerges; their engagement is cancelled; and Sidney is rushed into marriage with the weak spendthrift Mr Arnold in order to avoid imputations that Faulkland rejected her for some nefarious flaw.

Like Sidney, Faulkland is a version of a sentimental hero, but rather a proto-Byronic one. He has one, sentimental weakness, a lax sexuality that, coupled with his amiable temperament, enables his seduction; and one fatal flaw, a quick, ungovernable temper which leads him to impulsive violence. This occurs twice. Early in the novel, his savage punishment of a drunken servant whose carelessness causes Sidney's fall from a horse and sprained ankle, leads to the servant's attempt at blackmail, the exposure of his one-night intrigue with Miss Burchell and her resulting pregnancy. The consequences are nothing short of catastrophic: Sidney's mother, leaping to the conclusion that he is a seducer, forbids the marriage, befriends the deserted mistress, who at the end we discover is a prostitute, compels him (with Sidney's influence) to marry her, and propels both sentimental lovers to lives of frustration, unhappiness and disgrace.

The second instance drives the end of the novel. In self-induced exile in Ireland with his wife, Faulkland discovers her in flagrante delicto with an acquaintance, Major Smyth; Smyth seizes one of a pair of pistols, and shoots at Faulkland, who 'in the first transports of his rage', seizes the other pistol and shoots Smyth, who in turn appears to shoot Mrs Faulkland.[19] Faulkland must flee Ireland to escape arrest, but the conviction of his crimes weighs on him so that, even when he discovers, bitter-sweetly, that Mrs. Faulkland merely fainted and that, although Smyth dies, he would be charged only with self-defence, it is a blow too much. His marriage, hastily arranged on his deathbed by Sir George to Sidney, is voided: his mind is broken, his spirits finally crushed and his heart fails. He dies in the night, without even a kiss from the woman he has spent his whole life adoring, obeying, attempting to help and protecting from afar.

Sidney's vulnerability (and her mother's) to fancied misrepresentations – such as the possibility of a rumour impugning her when her marriage to Faulkland is called off – reveals one of several flaws in her character. Sidney's system of virtue is based on the avoidance of even the slightest hint of impropriety, but, surrounded by malice and deceit, this is impossible, and not, in fact, within her control. Far from imperceptive, nonetheless she refuses to act on her own judgement – for example, her correct suspicions of Miss Burchell's honesty, and her knowledge that both her mother and her moral exemplar, the rigid Lady Grimston, err in their judgements. Her motivations seem blameless: most powerfully, absolute obedience to her mother, but also justice for Miss Burchell, piety and a determination to place others' happiness above her own. However, these principles plunge her into an ecstasy of self-denial, in which the reasons for refusing Faulkland grow ever more refined. Her filial obedience compels her to concede to her mother's wilful blindness in refusing to read Faulkland's explanatory letter, which would exculpate him from the charge of seducer, or to permit Sidney to see or hear explanations from him. She adheres inflexibly to her daughterly duty of obedience.

Sidney preserves this phantom honour in the face of her better knowledge. She knows that Mrs Bidulph, whatever her professed Christianity, is driven by a hatred of men occasioned by her own disappointment at the altar, but repeatedly (and unconvincingly) excuses her mother's 'despotic . . . government' over her, and declares, 'even her errors proceed from virtue' (I, 45). While this demonstrates her perfect daughterly duty, it also highlights the flaws in a moral system that assigns absolute authority over one person's body to another. Repeatedly, the possibility of the union of Sidney and Faulkland arises only to be felled by Mrs Bidulph's interference and insistence on Sidney's scruples; Sidney's compelled marriage to Mr Arnold, a man to whom she is indifferent and who wastes his fortune on an affair with Miss Burchell's whorish aunt, reducing her at one point to banishment, destitution and near-divorce; and, worse of all, emotionally blackmailing Faulkland into marrying Miss Burchell, 'that monster, a female libertine, a rake in the worse sense of the word' (III, 355), enjoyed by – among others – Sir George. Even when Faulkland, apparently a widower, begs for her hand, she hesitates 'to receive a hand stained with – [blood]' (III, 401). Her delicacy results in misery for both.

Sheridan reveals that this delicacy derives not merely from Sidney's excessive conscience, but from her pride. Even as Sidney grows more and more religious, her Christian submission and selfless heroism retain this taint and turn her apparently 'masochistic' passivity, which has maddened many feminist critics, into a form of self-admiration.[20] She confesses that the thought that it might appear that Faulkland withdrew from their marriage, rather than the reverse, 'would a little hurt my pride', and admits 'our pride sometimes stands in the place of virtue': that what appears an action done for honour actually reflects self-love (I, 49). After Arnold dies, and she is left widowed, the mother of two 'faded with grief', she still refuses to marry Faulkland because 'My own honour (scrupulous you might call it) would not suffer me to let the man succeed Mr Arnold in my love, who was the occasion of so much uneasiness to him, and the cause of my being suspected in my fidelity. Would it not be an insult to his memory?' (II, 294). Later, she returns the money Faulkland secretly sends her under cover of his relative, declaring, 'my soul has still too much pride, or let me call it delicacy, to submit to this' obligation to him (II, 295). She even disapproves her mother's imprudent 'impulsiveness' in openly reporting their family's affairs (I, 95; II, 176). Sidney's prudence raises reputation above happiness. This pride rests in an adherence to excessively quixotic principles of self-denial: the determination to put anyone else's happiness before her own. Faulkland himself derides her 'obstinate punctilios' (III, 410), and even her friend Cecilia questions 'those punctilios, which ... *might* have been got over' (III, 310). By detailing the conflicts between worldly opinion and sentimental delicacy, and the triumph of malicious rumour, greed and selfishness over self-conscious virtue, Sheridan writes essentially a satirical critique of both: a world indifferent to injustice and a sentimental philosophy that feeds on pain.

The differences between Faulkland's and Sidney's forms of feeling reflect a gendered cliché. Sidney's feelings are more gentle than passionate; the blamelessness of her self-opinion supersedes passion. This feminine delicacy leads to abnegation of responsibility: 'Fain would I bring myself chearfully to conform to my mother's will', she declares, 'for I have no will of my own. I never knew what it was to have one, and never shall, I believe' (I, 78). She claims, unconvincingly, to reason her way out of love with Faulkland and into love with Mr Arnold, and her cruelty to Faulkland justifies his declaration that only his death will satisfy her. Indeed, when they finally wed – a marriage immediately invalidated by Faulkland's wife's survival – Sidney justifies it in terms that suggest she prefers bestowing to receiving favours:

> I beheld him now ... in a light in which I never before viewed him; overwhelmed by misfortunes, of which I accused myself of being the author. I saw him an exile, likely to be deprived of a noble fortune, his heart pierced with remorse for an involuntary crime. I saw too that he loved me; loved me with a fervent and unconquerable passion ... Shall I own it to you, my Cecilia, I think I never loved him as I did in that moment. My heart was at once assailed by a variety of passions; amongst which, gratitude, and the softest compassion, were predominant.
>
> (III, 416)

Desire is melted into gratitude at his love of her, a devolution that hints again at pride. In the end, she believes her fate shows God's will; thinking herself 'a Heroine' (I, 49), she, like Richardson's Clarissa, becomes a kind of saint through her submission to fate and Christian resignation. Her maid Patty observes, 'Piety, meekness, and patience, were ever Mrs Arnold's characteristics', and Sidney herself asserts, "'I have been set up as a mark, my Cecilia; let me fulfil the intention of my Maker, by shewing a perfect resignation to His will'" (III, 423).

In addition, Sidney denies her feelings. She falls in love with Faulkland, and never falls out of it, but she protests to herself and Cecilia repeatedly that she is perfectly indifferent to him. While attempting to persuade herself that she can love Mr Arnold, she writes,

> I have been searching my heart . . . to try if there remained a lurking particle of my former flame unextinguished; a flame I call it . . . but it never rose to *that*: it was but a single ray, a gentle glow that just warmed my breast without scorching . . . I have the satisfaction to find, that the short-lived fire is quite extinct.
>
> (I, 78)

As Jean Coates Cleary points out,

> When she finds herself unexpectedly close to Faulkland in a theatre, the building itself bursts into flames . . .. Sidney's assertions about her feelings for Faulkland, invariably prefaced by such statements as 'I call that being to witness who knows the secrets of all hearts' or 'if ever I knew my own heart', attest both to the good faith in which her assertions are made and to the double bind in which she is caught. She cannot see what she has been taught must not exist.[21]

Only at the very end, when her benefactor Mr Warner declares, 'I . . . know that at the bottom of your heart you *love* Faulkland . . . notwithstanding all your pretended demurs', she finally admits, 'I should be disingenuous to deny it', with the involuted language of the double negative registering her reluctance (III, 400).

Although Sidney may be the sentimental protagonist in the novel, in many ways it is Faulkland who is the sentimental hero, feminized into passive suffering.[22] She suffers the trials of living in society, but he is a 'hopeless wanderer', exiled and alone, as much obsessed by passion for his icy maiden as a chivalric knight (II, 214). Their difference in gender determines their difference in temperament and in destiny. Sidney early on observes, 'Mr Faulkland is of too warm a temper; yet I am not alarmed at the discovery; you know I am the very reverse', adding that 'His own good sense and good nature must incline him to wish it corrected . . . he has often lamented this vice of his nature' (I, 32). Strong passions, especially sexual passion but also the passion for acting honourably and generously, drive Faulkland and, accordingly, lead to his vulnerability to the seductress Miss Burchell, and thus to his Romantic death from frustration, remorse and despair.

Conclusion

These three novels describe sentimental heroes – women or feminized men – seeking love and friendship in contention with a cynical society, where malicious rumour and misunderstanding cloud perception, and where absolute principles of right and wrong collide with the realities of a world of compromise. Through improbable plot twists and sudden rescues by a *deus ex machina*, all three novels highlight the unlikeliness of virtue succeeding against selfishness. They also present a critique of sentimentalism as both impractical and self-indulgent: the inability or refusal to apply reason and discipline to the feelings. The result is a double-edged condemnation of injustice and evil, and a fatalistic exposure of sentimental folly. Each of these sentimental characters also grapples with a fundamental problem at the heart of sentimentalism: the paradox of empathy – the imaginative and emotional identification with others – as opposed to a perception that recognizes difference: these characters see others as mirrors of themselves, and thus attribute to them impulses and desires identical to their own. This blinds them not only to the possibility of others' deceit, but also to their own self-delusions.

Gendered differences in attitudes towards sexual commitment and fidelity also mark both the heroes and the authors' approach to one of the main themes of these three novels. Whereas *David Simple* largely sinks sexuality into sentimentality, *Amelia* presents men as fools of their physical desires when unimpeded by correlative emotional commitment; *Sidney Bidulph*, on the other hand, finds sexual impulse a threat to reason and morality. In each novel, the protagonists attempt to construct an ideal family with like-minded intimates, relatives and offspring to counter the harshness of an unsympathetic world. Through satire and sentiment, they examine similar themes: friendship, romantic love, gender roles, injustice, greed, hypocrisy, envy, cruelty, malice and, especially, selfishness. Although women appear generally more vulnerable than men because of their fragile frames and sensibilities, both genders are weakened and effeminized by the delicacy of their feelings. The solution for each is retreat, even if temporarily, from urban complexity to a simple rustic life, but only in *Amelia* does this solution end the story. The picture these novels paint owes as much to Augustan misanthropy as to Shaftesburyan sentimental philosophy.[23] The portrait is grim indeed.

Notes

1. Sarah Fielding, *The Adventures of David Simple*, ed. Malcolm Kelsall (Oxford University Press, 1987), I, 3, 27. All citations refer to this edition.
2. Simon Dickie, 'Novels of the 1750s', in *The Oxford Handbook of the Eighteenth-Century Novel*, ed. J. A. Downie (Oxford University Press, 2016), 253; see Mika Suzuki, 'Sarah Fielding and Reading', in *The Eighteenth-Century Novel*, vol. 11, ed. Albert J. Rivero and George Justice (New York: AMS Press, 2002), 91–112.
3. Bill Knight, '*David Simple* and the Ethics of Genre', *Genre* 50 (2017): 267–8; Tera Pettella, 'Devotional Reading and Novel Form: the Case of *David Simple*', *Eighteenth-Century Fiction* 24 (2011–12): 279–80.
4. Deidre Lynch, *The Economy of Character: Novels, Market Culture, and the Business of Inner Meaning* (University of Chicago Press, 1998), 39.
5. Janet Todd, *Sensibility: an Introduction* (London: Methuen, 1986), 4.
6. James Kim, 'Mourning, Melancholia, and Modernity: Sentimental Irony and Downward Mobility in *David Simple*', *Eighteenth-Century Fiction* 22 (2010): 477–502.
7. Bryan Mangano, 'Ideal Friendship and the Paradoxes of Narration in Sarah Fielding's *David Simple*', *Eighteenth-Century Fiction* 26 (2013–14): 165–88.
8. Todd, *Sensibility*, 5–6, 125.
9. Henry Fielding, *Amelia*, ed. David Blewett (New York: Penguin 1987), 12, 9, 545. All citations refer to this edition.
10. R. F. Brissenden, in *Virtue in Distress: Studies in the Novel of Sentiment from Richardson to Sade* (London: Macmillan, 1974), identifies the 'Comic, Pathetic and Tragic Versions of the Distressed and Virtuous Hero' in later eighteenth-century fiction (243).
11. Scott Black, 'Henry Fielding and the Progress of Romance', in Downie, *Oxford Handbook*, 249.
12. John Mullan, *Sentiment and Sociability: the Language of Feeling in the Eighteenth Century* (Oxford: Clarendon Press, 1988), 124.
13. Terry Castle, *Masquerade and Civilization: the Carnivalesque in Eighteenth-Century English Culture and Fiction* (Stanford University Press, 1986).
14. Deidre Lynch, 'Personal Effects and Sentimental Fictions', *Eighteenth-Century Fiction* 12 (2000): 345–68; Lynn Festa, *Sentimental Figures of Empire in Eighteenth-Century Britain and France* (Baltimore: Johns Hopkins University Press, 2006), 75.
15. Jean Coates Cleary, 'Introduction', in Frances Sheridan, *Memoirs of Miss Sidney Bidulph*, ed. Patricia Koster and Jean Coates Cleary (Oxford University Press, 1995), xxiii.
16. Sheridan wrote a continuation of the novel entitled, *Conclusion of the Memoirs of Miss Sidney Bidulph* (1767), which resumes the story years later to follow the children, Orlando and the two Miss Arnolds, as they prepare to leave home. See *Conclusion of the Memoirs of Miss Sidney*

Bidulph, ed. Nicole Garret and Heidi Hutner, with an Introduction by Nicole Garret (Peterborough, ON: Broadview Press, 2013); John C. Traver argues that the sequel exposes 'the first novel's failure adequately to condemn male partiality and rigidity' in 'The Inconclusive Memoirs of Miss Sidney Bidulph: Problems of Poetic Justice, Closure, and Gender', *Eighteenth-Century Fiction* 20 (2007): 36.

17. Todd, *Sensibility*, 4.
18. Tim Parnell, 'Sterne's Fiction and the Mid-Century Novel: the "Vast Empire of Biographical Freebooters" and the "crying Volume"', in Downie, *Oxford Handbook*, 280.
19. Frances Sheridan, *Memoirs of Miss Sidney Bidulph*, with Introduction by Sue Townsend, 3 vols. in 1 (London: Pandora, 1987), III: 397. All citations refer to this edition.
20. Cleary, 'Introduction', xxix; Patricia Meyer Spacks, *Desire and Truth: Functions of Plot in Eighteenth-Century English Novels* (University of Chicago Press, 1990), 136–7; Margaret Anne Doody, 'Frances Sheridan: Morality and Annihilated Time', in *Fetter'd or Free? British Women Novelists, 1670–1815*, ed. Mary Anne Schofield and Cecilia Macheski (Athens, OH: Ohio University Press, 1986), 345; Janet Todd, *The Sign of Angellica: Women, Writing, and Fiction, 1660–1800* (New York: Columbia University Press, 1989), 167.
21. Cleary, 'Introduction', xxxiii.
22. Kathleen M. Oliver, 'Frances Sheridan's Faukland, the Silenced, Emasculated, Ideal Male', *Studies in English Literature, 1500–1900* 43 (2003): 683–700, esp. 697–8.
23. Michael Genovese, '"A Mixture of Bad in All": the Character of Self-Interest in Sarah Fielding's *David Simple*', *The Age of Johnson* 22 (2012): 207–31.

CHAPTER 5

Sentiment from Abroad: French Novels after 1748

Gillian Dow

In 1748, Richardson's *Clarissa* was published in England. Three years later, in 1751, Antoine François Prévost published a very free translation of it. He omitted several crucial passages, including a large portion of the narrative after Clarissa Harlowe's death. Anna Howe's lament over her friend's corpse, Sinclair's death, and a great many letters between Lovelace and Belford are all left out of Prévost's recasting. Prévost shaped Richardson's novel to suit the tastes of his countrymen and with a keen eye for the market. Despite claims in his preface that he published simply for pleasure, Prévost – as Thomas O. Beebee and others have pointed out – was constantly in need of money, and most of his translations were published for financial reasons.[1] As Richardson himself wrote in a June 1753 letter to his Dutch translator, Johannes Stinstra, Prévost was also well known for having written 'several Pieces of the Novel Kind'.[2] Richardson's dismissive reference to Prévost's prior publications damns the French novelist not with faint praise, but with mid-eighteenth-century anxieties about the novel genre. It is clearly much worse to be the author of a kind of novel than of a novel proper. Richardson's knowledge of Prévost's fiction hinges, almost certainly, on the popularity and success of the Frenchman's *Histoire du Chevalier des Grieux et de Manon Lescaut* (1731). This was a tale of passion focusing on a beguiling heroine who becomes a prostitute, told through her lover's eyes. It was considered by a great many readers across Europe to be both amoral and immoral.

Anne C. Vila has argued that the eighteenth-century cult of sensibility differed in France from elsewhere in Europe, distinguishing 'French' sensibility from 'English' versions, and thus distancing her account from models provided by Barker-Benfield and others. Vila notes three major differentiating factors, and she is worth quoting at length:

> First, sensibility and sentimentalism were closely associated in France with the process of secularization that the philosophes were intent on

> advancing. Second, French writers did not polarize sensibility in relation to sex and gender nearly as much as did their British counterparts, at least not until the last few decades of the century; rather, even the most hard-boiled philosophes prided themselves on their sensibility and saw nothing unmanly about cultivating this quality. Finally, sensibility was standardly imbued by French writers with a pronounced physicalist or materialist undertone, without provoking any major outcry from the defenders of morality and religion.[3]

If we accept Vila's three defining characteristics for the French vogue for sensibility, it seems somewhat strange that the French *philosophes* were among Richardson's most enthusiastic, and vocal, readers. Indeed, the great triumvirate of Voltaire, Rousseau and Diderot commented extensively on Richardson, and all three published fiction inspired by the English author's novels. Most interestingly, although Voltaire and Diderot in particular made extensive use of parody and satire, their 'Richardsonian' fictions were not parodic or satirical. They were rather, as James Fowler has explored in *Richardson and the* Philosophes, 'serious attempts to appeal to the kind of (ideal) reader who rejoiced to see Pamela rewarded or wept at the sufferings of Clarissa'.[4] Richardson had many readers in France, and was lauded by *philosophes* and anti-*philosophes* alike: these early French readers seem to have been peculiarly sensitive to both Richardson's sentimentality and his moral sentiment.

Rousseau's *Julie, ou la Nouvelle Heloise* (1761) is the most notable example of French Richardsonian fiction. It is also the most discussed, both on first publication and today. There is one direct reference to Richardson, and many more indirect comparisons between the heroines Julie and Clarissa, in the text itself. It is tempting to read the eighteenth-century French bestseller as Rousseau's homage to his English counterpart. Certainly, classic sentimental themes are shared, notably, that civilization corrupts, and prevents natural feelings, and that primitive society restores such feelings. Rousseau, however, takes pains to emphasize the differences between his and Richardson's heroines: *Julie* is no straightforward tribute, nor was the novel read as such, on either side of the English Channel. Indeed, Rousseau's imposing figure can be seen in much of the sentimental fiction published in Britain post-1761, and his influence only increased after his death in 1778. Translated by William Kenrick, and published in 1761, there were at least fifteen English editions of *Julie* before 1815. It inspired literary pilgrimages to the Swiss Alps and a great many re-workings in English fiction too, from Henry Mackenzie's *Julia de Roubigné* (1777) to Helen Maria Williams's *Julia* (1790).

Denis Diderot, one of the brilliant minds behind the *Encyclopédie*, is known to the scholar of Richardson and English sensibility largely for his *Éloge de Richardson* (1762). This is a complex work of criticism that takes as its starting point the fact that the French reader who has only read Richardson via Prévost's mediation – 'que dans votre elegante traduction' – has not read the full and moving tale of Clarissa's burial.[5] Diderot's famous account of his feeling friend's response to reading of Clarissa's fate – complete with free-flowing tears, sobs, screams, pacings and railings against the entire Harlowe family – remains one of the most evocative accounts of an affective eighteenth-century reading experience. Diderot also wrote a remarkable epistolary novel, *La Religieuse*, inspired in part by Richardson's and Rousseau's sentimental fictions. Completed around 1780, *La Religieuse* was only published posthumously, in 1796. Diderot's heroine, a nun named Suzanne, is a first-person narrator, writing her memoirs. Through her, the author creates a Richardsonian illusion of reality: the reader is encouraged to trust and sympathize with the young novice. Indeed Suzanne, in her convent, follows a seduction narrative that is very like Clarissa's own trajectory. The passages dwelling explicitly on the young nun's body and its involuntary reactions during the notorious seduction scene between Suzanne and the Mother Superior have led a more recent French editor, Robert Mauzi, to situate *La Religieuse* between Richardson and the Marquis de Sade – a not incompatible pairing, for which Diderot provides the ideal transition.[6] Indeed, Diderot's triumph is his success in writing a Richardsonian-style novel which not only damns the convent, but is explicitly critical of Christianity, and, implicitly, of revealed religion in general.

Another landmark French novel where the Richardson reference is explicit is Laclos's magisterial multivocal novel, *Les Liaisons Dangereuses* (1782). When the libertine Valmont receives a letter from his valet Azolan describing Madame de Tourvel – at a critical moment in her own seduction narrative – reading a volume of *Christian Thoughts* alongside *Clarisse*, the alert reader knows exactly how to read the reference.[7] Indeed, Tourvel's reading foreshadows the conclusion of Laclos's novel. Between them, Laclos's sentimental heroine, Madame de Tourvel, and her callous seducer, the Vicomte de Valmont, exemplify the extraordinary vogue for Richardson's novels in France: like Clarissa, death is the only proper atonement for Tourvel's loss of chastity; like Lovelace, Valmont dies as a result of injuries sustained in a duel.

Bernardin de Saint-Pierre's *Paul et Virginie* follows *Les Liaisons Dangereuses* a few years later in 1788, picking up on the Richardsonian and Rousseauvian critique of corrupting society and its class divisions. *Paul et Virginie* idealizes the 'child of nature' through its eponymous hero and heroine. The exoticism of the setting – Ile de France, now better known as Mauritius – facilitates an explicit critique of slavery, something that is far less sustained in sentimental fiction of the period than in poetry or polemic, as Brycchan Carey points out in his chapter in this volume (see Chapter 8). Other sentimental themes employed by Bernardin de Saint-Pierre are classic, and instantly recognizable. Virginie herself is doomed to the fate of so many sentimental women in fiction. They are often swooning, distracted by physical sensation (in Virginie's case, sexual awakening due to puberty), frequently ill and, in the novels' conclusions, dead.

Rousseau's *Julie* (1761), Diderot's *Éloge de Richardson* and *La Religieuse*, Laclos's *Les Liaisons Dangereuses* (1782), Bernardin de Saint-Pierre's *Paul et Virginie* (1788): these are all vitally important works of sensibility in the French tradition, all published after Richardson and – it could certainly be argued – all indebted to the characters he created and the themes he explored. For the remainder of this chapter, however, I do not attempt to present an established and recognizable canon of French works of sensibility. Nor do I wish to set out a line of work 'indebted' to Richardson, reducing those who followed him across the Channel to 'disciples'. I wish rather to look at cross-Channel sentimental exchange in the fiction of the latter half of the long eighteenth century. Where it might be tempting to view the French sentimental novels that found a market and readership in Britain after 1748 as inspired, largely, by Richardsonian fiction (notably *Clarissa*), cultural exchange is more complex. Indeed, adopting a cross-Channel approach complicates arguments that examining national traditions is the best way to interrogate the literature of the eighteenth and early nineteenth century.

Cultural transfer, as developed by Michel Espagne and Michael Werner, argues that nations or cultural areas must be modelled as dynamically interrelated systems. What is sometimes believed to be an authentic part of a national tradition turns out, on closer investigation, to have been imported, and vice versa.[8] For the sentimental novel, rather than seeing distinct national traditions of sentimentalism, I wish to pick up on Lynn Festa's argument that 'the sentimental text represents forms of interpersonal communion that transcend national boundaries to embrace all humankind; it produces a community of weeping readers united across cultural and geopolitical barriers by shared tears'.[9] Anne C. Vila's account of the *differences* between the French and the British traditions seems to have mattered much less for the eighteenth-century publishers, translators and indeed readers of the sentimental novel than for twentieth-century critics. As Festa puts it, not all sentimental feeling has a national side. Although later British readers note a type of sentimental French novel that is morally suspect, earlier readers welcomed the addition of French sentimental fiction to their native fare, just as 'le divin Richardson' was welcomed into the accepted French canon of eighteenth-century novelists as one of their own.

Re-examining the Sentimental Marketplace

As a wide range of predominantly Anglo-American critics, working on the Anglo-American tradition, have argued, the canon-forming attempts – invariably nationalist endeavours – of the nineteenth and early twentieth century have had a dramatic influence on telling the story of the rise of the eighteenth-century novel. This is as true for the sentimental novel as it is for the picaresque, the libertine and the Romance. The success of nineteenth-century realist and naturalist French novelists such as Stendhal (1783–1842), Honoré de Balzac (1799–1850), Victor Hugo (1802–85), Gustave Flaubert (1821–80) and Emile Zola (1840–1902) has led to a neglect of their predecessors. Scholarship looks forward to Proust, Gide and Camus, rather than looking back to Scudéry and La Calprenède, and the emphasis on the eighteenth-century *philosophe* thinkers is to the detriment of the *romancière* (I use the feminine form of the noun advisedly here). When we consider the 'Great Forgetting' of French women writers of the late eighteenth and early nineteenth century in British literature – to appropriate a phrase used by Clifford Siskin for eighteenth century and Romantic-period British women writers – sentimental fiction takes centre stage.[10] Margaret Cohen has argued, in her suggestive study of the French nineteenth-century novel, *The Sentimental Education of the Novel* (1999), that French novelists Balzac and Stendhal carved out their own place in the literature of the nineteenth century via 'a hostile takeover of the dominant practice of the novel . . . sentimental works by women writers'.[11] Cohen's work has implications for the study of sentimental fiction more generally, and in particular across the Channel in Britain, where the sentimental works by the French women writers that she champions had a clear market, both in the original French and in English translation. Taking account of the once hugely popular novels of Marie-Jeanne Riccoboni (1713–92), Isabelle de Montolieu (1751–1832), Germaine de Staël (1766–1817) and Sophie Cottin (1770–1807) enables us to remap the sentimental novel in

Britain, and to redraw the temporal boundaries of the switch in popularity to the realist and naturalist novel.

Josephine Grieder, in her valuable study and bibliography *Translations of French Sentimental Prose Fiction in Late Eighteenth-Century England: the History of a Literary Vogue*, claims that the fashion for English translations of sentimental novels from the French can be dated from the 1760s, peaking in the 1780s and early 1790s, and then declining rapidly. Grieder's cut-off date of 1800 seems somewhat arbitrary, not least because several of the French authors she identifies as highly fashionable in the Britain of the 1780s and 1790s continued to publish, and were translated, in the 1800–30 period.

Grieder claims that 'what doubtless killed sentimental fiction was the French Revolution itself', and that the novel of sensibility 'perished when the world for which it had been created disappeared'.[12] This makes for a convenient thesis. Taken to its logical conclusion, we might consider Bernardin de Saint-Pierre's *Paul et Virginie* (1788) as the last hurrah of the French sentimental novel, published, as it was, just one year before the storming of the Bastille. Helen Maria Williams completed her 1795 translation, *Paul and Virginia*, in France, amid the horrors of Robespierre's tyranny, which makes for a neat coda to the story of the production and reception of this pre-Revolutionary tale. But Grieder's thesis is not sustainable when one considers the continuing popularity of translated sentimental French fiction in the Britain of the opening decades of the nineteenth century. As Peter Garside notes in the introduction to his bibliographical survey of the prose fiction of the period 1800–29, new translations do not start to tail off until the 1820s.[13] Grieder's summary does not take stock of the continuing popularity in the 1800s of authors who first published fiction in the 1780s. Stéphanie-Félicité de Genlis (1746–1830) is a notable example. Genlis's novels of the early nineteenth century have been considered historical novels – and indeed that is how Genlis herself referred to them – but they cover a great many themes familiar to the reader of the sentimental novel. Where Grieder writes that her study of French sentimental fiction in English translation illuminates 'certain moments when the literary taste of two different nationalities coincides to a considerable degree', she is underplaying the extent to which the novel in the eighteenth century developed as a cross-Channel literary production.[14] A great many scholars, since Grieder, have charted this development, including myself. Edited collections of essays by Margaret Cohen and Caroline Dever, Hilary Brown and Gillian Dow, Nathalie Ferrand, and Jenny Mander re-examine the 'rise' of the novel in its pan-European context, and Mary Helen

McMurran's *The Spread of Novels* sites the eighteenth-century novel more specifically as a cross-Channel development.[15] Margaret Cohen even argues that the sentimental novel, as a transnational genre, was tasked, in the wake of the French Revolution, with improving the relationships between Britain and France.[16]

In the closing decades of the eighteenth century, earlier French sentimental novels were also resurrected by new English translations. Charlotte Smith's translation of Prevost's 1731 *Manon Lescaut* attempted to breathe new life into the French novel's British reception in 1785 – somewhat unsuccessfully, since the translation was withdrawn almost immediately after publication, and only one copy is now extant. The splendidly named Radagunda Roberts published a translation of Françoise de Graffigny's 1747 *Lettres d'une Peruvienne* as *Peruvian Letters* in 1774 and Jeanne-Marie Leprince de Beaumont's 1748 *Le Triomphe de la vérité, et Mémoires de M. de La Villette* as *The Triumph of Truth; or Memoirs of Mr de La Villette* in 1775.[17] Roberts dedicated the latter to the Duchess of Devonshire, adopting in her 'Dedication' the standard 'defence' of the sentimental tale, by claiming it as a moral tale. Indeed, there is often something of a slippage between the two: *The Triumph of Truth* opens with the death of a twelve-year-old child from smallpox, and the resulting anguish of his playmate, and a great many sentimental tropes are deployed throughout. Roberts assures the dedicatee – and of course her readers – of the moral and improving aspects of the narrative. She insists that 'the Work in the Original' was 'stored with those sentiments of virtue and religion with which your Grace's illustrious ancestors have been peculiarly blessed'.[18] She remains confident that the Duchess of Devonshire 'would not disdain to patronise a work originally written, and since translated, by a woman'. Roberts's subsequent translator's preface is a lengthy one. She claims she does not wish to 'give a dissertation on Modern Romance', while damning those 'libertine' novels where the 'Man of Pleasure, is depicted in so pleasing a light, as to encourage that mistaken notion so readily received among young Women, that a reformed Rake makes the best Husband'. Interestingly, Roberts's concerns are not made specific to the French novel, or to an English tradition: she conflates the two, in terms of the common themes addressed by both. Roberts sees herself as serving a moral purpose, by accurately translating the best French works of moral sentiment for British consumption: there are dangerous 'men of pleasure' in both languages.

Radagunda Roberts was a frequent contributor of sentimental tales and translations from the French to *The Lady's Magazine* in its early years, a neat reminder that one must also look for the presence of French sentimental novels and authors in other places than in standard, novel-length translations published by British publishing houses. *The Lady's Magazine*, which ran from 1770 to 1830, included a great many original translations of moral and sentimental fiction, and French fiction was also serialized across a range of issues. The prefaces, and indeed the main body, of British sentimental tales can reference French sensibility. Such is the case in Henry Mackenzie's *The Man of Feeling* (1771), where the fictional editor describes himself 'a good deal affected by some very trifling passages in it; and had the name of a Marmontel, a Rousseau, or a Richardson, been on the title-page – 'tis odds that I should have wept'.[19] The inclusion of Marmontel alongside the two pillars of mid-eighteenth-century sentiment is worth commenting on. Jean-François Marmontel's 1761 *Contes Moraux* was enormously popular in Britain. His 1767 *Bélisaire* (condemned in France as heretical, thus setting it on the path to European celebrity) saw seven English editions in the year of first publication, and at least thirty by 1800. He was also a leading French sentimentalist in the pages of British periodicals and magazines. Alongside a great deal of Marmontel, a reader of *The Lady's Magazine* could find extracts from Le Sage, Genlis, Graffigny, Staël, Leprince de Beaumont, Rousseau and other named authors.

Many French authors, now obscure, loom large in the pages of the British periodical press alongside anonymous works purporting to be 'from the French'. Several of these authors, indeed, were compared by British critics to Richardson himself. The French writers often fared better through the comparison. In December 1783, the *European Magazine* described Baculard d'Arnaud – author of such works as *Les Épreuves du sentiment* (1775–78) and *Délassemens de l'homme sensible, ou Anecdotes diverses* (1783–7) – as 'one of the most pathetic and moral writers now in France', and stressed to their readers that he could be usefully read alongside 'the immortal author of *Clarissa*'.[20] Few are the readers who would now read these works comparatively. In the remainder of this chapter, I attempt to resituate these works within the context of the British literary marketplace of the late eighteenth and early nineteenth century, arguing for the French novel's inclusion in an exploration of British sentimental fiction of that period.

Reading the French Sentimental Novel in Britain

Marie Jeanne Riccoboni (1713–92), a French actress married to an Italian, became a tremendously popular author on retiring from the stage.

In January 1772, she wrote of the 'fureur' of sensibility that reigned supreme in France: 'nos dames veulent pleurer, crier, étouffer aux spectacles . . . le sentiment est la folie du jour'.[21] Riccoboni was describing what she felt was a specifically French scene to her good friend David Garrick, who must have recognized at least some of it from his experience of what was then popular on the English stage. Riccoboni's letter is, on the surface, derisory of the 'sentimental vogue'. But it was sentimental novels, published between 1757 and 1780, that made her name. And her name was a significant one, in Britain, as in her native France. Where Richardson is the novelist with the sixth-largest number of British editions in the period 1750–69, Riccoboni ranks at number seven.[22] The earliest chroniclers of the modern novel recognized Riccoboni's importance too. In Clara Reeve's *The Progress of Romance* (1785), Sophia brings up her name as 'a writer of great merit', and Euphrasia agrees that her work is, for the most part, 'in the first rank of Novels'.[23] Indeed, Riccoboni's continuation of Marivaux's *Marianne* became an accepted part of the English translation of the novel in the latter half of the eighteenth century.

Joseph Bartolomeo, in Chapter 10 in this volume, examines Frances Brooke's *The History of Emily Montague* (1769) as arguably the first Canadian novel, and certainly one of several sentimental novels exploring questions of national identity in the New World. Brooke's apprenticeship as a novelist was forged, however, in a cross-Channel context, through her activities as a translator of French sentimental fiction. Brooke published her popular translation of Riccoboni's *Letters from Juliet Lady Catesby, to her Friend Lady Henrietta Campley* in 1760. The questions of national identity, here, are curiously incidental. Riccoboni certainly attempted an 'English' framework for her novels, all of which are epistolary (mostly mono- or dialogic). On the whole, Riccoboni's characters are English, but of an oddly French Englishness. What must the original English readers have made of Riccoboni's first publication, the splendidly titled *Lettres de Mistriss Fanni Butlerd, a Milord Charles Alfred de Caitombridge, comte de Plisinthe, duc de Raflingth*, first published in Amsterdam [Paris] in 1757, purporting to be written in English in 1735 and translated into French by the fictional Adélaïde de Varançai in 1765. In *Juliet Catesby*, too, names are frequently pseudo-English; places such as 'Vinchester' and 'Amstead' are the setting. Frances Brooke changes Riccoboni's place names to 'Winchester' and 'Hampstead', and she makes a great many changes to characters' names, anglicizing them in the process.

Riccoboni's sentimental heroines invariably suffer from the inconstancy of their lovers. Juliet Catesby, for example, is a young widow, abandoned by her betrothed, Ossory, who swiftly marries another, for reasons the heroine cannot understand. After a series of letters, complicated plot twists and misunderstandings, it transpires that Ossory, in a moment of weakness, raped Fanny Montford, the young sister of his friend. As translated by Brooke, the moment of the seduction is rendered as follows:

> Abandoned to my senses, I forgot my love, my probity, the laws of honour which had always been sacred to me, the sister of my friend: a woman whom I ought to have respected, appeared to me at that instant, only as a female delivered up to my wishes, to that gross passion which has its source in instinct alone. Hurried away by an impetuous emotion, I had the cruelty to take advantage of the disorder and simplicity of a young imprudent, whose artless innocence alone occasioned her error.[24]

Fanny becomes pregnant, and – after her marriage to Ossory, upon which she becomes Lady Ossory – she gives birth to a daughter. Shortly after, Lady Ossory dies. Juliet laments her love rival's death to her friend Henrietta, the recipient of the majority of the letters in the novel, using heightened and sensational language. Lady Ossory's tale moves Juliet to tears, and she poses a series of rhetorical questions about the behaviour of Lord Ossory, who is to become her own husband by the end of the novel, just a few short pages later: 'Why did he not make her happy! . . . Why did he avoid her? Why afflict a heart so full of sensibility? Had she not a right to his tenderness? What cruelty to deprive her of it? I am shocked at the inhumanity of his behaviour, and cannot approve that unsocial chagrin, of which he made her the victim.'[25] The conclusion – which sees Juliet Catesby and the widowed Lord Ossory united at last – is haunted by the spectre of the first Lady Ossory. Frances Brooke may even give a suggestion of her own dissatisfaction with the treatment of this character in her translation. While the first Lady Ossory is dying, Brooke includes the introduction of a Dr Lewin (where Riccoboni uses 'Lereins'), a character whose very appearance makes the intertextual references to Richardson's *Clarissa* explicit: Dr Lewin is Clarissa's spiritual advisor. The first Lady Ossory may be read, then, as another Clarissa. But this is a reference that the original author – Riccoboni herself – may never have intended.

Connections between Riccoboni and Richardson's works were observed by another of Riccoboni's translators, who made the comparisons explicit. Percival Stockdale, the translator of Riccoboni's *Letters from Lord Rivers to Sir Charles Cardigan* (1778), dedicates the work to Mrs Shipley, wife of the Bishop, as deserving of the attentions of the serious and the good: 'their Author has given a moral Force to Reason, to Sentiment, and to the

Passions'.[26] Stockdale continues, in his Translator's Preface, to stress the moral sentiment of Riccoboni's work, by quoting Dr Johnson's praise of Richardson:

> Literary Glory is the first human Splendour; therefore *it is not to be sported with*. With a proper Distinction, however; with a proper Veneration of the Memory of Richardson, we may apply to Madame Riccoboni the noble Encomium with which *He* has been honoured by the illustrious Author of the Rambler – 'She hath enlarged the Knowledge of human Nature, and taught the Passions to move at the Command of Virtue'.[27]

Despite this seemingly high praise of Riccoboni, Stockdale has not been above 'little Additions' to his translation, where he feels that the original was 'defective in Argument, in Sentiment, or in Imagery'. His translator's notes, we read, have been annexed to correct some important errors, where Riccoboni was 'mistaken as a Philosopher; where she was misled by the Partiality of a Native of France; and by the Prejudices of a Woman'.[28] Stockdale writes, he tells us, for the benefit of his 'fair Countrywomen', seeing women readers as the ideal recipients of his 'improved' version of Riccoboni's text. This is common practice for a translator in the period.

Recent critics – notably Marijn Kaplan, Joan Hinde Stewart and Suzan van Dijk – have all stressed the feminist subtexts in Riccoboni's works.[29] In her novels, the sentimental heroines, thwarted in love, emphasize feminine sympathy and female friendship. Juliet Catesby, because of Lady Ossory's death, can marry the latter's widower, the man she loves, and indeed admire him for doing his duty to his late wife and daughter: a somewhat rare happy ending for the sentimental heroine. Other novels conform to type. Another of Riccoboni's heroines, Mme de Cressy, from the *Histoire de M. le marquis de Cressy* (1758), puts a powder in her tea on learning of her husband's inconstancy. She dies in his arms and M. de Cressy lives on, the author tells us, rich, exalted, but not happy.

Sophie Cottin (1770–1807), another near-contemporary sentimental novelist who used suicide and attempted suicide as a theme, has been almost entirely neglected, and yet her novels were popular in the first decade of the nineteenth century, and, in the case of *Elisabeth, ou Les Exiles de Sibérie* (1806), published in new English translations throughout the nineteenth century. In her short life, Cottin lived through events that would not be out of place in the sentimental novels that made her name. Indeed, the presentation of the *Critical Review*, using the biography of Cottin written by Boileau, is of a true heroine of fiction:

> The whiteness of her complexion, her large blue eyes, and the melody of her voice announced the beauties of her soul; the whole of her physiognomy bore the impressions of an excessive sensibility; and no man who has witnessed the smile of benevolence that played upon her lips, or the tears of compassion that trembled in her eye-lids, will ever lose the remembrance of her angelic sweetness.[30]

Cottin was born Sophie Ristaud, into a Protestant, bourgeois Bordeaux family, and married a banker, Paul Cottin, aged nineteen. Fleeing the Revolution, the young couple travelled to Spain, and then to England, returning to Paris in late 1793. Paul died in Paris, perhaps of a heart attack, perhaps – it has been suggested more recently – at his own hand. Sophie never remarried, turning down several proposals – one of her suitors committed suicide as a result of her rejection. Another suitor seemingly rejected her on learning of her infertility – a topic that has been seen, by the only full-length study of her novels to date, as crucial to her creativity.[31] She was part of a literary network of novelists that also included François-René de Chateaubriand, Germaine de Staël and Bernardin de Saint-Pierre, with whom she carried out extensive correspondences. Her death – aged only thirty-seven, of breast cancer – shocked literary society, for whom her novels *Claire d'Albe* (1799), *Malvina* (1801), *Amélie Mansfield* (1802), *Mathilde* (1805) and *Elisabeth, ou Les Exiles de Siberie* (1806) had proved tremendously popular. In Britain, Cottin's novels were translated by Elizabeth Gunning and Elizabeth Meeke née Allen, stepsister of Frances Burney, placing Cottin herself at the forefront of popular female-authored fiction of the age, and at the centre of a cross-Channel network of women novelists. Indeed, the popularity of the sentimental fiction of Sophia Lee and Burney's last novel, *The Wanderer* (1814) – read as 'historical anachronisms' by Melissa Sodeman in Chapter 11 in this volume – is far less anachronistic if the popularity of Cottin in Britain is also taken into account.

The influence of Rousseau's *Julie* on Cottin's fiction is undeniable, and was observed by contemporary readers. What has been less remarked on is the Wertherian influence – and yet this too was commented on in Britain. The comparison is explicit, in fact, through the attempted suicide of the heroine of *Amélie Mansfield*, who – believing she has been betrayed by her lover – throws herself into the Danube. The *Critical Review*, reviewing *Amélie Mansfield* in May 1804, describes the novel as 'truly affecting', and, as such, stresses that it 'nearly approaches Werter'. That said, the reviewer wishes such 'distressing scenes' not to be 'commonly circulated', despite the desire of 'the sentimental fair one' to 'be beguiled of her tears'.[32]

The sentimental fair ones in Britain do indeed seem to have appreciated Cottin's novels, and for several decades after their first publication. Accounts of reading her novels appear in the diaries of Elizabeth (Betsey) Fremantle (1778–1857) and Mary Shelley (1797–1851), although those readers do not comment on their responses at any length. One reader, Anne Lister (1791–1840), left a fuller account of her reading. The Yorkshire landowner, known now for her voluminous diaries documenting her lesbian affairs, subscribed to the library in Buxton for a month in August 1825. One of the first volumes she withdrew was *Amélie Mansfield*, although she records on 9 August that the language was 'poor ... after that of Rousseau' who 'spoils me for such language as Mme Cottin'. On 10 August, despite the poverty of language, Lister appears much absorbed in the sentimental plot: 'Too much interested in my book to leave it off. Cried over it almost all the time.' Writing to her correspondent, Maria Barlow, on 16 August, Lister documents her French reading: 'My leisure is passed in rummaging all over the French Novels the miserable public library here affords! I have just finished Amelie Mansfield. My Aunt fancies I read for the sake of keeping up my French.'[33] Notably, Lister hints here at the illicit pleasures of a French novel. There is a troubled relationship between keeping up one's French – an important accomplishment for a gentlewoman – and the dangerous reading that such an accomplishment affords. Indeed, several near-contemporary novels emphasize the dangers: more than one British heroine falls in love with an unsuitable man over a shared reading of Rousseau.

British critics suggest they were fighting a losing battle against the dangers of reading French sentimental fiction in the opening decades of the nineteenth century. In a review of Sophie Cottin's novels in 1809, the *Critical Review* observed that 'amidst all the language of exalted and virtuous sentiment, with which these works abound, there is in the avowed principle which inspired and pervades them, an insidious sophistry most dangerous to the heart, and most pernicious to the understanding of young and susceptible females'. The *Critical* reviewer, without the 'smallest hesitation', recommends to 'our daughters ... the works of Fielding, Smollett, or Sterne, in preference to the poisoned sensibilities of this *moral* writer'.[34] Not for the first time, the British critics warn away from dangerous French texts to apparently more wholesome, home-grown fare. The threat is unspecified, but it is certainly often to the detriment of French women writers, who cannot match their British male counterparts, in the eyes of the British reviewers. Anxieties hinge vaguely, too, on concerns about the depiction of sexual desire, which seem to be perceived as an oddly 'French' preoccupation, although I can find no clear evidence of separate trajectories for explorations of the theme in the French and English fiction of the period. What is much clearer is the British critics' nationalizing agenda which *claims* difference where very little exists. Attempts to differentiate between native literature and foreign imports appear in reviews of French sentimental fiction long before the true canon-forming publications of the later nineteenth century are published.

Transnational and Cross-Channel Sentimentality in 1816

The transnational settings of key French sentimental texts from the turn of the eighteenth and nineteenth centuries offer another reason to investigate fiction across borders, and can be usefully set against the great number of 'national' tales published in Britain in the first decade of the nineteenth century, before Walter Scott's *Waverley* (1814). The *roman d'émigration* is an example of a vogue that flourished in the immediate aftermath of the French Revolution, tracing displaced aristocrats across Europe and lamenting their plight.[35] Chateaubriand's *Atala* (1801) and *René* (1802) – both set among the Natchez Native American people, with episodes in Scotland (in the footsteps of Ossian), Italy and France – are celebrated examples of French fiction that crosses borders in the period. Benjamin Constant's *Adolphe* is another example of what I would term a 'transnational' French text. First published in 1816, although written largely in 1806, *Adolphe* is a somewhat neglected text both in terms of the history of the French novel and in the history of the sentimental novel more generally. Patrick Coleman, editor of the World Classics translation, sees it as belonging to 'a distinctive French tradition of concentrated first-person narratives or *récits* that includes such works as Gide's *The Immoralist* and Camus's *The Stranger*'.[36] The novel is, however, far better understood as a pan-European Romantic product, and should be read within the context of other European sentimental successes of the period: Goethe's *The Sorrows of Young Werther* (1774), of course, but also Germaine de Staël's *Delphine* (1802) and *Corinne* (1807).

Adolphe was written in French by a Swiss Protestant writer, and is set in provincial Germany and Poland. Constant's connections with European literary elites saw the novel a success even before publication. Lady Caroline Lamb tried to persuade John Murray II to publish it, attempting to use her relationship with both Constant and Murray to mediate its success. Murray had published Staël's *De l'Allemagne* in both French and English in 1810, and was the publisher of Lord Byron, who was connected to Constant, Staël and the Coppet circle. For reasons unknown, although presumably to do with his lack of emphasis on the novel genre in general (he famously declined to publish Mary Shelley's *Frankenstein*), John Murray declined the publication of *Adolphe*. The novel was eventually published in French, in London, then in translation in London – both by H. Colburn on Conduit Street – then in French in Paris. The *Critical Review*, in its account of the first French edition of *Adolphe*, noted that Constant was 'known as the translator of Schiller's Wallenstein, so beautifully rendered in English by Mr Coleridge', and observed that he 'has been allowed to fill the character of a French legislator at different periods of the Revolution, though, we believe, his birth was in Switzerland, and his family connections, and much of his early life, have been in Germany'.[37] Indeed, the pan-European literary scene plays out within the pages of the narrative. Adolphe and Ellénore are clearly members of a European literary elite. They 'read the English poets together' during the early stages of their love affair, and the novel insists on the disaffection of its titular hero, who is both a solitary wanderer and a Wertherian sentimental hero.[38]

British readers – several of whom heard the manuscript read by Constant himself after a dinner at the Bourkes in Cavendish Square – clearly responded to the tragedy of the lovers, which is, to an extent, the tragedy of the human condition. Mary Berry describes the end as 'so touching that it was scarcely possible to restrain ones tears': the effort she made to do so made her 'positively ill', and both she and her sister 'burst into tears' on their return journey home.[39] The pleasure of a sentimental novel has not diminished, and emotional affectivity appears to be unaffected by national agendas.

That said, the year 1816 can, with the benefit of hindsight, seem like something of a watershed in terms of the new direction British and French novels were to take in the nineteenth century. As we have seen, John Murray had declined to publish Constant's *Adolphe* in 1816. But he had published – in December 1815 – Jane Austen's *Emma*, the second novel on his list (the first was an English translation of Genlis's *La Duchesse de La Vallière*, published in 1804). *Emma* – that most English of English novels – can be read as a significant text in terms of the cross-Channel exchange in fiction. The French translation appeared early in 1816, anonymously translated for Paris-based publisher Arthus Bertrand, who seems to have had a keen eye on what Murray was publishing across the Channel. When, in 1816, *La Nouvelle Emma* was published, it was as a more or less straight translation of Austen's original, with a lengthy anonymous preface for the French reader. In it, the French reader would learn that Austen's work was not, in fact, a novel, but rather an ethnographic guide for the visitor to England. Bertrand was known as a publisher of sentimental fiction – indeed, one of his bestselling authors was Isabelle de Montolieu, the Franco-Swiss author of the sentimental novel *Caroline de Lichtfield* (1786), and the translator of Austen's *Sense and Sensibility*, which had appeared under Bertrand in 1815. Isabelle de Montolieu's translation of Austen's first-published novel as both a warning against excessively sensibility and a sentimental novel *par excellence* (complete with dramatic plot changes to Austen's original ending) tells us a great deal about the horizon of expectations of the reader in Continental Europe in 1815. The sentimental novel still dominated, and Montolieu's changes were just right for her intended audience, who would have appreciated a Marianne Dashwood (Maria, in Montolieu's French rendering) who swooned and sighed much more than the original.

Isabelle de Montolieu recognized that Jane Austen's path was quite a different one to her own. Montolieu's own novels, and indeed her translations, emphasized sensibility, and were designed to provoke dramatic responses in their readers. But her critical engagement with Austen's realism – from a fellow novelist – reminds us of nothing so much as Walter Scott's careful and sustained engagement with *Emma* in his *Quarterly* review of 1816. Montolieu's 1821 'Translator's Note', which appeared at the beginning of her *La Famille Elliot* – a translation of *Persuasion* – points out that readers who enjoy being violently moved ('être violemment émus') will be disappointed in Austen's prose, but equally Montolieu stresses that no one has captured natural scenes of real life as Austen has. When one considers the responses of Maria Edgeworth and Walter Scott to *Emma*, Montolieu's changes to *Sense and Sensibility*, and her comments on *Persuasion*, do not seem quite as startling as they might otherwise have done. Jane Austen and her celebrated French translator – whose reputation thoroughly eclipsed Austen's own in Europe throughout the nineteenth century – represent different perspectives on the role of sentiment, and indeed on the direction the modern novel was to take on each side of the Channel. Both France and England saw a move away from the sentimental novel to the realist novel, which was the more literary and prestigious form by the end of the nineteenth century.

What, then, remains to be explored through the cross-Channel sentimental novel? I conclude with an anecdote. On the death in May 1849 of salonnière and society beauty Juliette Récamier, an inventory of her books was made.[40] The list includes surprisingly little French fiction. As far as English-language texts are concerned, the usual historians, moralists and guides are present: Blair's Rhetoric; Johnson's English Poets; Hume's History of England; *The Spectator*; Pope's Homer. And one copy of Henry Mackenzie's *The Man of Feeling*, first published in 1771 – a work Mackenzie's compatriot Robert Burns said he prized 'next to the Bible'.[41] And yet Récamier must have had books elsewhere, uncatalogued. She must have borrowed fiction, from *cabinets de lecture* or less formally. She must have read the sentimental novels of her close friends Chateaubriand, Constant and Staël. Récamier's book inventory, that is, does not tell us much about anything other than what the person drawing up the inventory found worth recording – a canon, of sorts, registering mid-nineteenth-century preoccupations and interests.

In an age of scholarly preoccupation with big data as providing the 'truth' about literary fashions and taste, we must also pay close attention to what we find worth recording, and how we make those judgements. French sentimental fiction may not have appeared on Récamier's shelves, but we should certainly write these texts back into our accounts of literature of the period. Caroline Franklin writes in a recent study of the British novel of sensibility in the 1780s that 'sensibility should be seen as a long-lasting literary movement rather than an ephemeral fashion', pointing out that it can be detected in Anglo-American political drama as early as the Exclusion Crisis of 1679–81, and that it survived in the 'mid-nineteenth century lachrymosity of Charles Dickens and Harriet Beecher Stowe'.[42] Looking across the Channel, the story is similar: the roots of French sensibility can be seen in the romances of Scudéry and La Calprenède; its descendants in George Sand, and even naturalist Zola's heroines. No alert reader should come to Zola's account of the fate of Lalie – the child martyr in *L'Assommoir* (1877) – without being aware of her eighteenth-century sentimental ancestors, ancestors who appeared in both French and English fiction. Geoffrey Sill, in a chapter on British sentimental fiction in the recent *Oxford Handbook of the Eighteenth-Century Novel*, concludes that the future for studies of sentimental fiction might be not 'in uncovering reasons for its decline, but in discovering the ways in which the forms of sentiment have survived'.[43] Clearly, one of the ways the sentimental novel survived in the nineteenth century was in the popularity of translations of sentimental fiction, and the textual presence of the original works abroad: Rousseau, Riccoboni and Cottin in Britain; Richardson and Henry Mackenzie in France; Isabelle de Montolieu's version of Jane Austen's *Sense and Sensibility* across Europe. Perhaps we should work towards a broader definition of sentimental fiction in our readings of the eighteenth- and nineteenth-century novel. Certainly, we must continue to remap national accounts, and to look beyond borders. Only then will we uncover the full extent of this cross-Channel vogue.

Notes

1. Thomas O. Beebee, *Clarissa on the Continent: Translation and Seduction* (University Park: Pennsylvania State University Press, 1990). See Beebee's Introduction for comments on Prévost's career as a literary translator.
2. Quoted in ibid., 10.
3. Anne C. Vila, *Enlightenment and Pathology: Sensibility in the Literature and Medicine of Eighteenth-Century France* (Baltimore: Johns Hopkins University Press, 1998), 3.
4. James Fowler, *Richardson and the* Philosophes (Abingdon, Oxford, and New York: Legenda, Modern Humanities Research Association and Maney Publishing, 2014), 1.
5. Denis Diderot's *Éloge de Richardson* first appeared in the *Journal Étranger* of January 1762. Subsequent French translations invariably included Diderot's critique as a preface.
6. Denis Diderot, *La Religieuse*, ed. Robert Mauzi (Paris: Folio Classique, Gallimard, 1972) ; see Préface, 16.
7. Choderlos de Laclos, *Les Liaisons Dangereuses*, trans. Douglas Parmée (Oxford University Press, 1995), 239.
8. Stefanie Stockhorst provides an excellent introduction to Michel Espagne and Michael Werner's concept of 'cultural transfer'. See *Cultural Transfer through Translation: the Circulation of Enlightened Thought in Europe by Means of Translation*, ed. Stefanie Stockhorst (Amsterdam: Rodopi, 2010), 19–22.
9. Lynn Festa, *Sentimental Figures of Empire in Eighteenth-Century Britain and France* (Baltimore: Johns Hopkins University Press, 2006), 45.
10. Clifford Siskin, *The Work of Writing: Literature and Social Change in Britain, 1700–1830* (Baltimore: Johns Hopkins University Press, 1997), 193–227.
11. Margaret Cohen, *The Sentimental Education of the Novel* (Princeton University Press, 1999), 6.
12. Josephine Grieder, *Translations of French Sentimental Prose Fiction in late Eighteenth-Century England: the History of a Literary Vogue* (Durham, NC: Duke University Press, 1975), 15.
13. Peter Garside, James Raven and Rainer Schöwerling, *The English Novel, 1770–1829: a Bibliographical Survey of Prose Fiction Published in the British Isles*, vol. II: 1800–1829 (Oxford University Press, 2000), 99–101.
14. Grieder, *Translations of French Sentimental Prose Fiction*, ix.
15. See Margaret Cohen and Caroline Dever, ed., *The Literary Channel: the International Invention of the Novel* (Princeton University Press, 2002); Jenny Mander, ed., *Remapping the Rise of the European Novel* (Oxford: Voltaire Foundation, 2007); Nathalie Ferrand, *Traduire et illustrer le roman au XVIIIe siècle* (Oxford: Voltaire Foundation, 2011); Mary

Helen McMurran, *The Spread of Novels: Translation and Prose Fiction in the Eighteenth Century* (Princeton University Press, 2010).

16. See Margaret Cohen, 'Sentimental Communities', in Cohen and Dever, *The Literary Channel*, 106–32.
17. Radagunda Roberts was identified recently by Jenny DiPlacidi, part of the team working on *The Lady's Magazine* under the direction of Jennie Batchelor at the University of Kent: https://blogs.kent.ac.uk/ladys-magazine/2016/02/29/searching-for-r-a-collaborative-identification/.
18. Marie Leprince de Beaumont, *The Triumph of Truth; or Memoirs of Mr. de La Villette*, trans. Radagunda Roberts (London: T. Cadell, 1775), Dedication.
19. Henry Mackenzie, *The Man of Feeling* (London: F. Newberry, 1788), vii.
20. Quoted in Grieder, *Translations of French Sentimental Prose Fiction*, 21.
21. Quoted in Grieder, *Translations of French Sentimental Prose Fiction*, 8.
22. James Raven, *British Fiction, 1750–1770: a Chronological Checklist of Prose Fiction Printed in Britain and Ireland* (London: Associated University Press, 1987), 14.
23. Clara Reeve, *The Progress of Romance*, 2 vols. (Colchester: W. Keymer, 1785), 1: 132.
24. Marjin Kaplan, ed., *Translations and Continuations: Riccoboni and Brooke, Graffigny and Roberts* (London: Pickering and Chatto, 2011), 56.
25. Ibid., 63.
26. Marie Jeanne de Heurles Laboras de Mezières Riccoboni, *Letters from Lord Rivers to Sir Charles Cardigan*, trans. Percival Stockdale (London: T. Becket, 1778), Translator's Dedication.
27. Ibid., x–xi.
28. Ibid., xv–xvi.
29. See Marijn Kaplan, 'Marie Jeanne Riccoboni's *Lettres d'Elisabeth Sophie de Vallière*: a Feminist Reading', *Women in French Studies* 13 (2005): 25–36; Joan Hinde Stewart, *Gynographs: French Novels by Women of the Late Eighteenth Century* (Lincoln, NE: University of Nebraska Press, 1993); Suzan van Dijk, 'Lire ou broder: Deux occupations féminines dans l'œuvre de Mmes de Graffigny, Riccoboni et de Charrière', in J. Herman and P. Pelckmans, ed., *L'Epreuve du lecteur: Livres et lectures dans le roman d'Ancien Régime* (Louvain: Peeters, 1995), 351–60.
30. *Critical Review*, Appendix, 3rd series, 16 (JanuaryApril 1809): 502–11, 502.
31. See M. J. Call, *Infertility and the Novels of Sophie Cottin* (Newark: University of Delaware Press, 2002).
32. *Critical Review*, Appendix, 3rd series, 2 (May 1804): 114–15, 114.
33. Anne Lister, *No Priest But Love: Excerpts from the Diaries of Anne Lister, 1824–1826*, ed. Helena Whitbread (Yeadon, West Yorkshire: Smith Settle, 1992), 114.
34. *Critical Review*, Appendix, 3rd series, 16 (January–April 1809): 502–11, 511.
35. See Claire Jaquier, Florence Lotterie and Catriona Seth, eds., *Destins romanesques de l'émigration* (Paris: Desjonquères, 2007).
36. Benjamin Constant, *Adolphe*, trans. Margaret Mauldon, ed. Patrick Coleman (Oxford University Press, 2001), xxvi.

37. *Critical Review*, 5th series, 4 (July 1816): 9–15, 9.
38. Constant, *Adolphe*, 16.
39. Mary Berry, journal entry 14 February 1816, *Extracts of the Journals and Correspondence of Miss Berry from the Year 1783 to 1852*, ed. Lady Theresa Lewis, 3 vols. (London: Longmans, Green and Co., 1865), III: 70.
40. My grateful thanks to William Hines, Librarian at the University of Aberystwyth, for drawing my attention to Récamier's Inventory, which forms part of the Special Collections at the University of Aberystwyth.
41. Quoted in Geoffrey Sill, 'Developments in Sentimental Fiction', in *The Oxford Handbook of the Eighteenth-Century Novel*, ed. J. A. Downie (Oxford University Press, 2016), 426.
42. Caroline Franklin, 'The Novel of Sensibility in the 1780s', in *The Oxford History of the Novel in English*, ed. Peter Garside and Karen O'Brien (Oxford University Press, 2015), 166.
43. Sill, 'Developments in Sentimental Fiction', 438.

CHAPTER 6

Sterne's Sentimental Empiricism

Jonathan Lamb

> Sitting in my Study I hear a Coach drive along the Streets. I look through the Casement and see it. I walk out and enter into it. Thus, common Speech would incline one to think, I heard, saw, and touch'd the same Thing, *viz.* the Coach.[1]

Empiricism, the dominant philosophy of the New Science, provided guidelines not only for the age of experimental investigation but also for the social intimacies of the age of sensibility that followed. Both epochs relied on the evidence of the senses to determine what was happening to matter and to the self, whether it consisted in the reaction of elemental particles with the motions of other bodies or in impressions made on the nerves, heart and mind by human subjects sharing the same space. In either case the five organs of sense were regarded as the sole channels of whatever information was to be gleaned and sorted by the mind from encounters in the natural and social worlds. Thus experiment and experience proceeded from the same axiom, that knowledge and understanding, together with the less definitive faculties of the mind such as imagination and passion, had no other source for their actions, images and ideas but sensation. In this chapter I want to measure how strong and how homogeneous was the influence of empiricism on the development of aesthetics and fiction in the eighteenth century, using Sterne's two sentimental novels as specimens. Particularly I want to determine how extensively John Locke's brand of materialism affected the writing of both.

Epicurean materialism held considerable sway over scientific and literary production at this time and reinforced empiricist thought, being founded on the indisputable alliance and authority of the senses. In *De rerum natura* Lucretius asks, 'Can th'eare the sight denie? / Shall th'eare, or tast, the feeling sense oppose? / Or shall the eie, dispute against the nose?'[2] Much ingenuity was expended on improving the performance and receptivity of the organs of sense in the pursuit of knowledge, health and pleasure, such as microscopes and telescopes for the eye, hygrometers for the nose, megaphones for the ear, artificial skins for the penis and dildoes for the vagina. There was likewise much curiosity about the synesthetic cooperation of the senses, particularly the eye and the hand. Addison wonders in his first *Spectator* paper on the pleasures of the imagination (No. 411) whether sight is not 'a more delicate and diffusive kind of Touch'; while Berkeley's *A New Theory of Vision* (1709) is an extensive account of how intricately visual and tactile stimuli are combined.[3] For his part Robert Hooke maintained that the experience of a rough surface was not complete until the eye had studied a magnified image of it through the medium of a prosthetic eye.[4]

Sterne proclaims his empiricist credentials with comments and axioms which emphasize the importance of sense perception to the faculties of will and reason. In *Tristram Shandy* these positions are robustly announced: 'REASON is, half of it, SENSE'; 'Love, you see, is not so much a SENTIMENT as a SITUATION'; 'Our minds shine not through the body, but are wrapt up here in a dark covering of uncrystalized flesh and blood'; 'Rumple the one – you rumple the other.'[5] He is fond of referring to his body and his book as a machine or a vehicle in which the mind is conveyed, pleasantly or otherwise. In *A Sentimental Journey* the reciprocal influence of material and mental motions is more delicately broached and gradually migrates to a higher plane, but a sentimental scene, like a Shandean one, always begins in a *situation*, with an array of sensational stimuli acting on the sentient individual inside it. Equally for Tristram and Yorick a situation is first of all defined exactly as a space: a garden, a sentry box, a pair of stairs, a coach, a courtyard, a door, a passageway, a counter, a street, a bedroom framed by 'the projection of a chimney on one side, and a large beam which cross'd the room on the other'.[6] The eye is saluted as the premier organ of perception in *Tristram Shandy* whereas Yorick prefers the hand. Bodies traverse these spaces, glancing and touching in the course of what Sterne refers to as sentimental commerce. The pattern of the exchange is sometimes unpredictable. Yorick finds himself holding hands with a woman he has never met before, and hardly seen: 'Monsieur Dessein left us together with her hand in mine, and with our faces turned towards the door of the Remise ... such a cordial situation, as Friendship herself could scarce have atchieved.'[7] The mutuality of bodily circumstances and mental events in Tristram's situations, such as Walter's exasperation caused by reaching for his handkerchief with his right hand into a low-cut left-hand pocket, are sometimes far from cordial, and while generally of short duration, they are not necessarily brief. The bowling green situation of Toby and Mrs Wadman lasts five years. But they all illustrate the spontaneous implication of mind and spirit with body and matter. Emotions, ideas and intentions may be brought to bear upon it, but even with the most careful staging, 'the Situation, like all others, has notions of her own to put into the brain'.[8]

Yorick nearly loses his first situation because he doesn't understand this, or rather doesn't *feel* it. By the time he exclaims, 'Whatever is my situation – let me feel the movements which rise out of it, and which belong to me as a man', he has learned the lesson the lady taught him at the remise gate when he was unwise enough to use words and ideas to advert to the intimate position they found themselves in.[9] 'Your reflection upon it, shews how much, Monsieur, she has embarrassed you by the adventure. When the situation is, what we would wish, nothing is so ill-timed as to hint at the circumstances which make it so: ... who but an English philosopher would have sent notices of it to the brain to reverse the judgment.'[10] Then she removes her hand from his. When he recovers it, he silently attends to the beat of her pulse, and she to his, so that when they finally speak their sentiments flow from a common vibration arising from a common touch. From then on we hear no more of the classes and orders of travelling tabulated in the 'Preface in the Desobligeant'. The metaphor chosen for the contingent circumstances of travel is drawn from the first situation: 'What a large volume of adventures may be grasped within this little span of life by him who interests his heart in every thing, and who, having eyes to see, what time and chance are perpetually holding out to him ... misses nothing he can *fairly* lay his hands on.'[11] But the question is, what kind of English philosophy is the lady thinking of when she rebukes Yorick? Evidently not one where sensations proclaim instant loyalty to the situation, generating ideas and words entirely faithful to it, such as Yorick's situational metaphor of hands and handling. John Locke would find this a scandalous inversion of the order of cognition and communication, 'Words being intended for signs of my Ideas, to make them known to others, not by any natural signification, but by a voluntary imposition, 'tis plain cheat and abuse, when I make them stand sometimes for one thing, and sometimes for another.'[12] Why then is it Locke who is cited apparently so respectfully in Sterne's fiction as the authority for comic and sentimental situations?

No matter how broadly empiricist thought and practice had spread, both abroad and in Britain, it would be a mistake to suppose that there was consensus regarding the materialist doctrines it favoured. Its most powerful antagonist was Descartes. The great sceptical experiment of his *Meditations* is to suppose that all sense perceptions are hallucinations manipulated by a sinister genie. Resisting them requires an effort of intense thought to identify what remains in the mind of its very own. Upon reflection Descartes discovers in his a stock of innate ideas, pre-existent to all experience and sufficient to arm the mind with the one certainty it can grasp no thanks to empirical information, namely that it thinks. The identity of a human being is formed by knowing this. The passions and the senses, prone to irregularities and extravagances, are subordinate agents of this 'thinking thing', the soul. Descartes was sufficiently impressed by Lucretius to accept the fluid dynamics of *De rerum natura* as a governing principle of the aggregations and dissolutions of animate and inanimate matter, but regardless of the swerves, vortices and explosions of atoms in motion, all move beneath the purview of the Cartesian soul.

There was a much stronger influence than Epicureanism operating on Descartes, however, and that was Platonism. Descartes's hypothesis of the first and second *Meditations* finds its original in the *Republic* where Socrates teaches Glaucon that pure thought – fed by the demonstrable truths of mathematics and geometry – is the sightless vision of the intelligible world, where reason 'makes absolutely no use of anything perceptible by the senses: it aims for types by means of types alone'.[13] That is to say, symmetries visible to the mind, but not to the organ of the eye.[14] Cartesian dualism systematizes the distinction between belief and knowledge with a set of airtight partitions separating the representations of actual matter from the diagrams of types, the blur of empirical observation from the truth of numbers, and the futile work of becoming from the timeless entity of the soul.

It was owing to his desire for a mathematical standard of meaning, where ideas act like numbers, or algebraic symbols, delivering measurable quanta of meaning, that Locke was prepared to accommodate two of Descartes's insights regarding the location of sensible qualities and the transition of sensations into ideas. These are summed up in Descartes's introduction to his *Treatise on Light*, where he says,

> The first thing I want to draw to your attention is that it is possible for there to be a difference between the sensation that we have of [light], that is, the idea that we form of it in our imagination through the intermediary of our eyes, and what it is in the object that produces the sensation in us, that is, what it is in the flame or in the Sun that we term 'light'. For although everyone is commonly convinced that the ideas we have in our thought are completely like the objects from which they proceed, I know of no compelling argument for this.[15]

Here a wedge is driven between what Locke was going to call primary and secondary qualities, introduced by the denial of any material continuity between sensations and ideas. In its place Descartes wants to install sensation as an impulse or charge of energy that is converted into a signal sent via the cranial nerves to the brain. 'Why could not Nature', he demands, 'have established some sign which would make us have sensations of light, even if that sign had in it nothing that resembles this sensation?'[16]

When he improves this idea in his *Essay concerning Human Understanding*, Locke also deploys the analogy between the production of ideas from sensations and the production of meaning from words in order to emphasize the common lack of any resemblance between each pair:

> To discover the nature of our Ideas the better . . . it will be convenient to distinguish them, as they are Ideas or Perceptions in our Minds; and as they are modifications of matter in the Bodies that cause such Perceptions in us: that so we *may not* think (as perhaps is usually done) that they are exactly the Images and Resemblances of something inherent in the subject; most of those of Sensation being in the Mind no more the likeness of something existing without us, than the Names, that stand for them, are the likeness of our Ideas.[17]

Locke is intent on freeing ideas from the imprecisions of their material origins in sense perception in order that they can function as determinate referents of signs attached arbitrarily to them by common agreement. Ideas are not to be shaped by the accidental effects of matter actually in motion, but by its enduring abstract properties that the mind only may apprehend: 'Solidity, Extension, Figure, Motion, or Rest, and Number'.[18] These are primary qualities, and the secondary ones belong to everything we foolishly imagine is transferred directly from objects to the mind by our eyes, ears, palate, nose and fingers: what Thomas Willis calls 'the shaddow of the objected thing . . . marked as upon a white wall'.[19]

When Tristram says that Toby's life was put in jeopardy by words, it is not at first clear what he means – whether his uncle was fallible or the words obscure. Tristram insists the doors of perception are not at fault in his uncle's case; rather 'the unsteady uses of words which have perplexed the clearest and most exalted understandings'.[20] However, words attached to ideas that have a natural affinity to sensations are more appealing. Siege architecture is liberal with terms based on physical and domestic analogies – 'flank', 'place' and 'curtain' – not to mention words for identical objects which change according to their situation, such as a 'ravelin' and 'half-moon'. But the mathematics of pyroballogy yield a very different vocabulary, so specialized only mathematicians or geometricians can use it. Toby's solution to the problem is indexical; he carries words along with their ideas back to the shape and location of their referents so he can point with his finger at what he means. His object is the same as his nephew's, namely 'to convey but the same impressions to every other brain, which the occurrences themselves excite in [his] own'.[21] Locke has served to provide Tristram a catalogue of the indexical *failures* of words rather than their *abuse*, and he uses it to resituate language inside the situations in which impressions first formed the simple ideas that we name when we talk. The worst wound Toby gets from a word comes when trying to define the mixed mode 'humanity'. By way of sympathetic retaliation Tristram enjoys showing how words themselves are vulnerable: ''Twas plain to the whole court the word [whiskers] was ruined: La Fosseuse had given it a wound.'[22]

Toby's sieges become more imaginative the more their verisimilitude is enhanced; that is to say, their indexical function is outstripped by an aesthetic one. With the advent of the War of Spanish Succession Toby starts copying battles he never fought, yet all sorts of illusions – smoking guns, sentry boxes, ramparts and drawbridges – preserve the simulacrum of real action. There is a danger here that images and words will entirely float free of any situational anchor, and that the sentiment will rise to a height beyond the constraints of matter. In this respect, hobbyhorses and sentimental travelling illustrate a truth about empiricism pointed out by Plato that Sterne would not dispute, and it is this: 'The impression sense-perception has to give of an object is that it is no more X than the opposite of X.'[23] Plato's example is the sensation of softness, which can only be known in relation to hardness. The equilibrium to be sustained between what is lost and gained by situational sentiments – in effect between the pain they soothe and the pleasure they afford – runs parallel with the psychophysical correspondence from which they stem. Any attempt to ignore the mixture of mind and matter will result in a loss of balance. These are lessons enforced in *Tristram Shandy*, even upon the author himself, whenever the illusion that 'X' is simply 'X' gets too powerful. So when Toby thinks he is the Duke of Marlborough or that Mrs Wadman is a miracle of humanity, he moves up to a realm where the trials and triumphs of sentience evanesce into the sublime: 'Heaven! Earth! Sea! . . . ye never compounded so intoxicating a draught. . . . Heaven! Earth! Sea! – all was lifted up.'[24] Sterne knew himself to be capable of this mistaken enthusiasm. He wrote to John Hall-Stevenson after a bad pulmonary haemorrhage: 'One or two more escapes will make me believe I shall leave you all at last by translation, and not by fair death.'[25] Whenever Tristram is tempted to forget that the comic festival of his life is also a dance of death, he is soon reminded otherwise.

Things are managed differently in France. Although Yorick has been told by the lady to observe the 'rotation of movements to which the situation is incident', his most serious enthusiasms aren't tethered to the earth nor is he.[26] When he feels every vessel in his frame dilate and all his moving parts operate without the least hint of friction, he is positive he could confound 'the most physical *precieuse* in France: with all her materialism, she could scarce have called me a machine'.[27] This overweening confidence in his bodiless presence, exempt from the constraints of its situation and the shadow of its non-X, looks forward to his meeting with Maria, which concludes with 'such undescribable emotions within me, as I am sure could not be accounted for from any combinations of matter and motion'.[28] Here in an explicit revision of the Shandean original of the scene, Yorick lays waste to Hobbes's account of the origin of everything we discern by feeling: 'All of which qualities called Sensible are . . . but so many several motions of the matter, by which it presseth our organs diversly'.[29] And on its ruins he mounts a Cartesian certainty that the situation itself doesn't modify: 'I am positive I have a soul; nor can all the books with which materialists have pester'd the world ever convince me of the contrary.'[30] The subsequent scene of 'The Grace' confirms his belief that above the level of the body there are spiritual impulses that dignify physical experience, but are certainly not derived from it.

This crux in Sterne's sentimental thinking originates in Locke's Cartesian definition of primary qualities. Yet it is only Locke's distinction between wit and judgement that Tristram disputes. 'It was his glory to free the world from the lumber of a thousand vulgar errors; – but this was not one of them.'[31] Yet Locke's attitude to wit as an abuse both of reason and of language is of a piece with the whole *Essay*. Ideas that are accidentally allied with other ideas, or ideas so uncertainly defined they can be mistaken for other ones, are his aversion. Binding up 'X' with 'non-X' would provide a notorious example: 'You shall see the very place, Madam; said my uncle Toby . . . You shall lay your finger upon the place', says he, talking of his map while she is thinking of his genitals.[32] As for the accidental association of ideas on the casual grounds of contiguity, succession, resemblance or contrast (the idea of travelling recalling the idea of holding something, for instance, or the word 'gay' putting Tristram in mind of the word 'spleen'), it is held forth in the *Essay* as a species of madness.[33]

While Locke is adamant that minds are joined to bodies and that ideas derive from sensations, he is equally certain that an idea once formed is not to change its structure or meaning unless by alliance with another idea; the only modification it will undergo will be its successive conjunctions with other ideas comparably clear and definite, forming an architecture of abstract meaning that wit and other false associations cannot molest. As Locke allows no rational grounds for hybridized ideas, any more than he allows a word to have two meanings or a body to have two souls, so he denies that an idea may return to its original impression because an idea and a sensation share neither a common thoroughfare nor a resemblance.

In his *Treatise of Human Nature* Sterne's friend David Hume mounted a passionate critique of Locke's concession to Descartes's dualism:

> The fundamental principle of that philosophy is the opinion concerning colours, sounds, tastes, smells, heat and cold; which it asserts to be nothing but impressions on the mind, deriv'd from the operation of external objects, and without any resemblance to the qualities of the objects . . . Upon the removal of sounds, colours, heat, cold, and other sensible qualities, from the rank of continu'd existences, we are reduc'd merely to what are called primary qualities, as the only *real* ones, of which we have any adequate notion. Those primary qualities are extension and solidity, with their different mixtures and modifications; figure, motion, gravity and cohesion . . . I assert, that instead of its explaining the operations of external objects by its means, we utterly annihilate all these objects, and reduce ourselves to the opinions of the most extravagant scepticism concerning them. If colours, sounds, tastes, and smells be merely perceptions, nothing we can conceive is possest of a real, continu'd, and independent existence; not even motion, extension, and solidity.[34]

Instead of the X plus –X of empiricism, Hume locates in primary qualities, the modern version of intelligible forms, a total abolition of the sensible world, and by implication the reality and continuity of the sentient subject. He quotes Addison in the *Treatise*, so it seems likely he was familiar with Addison's reaction to Locke's onslaught on colour, anticipating his own. It comes in the 413th *Spectator* paper where Addison is forced to confirm a truth 'which has been proved incontestably by many Modern Philosophers': namely 'that Light and Colours, as apprehended by the Imagination, are only Ideas in the Mind, and not Qualities that have any Existence in Matter'.[35] In a melancholy reflection on the consequence of admitting such a truth, he cries, 'But what a rough unsightly Sketch of Nature should we be entertained with, did all her Colouring disappear, and the several Distinctions of Light and Shade vanish?'[36] On the authority of modern philosophy he is forced to conclude, 'In short, our Souls are at present delightfully lost and bewildered in a pleasing Delusion, and we walk about like the Enchanted Hero in Romance' – or, more to the point, like Descartes amid the hypothesis of his second Meditation, except that Addison is appalled to have to suppose such a terrible reality lurking behind the appearance of light, colour and the inventions of the imagination.[37] Just as his enchanted knight emerges from his trance into a barren heath or solitary desert, so the soul in the moment of our death, as all links with sentience are broken, will catch a glimpse of this bleak and unconsoling prospect: 'It is not improbable that something like this may be the State of the Soul after its first Separation, in respect of the Images it will receive from Matter.'[38]

Among the resources of the imagination he discusses in these ten papers on the pleasures of the imagination is what he calls in *Spectator* 414 the 'double principle' that he applies to all objects which strike the eye as exhibiting traces of design in what otherwise would be a work of chance. It is his answer to Plato's X plus –X, a fluid state of relativized impressions that serves not to falsify them but make the discrimination of them more present and vivid. Addison cultivates this oscillation in all situations of aesthetic pleasure, defining a spectrum of mingling sensations defined at one end by the darkness of death and at the other by the Platonic light that banishes all sensible forms. He engineers a route for experience where presence and representation are equally important and mutually exciting, where absorption and reflection nourish each other and defy annihilation. The hobbyhorse is an engine on the same principles operating between excessive light at one extreme and the cold obstruction of the grave at the other. Tristram's barren heath is discovered in his ejaculations, especially in the seventh volume: 'Sick! Sick! Sick! Sick! . . . Into what a delicious riot of things am I rushing? I – I who must be cut short in the midst of my days, and taste no more of 'em than what I borrow from my imagination.'[39] In the ninth even the line of beauty turns into a vanitas: 'Every letter I trace tells me with what rapidity Life follows my pen; the days and hours of it, more precious, my dear Jenny! than the rubies about thy neck . . . every thing presses on – whilst thou are twisting that lock, – see! It grows grey.'[40]

But for the most part Tristram maintains an equilibrium between accident and design he calls his digressive-progressive machine, by whose means a story is perfected by what thwarts it. 'Two contrary motions are introduced . . . and reconciled, which were thought to be at variance with each other.'[41] Tristram owns that the earth's 'elliptick orbit . . . that constitutes that variety and vicissitude of seasons we enjoy' suggested the thought,[42] recurring to the Apollonian definition of the ellipse, where two foci provide the twin centres of a figure that contains contrary outward and inward movements, leaving what might have been a circle in the shape of a slanted disc.[43] Tristram specifies the attributes of the centrifugal digressions as 'the sunshine; – they are the life, the soul of reading'; those of the centripetal narrative are not specified, but if they are non-X of digressions, then they tend towards 'one cold eternal winter'.[44]

The double principle and the digressive-progressive machine are elliptically making something out of what otherwise would have been nothing. The oscillation between the positive and negative, summed up by Socrates when he says to Glaucon of the empirical object, ' It is no more whatever it is said to be than it is not whatever it is said to be', provides Tristram with his most valuable discovery.[45] He sees all sorts of sentimental possibilities in the qualities of objects or propositions that make room for exceptions and intentions improved by chance. He has much respect, he says, for a chapter with '*only nothing in it*'. After all he is in many senses a child of nothing – 'nothing to found thy stamina in but negations' mourns his father; legal precedent has already decreed that his mother is 'nothing at all akin to him', and that same lamenting father 'still less than nothing'.[46] Why should he apologize then for enlarging upon the reasons that have nothing to do with Toby's difficulties with words?[47] Walter's treatise on education advances along the same elliptical lines as Tristram's narrative by means of two contrary motions more or less reconciled, that is by a dialectic of inspiration and resistance, writing by not writing. When Mrs Wadman falls in love with Toby she refuses to settle for the alternatives of a one-sided passion or no passion at all, electing instead to do neither one nor the other, seasoning the X of love with the non-X of indifference.[48] Equally relevant to the history of his obliquities is Tristram's accident beneath the sash-window when Susannah, having not considered that nothing was well hung in the Shandy family, makes her exclamation, 'Nothing is left – nothing is left – for me, but to run my country', where the ' – X' of nothing as a resource is nicely balanced with 'X' as annihilation.[49]

The set-piece of obtaining something from nothing is given to Yorick when he is left standing directly in front of a locked door in a wall, hand in hand with a strange woman whose face he has only just seen, whose name he does not know and whom he has never directly addressed. He finds himself endowed with all the effects of privacy and intimacy but none of their antecedents. 'When your eyes are fixed upon a dead blank – you draw purely from yourselves.'[50] What that means, Yorick has yet to find out, but his draft on fancy (that he is partnered by a goddess) is silly, while his reflection on the situation is an awkward introduction of ideas in advance of the sensations they are supposed to signify. Whenever Yorick senses this loss of equilibrium he blames his imagination or fancy for deceiving him. 'Thou art a seduced, and a seducing slut; and albeit thou cheatest us seven times a day with thy pictures and images, yet with so many charms dost thou do it . . . 'tis a shame to break with thee', and when he beholds Religion joining the dance at Mont Tarare, he confesses, 'I should have look'd upon it now, as one of the illusions of an imagination which is eternally misleading me.'[51] In these scenes Sterne is handling the very tricky issue of sensible transfers that preoccupied all empiricists and revolved around the question of whether it was possible not simply to recover an impression or sensation at its original pitch, but to accommodate as an image a sensation that you had never felt before. Locke's correspondence with William Molyneux revived debates about blind men who could feel colours and provoked many more examples of the triumphs and difficulties facing the newly sighted when confronted with three-dimensional shapes for the first time. The blank of 'The Remise Door' is an example of how the absence of visual stimuli can be compensated by touch provided the subject is willing not to set out by picturing instead of feeling it. 'The Temptation' is the opposite, being a scene which begins with a recognizable image that it is most important not an end in tangible corroboration.

It begins with a translocated blush as the room and the red bed, doubly reddening under the influence of the setting sun and the red curtains, introduce an idea of shame before there is any need to feel it:

> It was a fine still evening in the latter end of the month of May – the crimson window curtains (which were of the same colour of those of the bed) were drawn close – the sun was setting and reflected through them so warm a tint into the fair *fille de chambre*'s face – I thought she blush'd – the idea of it made me blush myself – we were quite alone; and that super-induced a second blush before the first could get off.
>
> There is a sort of pleasing half guilty blush, where the blood is more in fault than the man – 'tis sent impetuous from the heart, and virtue flies after it – not to call it back, but to make the sensation of it more delicious to the nerves – 'tis associated. – But I'll not describe it – I felt something at first within me which was not in strict unison with the lesson of virtue I had given her the night before.[52]

Hume provides us with an elliptical description of what is going on here. He calls it the double relation of impressions and ideas: 'When an idea produces an impression, related to an impression which is connected with an idea, related to the first idea, these two impressions must be in a manner inseparable, nor will the one in any case be unattended by the other.'[53] When the light suffusing the room causes Yorick to think that the *fille de chambre* is blushing, the idea of a blush uninflected by any further association changes into an impression coloured by the possibility that she is blushing for a reason that concerns him, and then he double-blushes with two contrary feelings in play, one of virtue and one of guilt, to which she responds with a solicitude that serves only to make the delicious feelings arising from the relation between good intentions and opportunity gradually less equivocal as opportunity begins to predominate.

It is fair to say that all situations in Sterne's two works of fiction are inconclusive, but it is particularly noticeable in *A Sentimental Journey*, where the breaking off of a flirtation is the whole point: a frisson that soothes Yorick's machine and reduces friction to a minimum is all that is required, not a fully social or sexual exchange and certainly no long-term consequences, despite what he sometimes hints. This scene is the closest he gets to sex, but it has none of Tristram's cheerful ambiguity about his ability to perform, just an exit into clumsy and shame-faced gestures at the doorway that will earn him a rebuke from the innkeeper not unlike the one he received at the outset of his travels. So having started by blushing for no reason but the association of impressions and ideas, he exits this rich spectrum of sensations by referring judgement to 'the father of spirits'.[54] That is to say, he is sending notices to a higher seat than the brain, but with the same intention imputed to him by Mme de L***. When he *thinks* he sees Religion joining in the peasant dance, and *believes* he was being misled by his imagination because he had never seen her so engaged, it is not certain whether he is renouncing the vision as a delusion or confirming the idea arising from such a singular event. But from previous efforts he has made to transcend the machinery of the secular world and to cleanse his ideas of traces of imagination, the latter is the buoyant inference; and what might have been a moment of joy like that experienced by Tristram when he danced in Provence is translated first into an allegory and then into a pious homily. That is to say, Yorick cannot suffer the vibration of an unprecedented feeling without wanting to refer it to an idea, a name and a world of light none of us can see.

The difference between the Cartesian assault on the reality of secondary qualities and the various empiricist attempts to revive at least the possibility of their existence might be schematized as these two hypotheses: 'What if I do know, I didn't?' and 'What if what I don't know, I did?' Descartes's *Meditations* is an example of the first, while the second is a more complex exercise, dealing not only with the transfer from an object to a sensation, and then a sensation to an idea, but also with the reversal of the sequence by the imagination so that someone in a dungeon, as Addison says, can entertain himself with landscapes.[55] Both hypotheses raise the question of whether it is possible to perceive a phenomenon, say a colour, which has not been seen. Hume, for example, wondered whether a person acquainted with all shades of blue but one, who was then shown a spectrum of all blues but the blank where the missing one should be, would be able to imagine the tint that had never been experienced; and he supposes that he would.[56] The correspondence that preceded Locke's incorporation of Molyneux's query into the 1689 edition of his *Essay* persuaded him that instant recognition would not take place because you cannot recognize an image you have never seen before owing to the lack of an optical code. Diderot disagreed, using the example of Nicholas Saunderson, the blind mathematician who did geometry with a modified tactile abacus.[57] On this theme of darkness, light and the synaesthesia of touch and sight, Hobbes and Locke entertained two contrary speculations, one about white and the other about black, which I hope will illuminate the difference between Tristram and Yorick on the nature of sentimental wisdom.

In his *Elements of Philosophy*, Hobbes observed with a sly litotes, 'the word nothing is not unuseful', adding,

> Positives were before negatives ... When the name of *white* was imposed upon certain things, and afterwards upon other things, the names of black, blue, transparent, etc. the infinite dissimilitudes of these with white could not be comprehended in any one name, save that which had in it the negation of white, that is to say, the name *not-white*, or some other equivalent to it. . . . And by these negative names we take notice ourselves and signify to others what we have not thought of.[58]

Hobbes proceeds in a direction similar to Tristram's, using nothing or a negative to reserve places for the subtlety of sensations of future positives instead of obliterating them. Tristram calls it hanging lights in the darkest passages of his work, a technique of which his digressive-progressive machine provides the fullest expression.[59] What is missing will contribute to what is found; the darkness of Addison's barren heath is answered by the glories of elliptical sunshine. The point is that the darkness must never be absolute.

When Locke proposed to himself the problem of the nature of darkness, it was not to imagine that he might be able by some means or other to cast a light on it. What he wished to see was darkness itself. Proceeding in a manner opposite to Hobbes, he entertained the ingenious idea that privation was essential to any idea of fullness, as shadow is to light, and chiaroscuro is to figure. He demands, 'Whether the shadow of a Man, though it consists of nothing but the absence of Light (and the more the absence of Light is, the more discernible is the shadow) does not, when Man looks on it, cause as clear and positive an Idea in his mind, as a Man himself, though covered over with clear Sun-shine?'[60] This curiously stark emphasis on two men, the one defined by the absence of light and the other totally irradiated, seems to anticipate Addison's own miserable conjecture that the enchantment of the living eye disporting itself in light will be followed after death by the departing soul's vision of the world reduced to a cinder. However this is meant, Locke goes on to say, 'Indeed, we have negative Names, which stand not directly for positive Ideas, but for their absence, such as *Insipid, silence, nihil*, etc. which Words denote positive Ideas; v.g. *Tast, Sound, Being*, with a signification of their absence'.[61] It is a risky speculation on two grounds. First, what would he do with negative names that have no positive opposite and already signify perfection, such as 'innocent' and 'immaculate' – explain that they denote ideas of corruption? Second, it sounds as if he might be making the same claim for the dialectics of chiaroscuro mounted by Ruskin in *Modern Painters* when he says that Turner attains brilliancy of light by 'clear and exquisite drawing of the shadows ... shadows sharp and clear'.[62] But that is not what Locke means, for the light is merely a foil to the solidity of darkness. He concludes his estimate of the positive product of privation with this remarkable statement: 'And thus one may truly be said to see Darkness. For suppose a hole perfectly dark, from whence no light is reflected, 'tis certain one may see the Figure of it, or it may be painted.'[63] This is what Eugene Thacker calls 'retinal pessimism' which he glosses as 'the showing of nothing ... this "nothing-to-see"'.[64] Hobbes makes his way from white towards black winning all sorts of opportunities for visual stimuli for which ideas and names do not yet exist. Locke is going in the opposite direction towards a dungeon, or a diagram, of lightless space from which any positive sensation of light has been expelled. Yorick, who was introduced into Tristram's narrative under the pall of a black page, edges towards the showing of 'nothing-to-see' when, being positive he has a soul, he finds himself at last in the dark with his hand touching something he can't identify.

Notes

1. George Berkeley, *Essay towards a New Theory of Vision* (Dublin, 1709), 51.
2. Lucretius in Lucy Hutchinson, 'Translation of Lucretius', in *The Works of Lucy Hutchinson*, ed. Reid Barbour and David Norbrook, 2 vols. (Oxford University Press, 2012), II: 251.
3. Joseph Addison and Richard Steele, *The Spectator*, ed. G. Gregory Smith, 8 vols. (London: Dent, 1907), VI: 56.
4. Robert Hooke, *Micrographia* (1665; New York: Dover, 2003), xii.
5. Laurence Sterne, *The Life and Opinions of Tristram Shandy, Gentleman*, ed. Melvyn New and Joan New, 2 vols. (Gainesville: University Presses of Florida, 1978), II: 593, 723; I: 83, 189.
6. Laurence Sterne, *A Sentimental Journey through France and Italy*, ed. Melvyn New and W. G. Day (Gainesville: University Press of Florida, 2002), 162.
7. Ibid., 21, 24.
8. Sterne, *Tristram Shandy*, II: 763.
9. Sterne, *A Sentimental Journey*, 124.
10. Ibid., 24.
11. Ibid., 36.
12. John Locke, *An Essay concerning Human Understanding*, ed. Peter H. Nidditch (Oxford: Clarendon Press, 1979), 492.
13. Plato, *Republic*, trans. Robin Waterfield (Oxford University Press, 1993), 239; René Descartes, *Discourse on Method and Meditations on the First Philosophy*, ed. David Weissman (New Haven: Yale University Press, 1996), 67–70.
14. Plato, *Republic*, 245.
15. René Descartes, *Treatise on Light*, in *The World and Other Writings*, ed. Stephen Gaukroger (Cambridge University Press, 1998), 3.
16. Ibid., 4.
17. Locke, *An Essay concerning Human Understanding*, 134.
18. Ibid., 135.
19. Thomas Willis, *Two Discourses concerning the Soul of Brutes*, trans. Samuel Pordage (London: Dring, 1683), 59.
20. Sterne, *Tristram Shandy*, I: 100.
21. Ibid., I: 400.
22. Ibid., I: 414.
23. Plato, *Republic*, 253.
24. Sterne, *Tristram Shandy*, II: 537, 793.
25. Laurence Sterne, *Letters of Laurence Sterne*, ed. Lewis Perry Curtis (1935; Oxford: Clarendon Press, 1965), 186.
26. Sterne, *A Sentimental Journey*, 20.
27. Ibid., 5.
28. Ibid., 151.
29. Thomas Hobbes, *Leviathan*, ed. Richard Tuck (Cambridge University Press, 2004), 14.

30. Sterne, *A Sentimental Journey*, 151.
31. Sterne, *Tristram Shandy*, I: 238.
32. Ibid., II: 772–3.
33. Ibid., II: 603.
34. David Hume, *A Treatise of Human Nature*, ed. David F. Norton and Mary J. Norton, 2 vols. (Oxford: Clarendon Press, 2007), I: 149–50.
35. Addison and Steele, *The Spectator*, VI: 65.
36. Ibid.
37. Ibid.
38. Ibid.
39. Sterne, *Tristram Shandy*, II: 578, 595.
40. Ibid., II: 754.
41. Ibid., I: 81.
42. Ibid.
43. Karl Marx, *Capital*, vol. 1, trans. Ben Fowkes (New York: Knopf, 1977), 198.
44. Sterne, *Tristram Shandy*, I: 81.
45. Plato, *Republic*, 201.
46. Sterne, *Tristram Shandy*, II: 785; I: 354; II: 393.
47. Ibid., I: 100.
48. Ibid., II: 669.
49. Ibid., I: 449–50.
50. Sterne, *A Sentimental Journey*, 21.
51. Ibid., 22–3, 151.
52. Ibid., 121–2.
53. Hume, *A Treatise of Human Nature*, I: 189.
54. Sterne, *A Sentimental Journey*, 124.
55. Addison and Steele, *The Spectator* (No. 411), VI: 56.
56. Hume, *A Treatise of Human Nature*, I: 10.
57. Denis Diderot, 'Letter on the Blind for the Use of Those Who Can See', in Kate E. Tunstall, *Blindness and Enlightenment: an Essay* (London: Continuum, 2011), 216.
58. Thomas Hobbes, 'Elements of Philosophy', in *The Works of Thomas Hobbes*, ed. William Molesworth, 16 vols. (London: Bohn, 1839), I: 18.
59. Sterne, *Tristram Shandy*, II: 558.
60. Locke, *An Essay concerning Human Understanding*, 133.
61. Ibid.
62. John Ruskin, *Modern Painters*, ed. David Barrie (New York: Knopf, 1987), 79–80.
63. Locke, *An Essay concerning Human Understanding*, 133–4.
64. Eugene Thacker, 'Black on Black', in *The Public Domain Review, Selected Essays, Vol.* III, ed. Adam Green (Cambridge: PDR, 2016), 25, 28.

CHAPTER 7

Virtue Not Rewarded: The Man of Feeling *and* The Sorrows of Young Werther

Maureen Harkin

'O how I envied him his feelings!'

'The Sword. Rennes', Sterne, *A Sentimental Journey* (1768)[1]

The eighteenth-century sentimental novel brims with detailed accounts of intense personal emotion, longings for new opportunities to experience these feelings, speculations about the emotions others may be experiencing, fears that one may be overwhelmed by feeling. Simply cataloguing the multiple ways in which the experience of intense sentiment preoccupies the Yoricks, Harleys, Werthers and other inhabitants of the genre would take up considerable space, and it is these protagonists' concerns with their own responses, the state of their own hearts, which constitutes the major focus and sets the tone of the sentimental novel.

To be sure, among the novelists grouped together under the rubric of sentimental fiction, there is considerable variety. The range runs from Sterne's Yorick, whose intense pleasure in sharing others' emotions and longing for repeat experiences borders on the addictive, to Goethe's depiction of Werther overwhelmed by suffering. But whatever the kind of emotion covered, all of this focus on feeling has come at a critical cost. It has not tended to raise the standing of the sentimental text. In fact quite the opposite: in the critical history of the sentimental novel the question of what the relation of all these feelings is to any action is usually broached to suggest that there is a problem here. From the earliest days of the sentimental novel a common, indeed almost irresistible critique was that the focus on *feeling* rather than action in the sentimental novel – 'action', in the senses both of internal plot event and of some larger extra-textual invitation to the sentimental reader to intervene in the social distresses that fill the pages of sentimental novels – effectively cut the sentimentalist off from actually *doing* anything about the deplorable situations that feature so prominently in these works. Indeed, sentimentalism throughout its critical career has typically been cast as a way of harmlessly venting concerns for real social problems, thereby doing away with the need for addressing them. Its substitution of intense but private fellow-feeling for any practical intervention in the novels' scenes of rapacious landlords, persecuted tenants, exploited slaves and suffering young women is understood as providing an innocuous, powerless outlet for otherwise potentially dangerous discontent.[2]

Henry Mackenzie himself provides some of the harshest comments in this vein in his own journalism from the 1780s. He may not *originate* the critique of sentimentalism as inadequate response to actual social problems and a self-deluding practice that has subjects mistaking their own fine feelings for effective response, but Mackenzie articulates the position with considerable energy, an especially striking circumstance considering that he had produced one of the genre's landmark works just a few years earlier:

> In the enthusiasm of sentiment there is much the same danger as in the enthusiasm of religion, of substituting certain impulses and feelings of what may be called a visionary kind, in the place of real practical duties . . . There are not wanting instances of refined sentimentalists, who are contented with talking of virtues which they never practice, who pay in words what they owe in actions; or, perhaps what is fully as dangerous, who open their minds to impressions which never have any effect upon their conduct, but are considered as something foreign to and distinct from it. This separation of conscience from feeling is a depravity of the most pernicious sort; it eludes the strongest obligation to rectitude, it blunts the strongest incitement to virtue; . . . That creation of refined and subtile feeling, reared by the authors of the works to which I allude, has an ill effect, not only on our ideas of virtue, but also on our estimate of happiness. That sickly sort of refinement creates imaginary evils and distresses, and imaginary blessings and enjoyments, which embitter the common disappointments, and depreciate the common attainments of life . . .[3]

Mackenzie's final point about the ill effects of these novels on readers indeed goes so far as to suggest that the problem with the sentimental novel is that it produces, in effect, a heightened or distilled version of the novel reading experience in general. This point is repeatedly made in a number of essays in his periodicals *The Mirror* and *The Lounger*, marking the dubiousness of stirring up reader sympathy for fictional sufferers, the insincerity of upper-class ladies more sentimental about their pets than their servants and so on.[4]

This auto-critique and unease with the characteristic tableaux of distress in sentimental fiction is strongly in line with twentieth- and twenty-first-century criticism of the genre, and indeed might be said largely to dictate its terms.

Markman Ellis, Thomas Keymer and many others have all given readings of the sentimental encounter as one of self-indulgence where the observing subject's feelings are the focus, not prevention or intervention in the suffering of the victim.[5] A variant of this argument about feeling as a kind of Barthes-ian inoculation against actually taking any action is the argument that 'men of feeling' are simply exemplars of maladaptation to 'the way things are', casting the genre as a mild, aestheticized and toothless kind of social protest that mobilizes reader indignation only to leave it with nowhere to go.[6]

To be sure, this is not the only reading. For example, Brycchan Carey in this volume (see Chapter 8) notes that sentimentalism regularly raises the topic of slavery for debate. Nonetheless the idea that the sentimental tableaux are to be evaluated by their effectiveness, or lack thereof, in spurring action still hovers over the genre. Added to the suspicion lingering over emotion's link to action, there has also been a longstanding wariness about encouraging readers' affective response to a text, seen as a displacement of a more properly literary interpretation attentive to form and making, ever since the publication of William Wimsatt and Monroe Beardsley's 'The Affective Fallacy' in the early days of the post-war, New Critical era of literary studies.[7]

In this situation the affective turn in the humanities over the past fifteen or twenty years might seem to create the possibility of a new perspective on the representation and communication of feeling in literature in general and sentimental fiction in particular – a moment where the lingering on the nuances of emotional response might look less like evasion and more like an intellectual exploration. Over the past couple of decades, across a range of disciplines, there has been a remarkable efflorescence of work on affect and emotion. One can point towards landmark works like the historical studies of William Reddy on the emotional regimes of Revolutionary era and nineteenth-century France; or that of Barbara Rosenwein on emotional communities in medieval and early modern Europe; accounts by psychologists like Silvan Tomkins and Paul Ekman on the physiological effects of exposure to certain kinds of emotional stimuli; and Brian Massumi's philosophical investigations of the nature of affect vs. emotion and its debt to Gilles Deleuze and Felix Guattari's pioneering *A Thousand Plateaux*.[8] The sheer amount and range of work being done is vast and expanding. It would seem that this is a propitious moment then for reconsidering how the figure of the 'man of feeling' functions and whether it is possible to get out from under by-now familiar critiques of the sentimental genre's tendency to substitute sentiment for action.

One thing shared by both recent writers on emotion and affect and authors of sentimental fiction is their focus on the workings of emotions that are intense, yet frequently in flux and difficult or impossible to translate into language. A word about terminology is in order here. I will be using the term 'emotion' to refer to feelings in this chapter, but the term 'affect' has also come to have wide currency, especially in the work of Brian Massumi. The distinction between 'affect' and 'emotion' in the work of Massumi in particular has come to indicate a difference in form and organization between feelings. Massumi argues that emotion requires a subject, and designates feelings given function and meaning, while affect remains 'unformed and unstructured'; it is feeling or intensity 'disconnected from meaningful sequencing, from narrative' and potentially from a subject.[9] While affect then seems to have acquired the sense of feelings radically untethered from conventional organization and plot, with a 'non-representational quality', giving it a wide range and intensity, some of this free-floating, untethered quality still adheres to emotion, and this is the term I will employ here.[10]

Sentimental writers in the later eighteenth century were engaged in a remarkably consistent series of experiments in representing feeling. As Stephen Ahern notes, it is

> as if collectively they are trying to grab hold of a truth about connections formed among feeling bodies that is always elusive, because diffuse, inchoate, always-becoming, more the circulation of affective forces than something that can be attributed to individual agency or even articulated in words . . . Narratives of sensibility, of the sensible body, are driven by an overarching imperative: to get at something profound but not quite reachable – hence the need to repeat, to rehearse as if obsessively, and without resolution, scenes of affective agitation.[11]

Ahern is insightful about sentimental novels' repetition of certain scenarios as a symptom of the difficulty of articulating something inchoate. However, his reading of Mackenzie tends to pick out only those episodes of Mackenzie's text that suggest possibilities for encounters that break through social conventions, rearranging the 'categories of difference that keep us apart – an effacing of socioeconomic, generational, gendered, racial, even species difference'.[12] Ahern, that is, reads Mackenzie's frequent moments of a kind of group emotional experience as opening up a space for at least the potential for some kind of political change. But I would argue that Mackenzie, despite occasional glimpses or moments of transcended boundaries, more typically refuses such visions, and indeed tends to offer explicit negatives to suggestions of such resolutions. There will be no new social and psychic arrangements due to sentiment in Mackenzie's version. Instead, let us look at the rather more marked ways in which sentimentalism as handled by Mackenzie, and after him Goethe, focuses on an intense kind of dysphoric non-action for its own sake.

Dysphoria is certainly the essential atmosphere of *The Man of Feeling*. The dominant tone of the text is one of futility and exhaustion, and this is established right from the outset, in the Introduction by the putative editor. Unlike Laurence Sterne's robust protagonist Yorick and the euphoric scenes of sentimental communion that dominate *A Sentimental Journey*, the predecessor and evident immediate antecedent for *The Man of Feeling*, Mackenzie introduces us here to the weary and disappointed editor, who in turn presents the demoralized narrator and the diffident, self-doubting Harley: a gallery of self-abnegating male characters in an entirely different mode from Sterne.

This state of dysphoria is beautifully limned in the opening act of the novel, the hunting dog's point:

> It was a false point, and our labour was in vain: yet, to do Rover justice, (for he's an excellent dog, though I have lost his pedigree) the fault was none of his, the birds were gone; the curate shewed me the spot where they had lain basking . . . There is no state where one is apter to pause and look round one, than after such a disappointment. It is even so in life. When we have been hurrying on, impelled by some warm wish or other, looking neither to the right hand nor to the left – we find, of a sudden that all our gay hopes are flown; and the only slender consolation that some friend can give us, is to point to where they were once to be found. And lo! . . . we look round and say, with the nauseated listlessness of the king of Israel, 'All is vanity and vexation of spirit'.[13]

Mackenzie economically sketches an almost encyclopaedic catalogue of failures here: the false point, lost pedigree, vain labour, flown hopes, and generalized disappointment, listlessness and vexation – a veritable grammar of discontent and disillusionment.

These first lines effectively set the scene for what is to come in Mackenzie's novel: sensibilities exquisitely attuned to pain, disappointment, especially in love, and crucially, numerous representations of a profound inability to successfully negotiate the hierarchies, duplicities and scheming of social life. This opening, that is to say, clearly foreshadows the plotting of the novel, but more importantly it establishes a consistent *tone*, one of dejection.[14]

Mackenzie supplies abundant examples of these detailed representations of failure and unhappiness throughout the novel: Harley's unsuccessful embassy to London, the paired stories of the sufferings of Miss Atkins and her father, the various sufferings and losses of Old Edwards, etc. It is these episodes in the novel, I would argue, that are its most definitive, tone-setting moments, rather than the more Sternean passages where feelings are shared (with Ben Silton in chapter XXXIII or Old Edwards in chapter XXXIV). Mackenzie's novel looks less like an attempt to raise 'imaginary blessings and enjoyments' and more like an exploration of the 'common disappointments of life'. His novel, that is, defies his own critique of sentimentalism. It is this tendency to dwell on feelings of dejection, rather than on feelings of shared, communal sympathy, that dominates Mackenzie's novel and gives the book its distinctive character; making this experience of isolation and depression visible is what constitutes the novel's single most important accomplishment. By doing so, Mackenzie displaces the model of Sterne's compulsive communions with scenes of *dis*connection between the central subject of the sentimental text and his society as the point of focus.

Mackenzie has a particular predilection, for example, for representations of thwarted action and feelings that simply seethe, more or less pointlessly, in *The Man of Feeling*. A notable instance is the lament over the ruined schoolhouse in chapter XXXV, where Harley immediately, and correctly, deduces that some rapacious landlord has been behind the destruction of the village school. Harley unleashes an impassioned outburst, concluding with a string of curses on the perpetrator when a passer-by confirms Harley's suspicion that the local squire has pulled it down 'because it stood in the way of his prospects':

> Harley . . . looked stedfastly on the mouldering walls of a ruined house that stood on the road-side. 'Oh heavens!' he cried, 'what do I see! silent, unroofed and desolate! Are all thy gay tenants gone? do I hear their hum no more? Edwards, look there, look there! the scene of my infant joys, my earliest friendships, laid waste and ruinous! . . . Curses on his narrow heart . . . that could violate a right so sacred! Heaven blast the wretch! "And from his derogate body never spring / A babe to honour him!"' (*MOF*, 112–14)

Yet after this condemnation of the man's hard-heartedness, Harley – fellow landowner and presumably neighbour of the unnamed offending proprietor – immediately drops the matter, apparently somewhat embarrassed by the intensity of his own feelings, and explicitly reassigns agency in punishing this misdeed to the workings of a larger providence: 'But I need not, Edwards, I need not, (recovering himself a little) he is cursed enough already: to him the noblest source of happiness is denied, and the cares of his sordid soul shall gnaw it . . . ' (*MOF*, 114)

Similarly, in the fragment 'The Man of Feeling talks of what he does not understand – An incident', Harley offers a passionate and, for him, lengthy critique of oppressive British colonial rule in India, working up to a fine rhetorical pitch: 'You describe the victories they have gained; they are sullied by the cause in which they fought: you enumerate the spoils of those victories; they are covered with the blood of the vanquished!' (*MOF*, 118–19) Yet once more, immediately after delivering the speech to a highly receptive Old Edwards, Harley backs off, again explicitly shifting the ground from *acts* to concentrate on feelings. The episode closes with Harley commenting to his friend, 'the feelings are not yet lost that applaud benevolence, and censure inhumanity. Let us endeavour to strengthen them in ourselves; and we, who live sequestered from the noise of the multitude, have better opportunities of listening undisturbed to their voice' (*MOF*, 119).

This move from impassioned critique to asserting the necessity of resignation and retreat is a familiar one. At this point in the text it has been made quite clear, both from the view of the ruined schoolhouse and from the experiences of Old Edwards and his family at the hands of his landlord, that living withdrawn from 'the multitude' offers little if any protection from being subjected to acts of inhumanity. Hence Harley's closing reference to solitude and retreat is a choice to focus on an *internal* process, and not a suggestion that a rural community might offer a haven from such behaviour.

Once again we have a pullback from action, or at least the threat of public speech, to a focus on cultivating a private sensibility. The effect created here is, I stress, not just the oft-noted one of sentimental fiction's tendency to dwell on the feelings of the observing subject rather than on an intervention that might solve a problem or end someone's suffering. Rather, Mackenzie's strategy – in the Introduction, in the schoolhouse episode and in the withdrawal from the critique of colonialism – is consistently to highlight a refusal to find comfort, to assert the powerlessness of feelings or analysis, and to suggest a profound disconnection between action and feeling *in general.*

What are we to make of this fascinated lingering on episodes of dissatisfaction, depression and doing nothing? Sianne Ngai has pointed out in her reading of Bartleby the Scrivener, Harley's distant descendant, the unease that is provoked by fictional accounts of passivity and inaction like that of Melville's celebrated non-actor.[15] According to

Ngai, this is to do with the fact that such representations of 'ambivalent situations of suspended agency' have the effect of drawing together two competing and conflicting conceptions of humanity and action: 'Hannah Arendt's claim that "what makes a man a political being is his faculty of action" and Baruch Spinoza's description of emotions as "waverings of the mind" that can either increase or diminish one's power to act'. This conflict between the imperative to act and the lingering in the shoals of feeling serves to draw attention to the nature of the feelings that lead to these hesitancies and 'suspensions'. Her suggestion is that literary texts like Melville's – and we would add, Mackenzie's – which represent situations of blocked action are freighted with a particular political significance: 'These situations of passivity . . . can . . . be thought of as allegories for an autonomous or bourgeois art's increasingly resigned and pessimistic understanding of its . . . relationship to political action.'[16] This is a claim at once both glum and ambitious, suggesting that literary works that stage such accounts of powerlessness have, perhaps paradoxically, a unique power to disturb readers and force awareness of the limitations placed on the aesthetic.

This account of literary works that stage their own inability to link feeling to actions, the aesthetic to the political, clearly challenges the vision of sentimental fiction as having the ability to transcend or overcome boundaries, the possibility suggested by Ahern above. But as Ngai also shrewdly observes, there is a force to this inability: 'one could argue that bourgeois art's reflexive preoccupation with its *own* "powerlessness and superfluity in the empirical world" is precisely what makes it capable of theorizing social powerlessness in a manner unrivalled by other forms of cultural praxis'. Literature, she argues, may offer the ideal space 'to investigate ugly feelings that obviously ramify beyond the domain of the aesthetic proper, since the situation of restricted agency . . . is one that describes art's own position in a highly differentiated and totally commodified society'.[17] The possible political benefit of Mackenzie's version of sentimentalism, in this light, would be the opportunities it offers, or rather forces on us, to simply sit with a storm of emotion that can have no possible resolution in action. In short, Ngai's apparently more modest estimate of how literary representations of inaction work gives us a better account of what sentimental fiction can accomplish in the realm of the political imaginary than do accounts of sentimentalism as potentially boundary-breaking transcendence.

The emotions that Mackenzie describes in *The Man of Feeling* are indeed not the ones typically associated with political action. Rather than the anger or fear driving men into political associations in Hobbes (or motivating reactions in Silvan Tomkins's and Paul Ekman's schemas), Mackenzie's emotions are less sharply defined, more of the nature of a non-specific discontent, displeasure, distaste or exhaustion. But, as Ngai suggests, it is precisely this kind of non-specificity, this lack of a goal in action, that gives them a certain power to identify or categorize situations, and situations marked by blocked or thwarted action in particular.[18]

I say Mackenzie's version of sentimentalism, but Goethe too traffics in these dysphoric scenes, in part borrowing from Mackenzie's example. Goethe's praise for the work of English sentimental novelists like Sterne and Goldsmith is well known.[19] But it is in fact the influence of Mackenzie that we notice in certain episodes from *The Sorrows of Young Werther*: for example, Werther's mild effusion when he notices on his return to his birthplace that the village schoolroom he attended – albeit rather less happily than Harley – has been turned into a shop.[20] More pointedly, Werther appears to channel Harley's rage at the destructive meddling of landed proprietors in his furious reaction to the news that the two grand old walnut trees standing before the manse of the pastor in St. have been chopped down: 'Chopped down! I shall go mad with rage. I could murder the wretch who first raised the axe against them. I who could grieve to death if two such trees grew by my house and one of them died of age – I have to witness this!' (*SOYW*, 72). And, just as in Mackenzie, such impulses to immediate condemnation and action rapidly slide into wishes for a rather feeble providential punishment of the offender: 'But one thing, dearest friend – some human feeling: the whole village is angry, and I hope the Pastor's wife will feel in the scanting of butter, eggs and other signs of goodwill just what a wound she has dealt her parish' (*SOYW*, 72).

Nonetheless, these episodes, especially Werther's initial vehemence in his reactions to the lost walnut trees, reveal the way in which both Mackenzie and Goethe appear to work with the older model of the *passions* rather than the emotions, a model which tends to position the subject as one who is acted upon rather than autonomous, subjected to being seized by more or less violent passions.[21] For example, Werther is described by the 'editor' thus: 'Grievance and unhappiness rooted deeper and deeper in Werther's soul . . . and at length took possession of his whole being . . . ' (*SOYW*, 83). This sort of 'possession' is more obvious in Goethe than in Mackenzie, partly because these occasions of passions seizing hold of Werther come into play so frequently, not only in his hopeless love for Lotte, but in far more banal social exchanges. It is also in part because Werther tends to give way to more intense and even violent verbal outbursts than we see in the comparatively mild-spoken Harley. Harley – frequently patronized by more knowing figures in his embassy to London – usually takes such condescension more or less in stride (*MOF*, 66, 82, 84). By contrast, Werther, asked to leave Count C's soiree, is overpowered by emotion, tormented by the thought that others enjoy his social humiliation, and he gives vent to his feelings in the strongest possible terms: 'God damn them! ... It was like venom in me ... when I hear that the envious are now triumphant and are saying, see what happens to those who get above themselves ... – it's enough to make you thrust a knife into your heart!' (*SOYW*, 61)

The intensity of the emotion that rules Werther makes even more palpable the disconnection between his rages and his (in)action. But perhaps nothing brings this disconnection into focus quite as forcefully as the death scenes in both novels. The climactic death and graveyard scenes that dramatically conclude both *The Man of Feeling* and *The Sorrows of Young Werther* give striking accounts of the lack of a clear place in the social world for intense emotion; and in their different ways, they bring up the notion of conventional gestures of comfort and resignation only to refuse and undermine them.

Death scenes in sentimental literature might initially be seen as offering prime opportunities for communal solace in shared tears; the potential, as Ahern puts it, for 'charged encounters to somehow act as a cure all'.[22] There are plenty of examples of such scenes in the genre; one thinks of Sterne's captive wasting away in a dungeon in *A Sentimental Journey* (11: 30); the narrator's tears over Ben Silton in chapter XI of *The Man of Feeling* (*MOF*, 51); or Lotte's recounting of her mother's death at the close of book one of *Werther* (*SOYW*, 49). Such scenes conform to what Franco Moretti, in his essay on later sentimental literature, has described as the typical function of the tear-soaked death and funeral of their protagonists: that these operate as a form of conciliation with social norms. Stressing the point-of-view shift that occurs with the death of the central character in a series of examples of nineteenth- and early twentieth-century 'moving literature', Moretti observes that the function of the protagonist's death in these works is to make the irreversibility of time more perceptible, and notes that this is felt that much more strongly if there is no doubt about the difference in the outcome of events one would have liked to see. It is this powerlessness, he argues, which makes the readers of sentimental scenes cry. Tears are indices of two conflicting truths: 'that the present state of things should be changed – and that change is *impossible*'.[23]

In effect, these tears ultimately perform a quite precise social task, of accommodating the mourners to the way things are, converting rage against injustice, anger and critique into some form of acceptance and a kind of compromise:

> Being moved – and crying, which is its most complete manifestation – is the exact opposite of being angry. Anger divides; tears *unite*. But to whom do they unite us? Not to the protagonist victim ... Our identification slides, imperceptibly yet inexorably, towards the others, the survivors. As at a funeral, the death of the protagonist manages to rebuild the community of those who remain. Through communal weeping, all rancour, all injustice, all blame is abolished. It is a ritual of reciprocal collective absolution.[24]

Yet it is notable that, while this model of death scenes laying anger to rest may apply to each example of the minor figures we gave above, it does not at all account for the deaths of Mackenzie's or Goethe's protagonists. Most dramatically, the death and funeral of Werther at the conclusion of Goethe's novel is very far from conforming to any pattern of tearful resolution. After the reading of Werther's suicide note, the text abruptly concludes with details of his violent end and protracted suffering. The funeral scene is one of unremitting desolation:

> The old Land Steward came post-haste at the news, he kissed the dying man in a passion of weeping. His eldest sons followed soon after on foot, they fell down by his bed, quite at the mercy of their grief ... He [Werther] died at twelve noon. The presence of the Land Steward and the measures he took hushed up any public outcry. At night, towards eleven, he had him buried in the place he had chosen for himself. The old man followed the coffin with his sons, Albert could not do it. They feared for Lotte's life. Working-men carried him. No priest attended. (*SOYW*, 111–12)

Very specifically without absolution or reconciliation, the closing scene represents unrelieved grief, unresolved division, tears that do not dissolve anger. *The Sorrows of Young Werther*, then, clearly avoids, in fact dramatically refuses, the work of compromise, acceptance or resignation, and marks a moment when, even if change in the state of things is impossible, it can still be resented, represented as a cause for 'outcry' rather than accepted.

Turning back to Mackenzie, we can also ask: what is accomplished through the death of *his* protagonist? The usual answer is that through this means Harley is established as a figure too sensitive and uncompromising to endure the harshness and moral ambiguities of the real world, and in that sense fits the story of the sentimentalist, the story of a *Bildung* that has failed to occur.[25]

But one has to say first that what is striking about Harley's death is its very ambiguous status: it is hard to say for sure whether it is due to illness or to a willed act of suicide. This issue of agency is important, not least because the man of feeling is generally not understood as victimized by social conditions.[26] It is notable that Mackenzie goes to great lengths to suggest *both* that Harley dies from a mysterious, unspecified illness and that his death is a suicide.

The antepenultimate chapter of the novel has the narrator visit Harley, who, though ill, is not yet considered in any serious danger by his physician. But as soon as he enters Harley's room the narrator is confronted by Harley's sense, or decision, that his death is both imminent and welcome: 'His look had . . . a gentle triumph in it.' When the narrator gives Harley the good report he 'had had from his physician, [Harley responds] "I am foolish enough," said he, "to rely but little in this instance upon physic: my presentiment may be false, but I think I feel myself approaching to my end, by steps so easy, that they woo me to approach it"' (*MOF*, 136) – a fascinating turn of phrase that mingles inclination with invitation, and suggests that Harley is making a decision to die, though he is careful to suggest that this is based on his intuiting the Divine will. Similarly, when Miss Walton attempts to strengthen Harley's belief that he will recover, he acknowledges his attachment to her and to life, but still asserts 'To meet death as becomes a man is a privilege bestowed on few. I would endeavour to make it mine' (*MOF*, 137). The subjunctive phrasing does not quite eliminate the idea of Harley's intent here.

What are we to make of this deathbed scene? It would seem that, with all due allowance for ambiguity, Harley is responsible for his own death. If Harley then really 'endeavours to meet death', the consequence would be that the responsibility for this death *is* actually laid at the feet of the society that has rendered the prospect so attractive to him. Indeed it is Harley's own conclusion that he is not a good fit for this world, explicitly denominating it as too hostile to feeling: 'There are some feelings which perhaps are too tender to be suffered by the world. The world is . . . selfish . . . and throws the imputation of romance or melancholy on every temper more susceptible than its own . . . I cannot think but in those regions which I contemplate . . . that these feelings will subsist; . . . there . . . in heaven' (*MOF*, 136). For all the overt resignation here, a clear sense of injustice and injury persists.

Similarly, the novel's final paragraph, while it appears torn between two competing visions of peace and unrest, allows a certain anger to surface, though it is quickly tamped down again:

> I sometimes visit his grave; I sit in the hollow of the tree. It is worth a thousand homilies! Every nobler feeling rises within me! Every beat of my heart awakens a virtue! – but it will make you hate the world – No: there is such an air of gentleness around, that I can hate nothing; but as to the world – I pity the men of it. (*MOF*, 139)

In this visible struggle between pity and active hate, the highlighting of divided responses to the meaning of the events of Harley's life and death, *The Man of Feeling* indicates that the sentimental novel of the 1770s has a political charge, but one that does not lie in commingled consolatory tears, or gestures towards some emancipatory overcoming of difference. Rather, Mackenzie's and Goethe's novels have impact by recording a sense of hopelessness, representing the authors' sense not only that the feelings cultivated by sentimental fiction do not benefit their objects, but that there is no direct relation to action or a public sphere at all. Mackenzie's example in particular makes it clear that we can shelve old questions about whether the representation of sentiment encourages or discourages the solving of social problems by showing that the relationship of feeling to acting is such a tenuous one. Feelings are in fact rarely direct preliminaries to action. Instead, emotions in Mackenzie and Goethe document the experiences of powerlessness, lack of control, and the psychic toll that takes. The impact of such documents will perhaps always be diffuse, uncertain and barely perceptible – but with the potential to expand a particular society's emotional regime by delineating its rough edges and hard limitations.[27]

Notes

1. Laurence Sterne, *A Sentimental Journey through France and Italy*. By Mr Yorick. 2 vols. (London, 1768), II: 59.
2. See, for example, John Mullan, *Sentiment and Sociability: the Language of Feeling in the Eighteenth Century* (Oxford: Clarendon Press, 1988); 119–30; John Dwyer, *Virtuous Discourse: Sensibility and Community in Late Eighteenth-Century Scotland* (Edinburgh: J. Donald, 1987), 147–54; Janet Todd, *Sensibility: an Introduction* (London: Methuen, 1986), 95–104. More recently George Boulukos has shifted the terms of the argument on slavery, for example, describing the link between attention to the suffering of slaves in sentimental texts and agitation for abolition as a very loose one: 'sentiment . . . turns out to be a cultural form without a predetermined content' (*The Grateful Slave: the*

Emergence of Race in Eighteenth-Century British and American Culture (Cambridge University Press, 2008), 14). Another useful recent analysis that opens up the problem of sentiment and action is Csengei's account of *The Man of Feeling* as a self-conscious training in reading. See Ildiko Csengei, '"I Will Not Weep": Reading through the Tears of Henry Mackenzie's "Man of Feeling"', *Modern Language Review* 103 (October 2008): 952–68.

3. *The Lounger*, No. 20 (Saturday, 18 June 1785), in *The Works of Henry Mackenzie*, ed. Susan Manning, 8 vols. (London: Routledge/Thoemmes Press, 1996), V: 181–4.
4. See also *The Lounger*, No. 90 (Saturday, 21 October 1786), in which Barbara Heartless recounts the extreme tender-heartedness of 'Mrs Sensitive' to her pets, in sharp contrast with her cold treatment of husband, servants and poor relations (Mackenzie, *Works*, VI: 302–13).
5. See Markman Ellis's comments in chapter 3 of *The Politics of Sensibility: Race, Gender, and Commerce in the Sentimental Novel* (Cambridge University Press, 1996), on the propensity of sentimentalist texts treating slavery to eschew abolitionist stances in favour of reforming slavery via humane plantation-owners (Sarah Scott's Sir George Ellison, Savillon in Mackenzie's *Julia de Roubigne*). See also Thomas Keymer's observations that sentimental fiction tends to 'highlight symptoms of social and economic inequality while effacing the underlying causes', quoted in Eric Parisot, 'Suicide Notes and Popular Sensibility in the Eighteenth-Century British Press', *Eighteenth-Century Studies* 47 (2014): 285.
6. 'One inoculates the public with a contingent evil to prevent or cure an essential one' ('Operation Margarine'), in Roland Barthes, *Mythologies*, trans. Annette Lavers (New York: Noonday Press/Farrar, Straus and Giroux, 1991), 42.
7. See William K. Wimsatt and Monroe C. Beardsley. *The Verbal Icon: Studies in the Meaning of Poetry* (Lexington: University Press of Kentucky, 1989).
8. William Reddy, *The Navigation of Feeling: a Framework for the History of Emotions* (Cambridge University Press, 2001); Barbara Rosenwein, *Generations of Feeling: a History of Emotions, 600–1700* (Cambridge University Press, 2016); Silvan Tomkins and Bertram Karon, *Affect, Imagery, Consciousness* (New York: Springer, 1962); Paul Ekman, *Emotions Revealed* (New York: Holt, 2003); Brian Massumi, *Parables for the Virtual: Movement, Affect, Sensation* (Durham, NC: Duke University Press, 2002); Gilles Deleuze and Félix Guattari. *A Thousand Plateaus: Capitalism and Schizophrenia* (Minneapolis: University of Minnesota Press, 1987). Also see the very useful overview of the field in Jan Plamper, *The History of Emotions: an Introduction* (Oxford University Press, 2017).
9. See Massumi, *Parables for the Virtual*, 25, 28.
10. See also discussions by Sianne Ngai, *Ugly Feelings* (Cambridge, MA: Harvard University Press, 2004), 26; Stephen Ahern, 'Nothing More than Feelings?

Affect Theory Reads the Age of Sensibility', *The Eighteenth Century* 58 (2017): 281–95; and especially Ruth Leys's incisive essay, 'The Turn to Affect: a Critique', *Critical Inquiry* 37 (2011): 434–72.

11. Ahern, 'Nothing More than Feelings?', 286.
12. Ibid., 287.
13. Henry Mackenzie, *The Man of Feeling*, ed. Maureen Harkin (Peterborough, ON: Broadview Press, 2005), 47. Hereafter cited as *MOF*.
14. Here I draw on Sianne Ngai's elaboration of tone: the text's 'global or organizing affect, its general disposition or orientation toward its audience and the world . . . the formal aspect of a literary work that makes it possible . . . to describe a text as, say, "euphoric" or "melancholic"' (Ngai, *Ugly Feelings*, 29–31). The term is not without its ambiguities and problems, as Ngai acknowledges (who is the subject of this euphoria or melancholy: the narrator? the reader?), but the concept of tone as a means of capturing a consistently evoked atmosphere is essential. See also the foundational discussion of tone and meaning in I.A. Richards, *Practical Criticism: a Study of Literary Judgment* (New York: Harcourt Brace, 2014), 173–81.
15. Ngai, *Ugly Feelings*, 2.
16. Ibid., 3.
17. Ibid., 2.
18. Ibid., 26–7.
19. Goethe owned himself indebted to the novels of Oliver Goldsmith and especially Laurence Sterne, writing in a letter of 25 December 1829: '[They] influenced me in the main line of my development. Their goodwilled irony, their justness along with all their broadness of view, their gentleness in all adversity, their constancy in all change, and whatever other related virtues, taught me much; and in the end it is such attitudes that finally lead us back from the false starts in our lives.' *Essays on Art and Literature,* in Johann Wolfgang von Goethe et al., *Goethe's Collected Works*, 12 vols. (Princeton University Press, 1994), III: 256.
20. Johann Wolfgang von Goethe, *The Sorrows of Young Werther*, trans. David Constantine (Oxford University Press, 2012), 65. Hereafter cited as *SOYW*.
21. See Thomas Dixon, *From Passions to Emotions: the Creation of a Secular Psychological Category* (Cambridge University Press, 2003), 98–134.
22. Ahern, 'Nothing More than Feelings', 288.
23. Franco Moretti, 'Kindergarten', in *Signs Taken for Wonders: Essays in the Sociology of Literary Forms* (London: Verso, 1997), 162.
24. Ibid., 173.
25. Harkin, Introduction, *The Man of Feeling*, 17–18.
26. See G. J. Barker-Benfield, *The Culture of Sensibility: Sex and Society in Eighteenth-Century Britain* (University of Chicago Press, 1992), 139–44.
27. See Reddy's discussion of emotional regimes in *Navigation of Feeling*, 122–7.

CHAPTER 8

Slavery and the Novel of Sentiment

Brycchan Carey

The engagement of the novel of sentiment with the late eighteenth-century debate about slavery and the slave trade was never as sustained as the response in poetry and polemic. Nevertheless, several sentimental novelists rose to the challenge. They were by no means unified, either in their political or in their aesthetic aims, and addressed the problem of slavery in extremely varied ways and with differing degrees of effectiveness. Some merely invited a self-indulgent tear – and were criticized both by contemporaries and by posterity for doing so – but others encouraged an 'active sensibility' that prompted their readers to genuine engagement with the abolition movement. Some arguably strengthened the planters' hand, by arguing for plantation reform rather than abolition. While the novel of sensibility was not by itself responsible for the slavery debate in the late eighteenth century, and while its representation of enslaved Africans is frequently problematic, it is nevertheless now widely accepted that sentimental novelists played at least a small part in fostering public discussion. This chapter accordingly reviews their role in challenging public perceptions of slavery and the slave trade. It surveys some of the most important representations of slavery in sentimental novels of the period, noting that while some clearly advocated an end to slavery, or at least the slave trade, others were more interested in ameliorating rather than abolishing either. The final part of the chapter offers a focused study of the ways in which slavery was represented in works by Laurence Sterne and those who were inspired by him – in particular, Ignatius Sancho, Susanna Rowson and the anonymous author of *Memoirs and Opinions of Mr Blenfield*. While the discussion of Sterne and his followers gives us a good sense of how Shandean sensibility could be harnessed in the service of abolition, the chapter overall demonstrates the sentimental novel's shifting and unreliable nature as a political tool.

The sentimental novel may arguably reflect a society increasingly interested in refined manners and empathetic behaviour, but it coincided with one of the most brutal practices in modern British history. Slavery was nothing new in the eighteenth century. Throughout history, many societies have enslaved parts of their population and forms of slavery remain widespread and common today, despite being illegal. The Atlantic slave trade and the system of plantation slavery which it serviced were, however, unusual both for their scale and for their inhumanity. British slave traders, who had operated at the margins of the Spanish Empire for much of the seventeenth century, secured by treaty the right to supply slaves to the Spanish in 1713 and for the next century Britain became the world's largest slave-trading nation. The height of the British slave trade coincided closely, therefore, with the rise in popularity of sentimental literature. From the start, however, there were those who felt that the slave trade was contrary both to British notions of liberty and to the Christian Golden Rule, as well as increasingly difficult to reconcile with the imperative to relieve suffering as it was expressed in sentimental literature and philosophy. Quakers led the way in banning slave trading throughout their worldwide community in 1761 and set about persuading others to do likewise. Over the next quarter of a century, the trickle of anti-slavery voices became an abolitionist movement – indeed, a mass movement in the years 1787 to 1792. Conservative reaction to the revolutions in France and Haiti muted the campaign for a while, but the British slave trade was finally outlawed in 1807. A generation later, in 1833, Parliament voted to make slavery illegal throughout the British Empire.

Scholarly attempts to understand why the British turned their backs on slavery have given rise to one of the most contested debates in recent historiography. In crude terms, opinion is divided between those who see abolition as a cynical response to declining plantation profits and those who see it as the enlightened act of a nation which had undergone profound moral and cultural change. The reality is more complex, but few historians today insist on a purely economic explanation, with most accepting that some sort of cultural transformation had indeed taken place. The culture of sensibility is clearly correlated with that transformation, but the lines of causation are harder to discern. In *Guinea's Captive Kings* (1942), Wylie Sypher expressed a profound distaste for what he saw as the insincere emotionality of abolitionist 'propaganda', with its 'delectable anti-slavery tear', but nonetheless saw the anti-slavery movement as a 'phase of the enlightenment . . . the protest is really one in the name of a dry "enlightened" theory, the rights of man'.[1] Although excoriating the moist sentimentality of anti-slavery literature, Sypher firmly established a strong relationship between sentimental literature and the anti-slavery movement, and this observation has informed all later studies. David Brion Davis's *The Problem of Slavery in Western Culture* (1966) and *The Problem of Slavery in the Age of Revolution* (1975) also lay at the root of the investigation. Davis responded to the then prevailing sense among historians that economic rather than ideological imperatives drove abolitionism by arguing instead that 'the emergence of an international antislavery opinion represented a momentous turning point in the evolution of man's moral perception'. This ideological shift 'emerged from a convergence of complex religious, intellectual, and literary trends', among which Davis recognized the importance of 'the popularization of an ethic of benevolence, personified in the "man of feeling"'.[2]

Sypher and Davis laid the essential groundwork, but few scholars came forward to build on their foundations until late in the twentieth century. The key text was *The Politics of Sensibility* (1996), in which Markman Ellis argued that 'the sentimental novel effectively created a new political role for literature' by focusing on 'youth, simplicity and "natural feeling"' and engaging with debates around prostitution, canals and commerce, as well as with slavery and the slave trade.[3] Ellis demonstrated the sentimental novel's role in the latter through important readings of Laurence Sterne and Ignatius Sancho in the context of the anti-slavery movement, and Sarah Scott and Henry Mackenzie in the context of the earlier debate about the amelioration of slavery. Ellis's discussion was the first, and still one of the most significant, of a dozen or so critical studies of slavery and sentiment to appear over the next twenty years. Some, like Marcus Wood's *Slavery, Empathy, and Pornography* (2002), essentially continue Sypher's argument that the sentimental novel misrepresented the enslaved Africans for whom it purported to act, and that the novels' emotionalism was both disingenuous and dangerous; 'the dangers of playing sentimentally with the suffering of the slave', Wood warns, 'are immense and uncontrollable'.[4] George Boulukos explored those dangers in depth in *The Grateful Slave* (2008). Examining the frequent representation of enslaved people showing gratitude to their enslavers for ostensibly humane treatment, he argued that the 'sentimental, reformist scenario of the grateful slave, represented in fictional narrative, was far more engaging to the values of its metropolitan audience than were the explicit arguments put forth in the polemics of apologists for slavery'.[5] Thus, the sentimental novel, by arguing for the amelioration of slavery rather than its abolition, in a language acceptable to readers with little direct experience of the plantations, could become a powerful advocate for sustaining the system of plantation slavery. Worse still, sentimental representations of 'humane' white masters and 'grateful' black slaves fuelled the ideology of racial difference that would lead to full-blooded pseudoscientific racism. The sentimental novel, in this analysis, entrenched slavery rather than challenged it.

Several studies have emphasized the importance of sentimental tropes and rhetoric to the development of anti-slavery opinion. Lynn Festa, for example, in *Sentimental Figures of Empire in Eighteenth-Century Britain and France* (2006), argues that 'in an era in which imperial reach increasingly outstripped imaginative grasp, sentimental fiction created the tropes that enabled readers to reel the world home in their minds'.[6] In my own *British Abolitionism and the Rhetoric of Sensibility* (2005), I called this trope the 'sentimental parable', and noted that 'a human story on a human scale is more likely to move, and more likely to persuade those who are moved'.[7] In a series of close readings, I went on to outline this and the other main tropes of sentimental rhetoric, and to show how they were deployed in a wide range of abolitionist writing, from the novel to parliamentary reportage. In her wide-ranging *Debating the Slave Trade* (2009), Srividhya Swaminathan shows that abolitionist rhetoric was associated more generally with the emergence of modern British national identity. While sentimental rhetoric was a part of this, however, Swaminathan showed that it was only one element. What she calls 'a brilliant mishmash' of sentimental, enlightenment and Romantic ideas 'allowed for the development of nationalist rhetoric from this particular social, political, moral movement'.[8] Swaminathan's reminder that anti-slavery discourse – indeed, all discourse – is a mishmash of ideas marks the start of a mature phase of enquiry in which the contribution of sentimentalism to the development of abolitionism is neither under- nor overemphasized. Indeed, as Stephen Ahern has pointed out in his introduction to *Affect and Abolition in the Anglo-Atlantic* (2013), the first major review of the field, 'the political implications of sentimental discourse depend in complex ways on the agenda of the writer and the preconceptions of the reader'.[9] This chapter hopes to show how some of those 'complex ways' played out, not in sentimental discourse as a whole, but in the narrower confines of the novel of sentiment.

Sentiment and Amelioration

The problem of slavery crops up in the very earliest novels in English, as readers of Aphra Behn and Daniel Defoe know well, and continues to appear in the novel throughout the eighteenth and nineteenth centuries. Many of these are associated with the high-water marks of both sentiment and abolitionism; Wylie Sypher lists more than twenty novels engaging with the slavery debate between 1785 and 1795, most of which can only be loosely categorized as anti-slavery literature.[10] Not all eighteenth-century novels that mention slavery are sentimental. The anonymous *Adventures of Jonathan Corncob* (1787), for example, offers a critique of slavery in Barbados embedded in a parody of the novel of sentiment. Maria Edgeworth's *Belinda* (1801), which caused controversy in its day for its depiction of the African figure of Juba and his interracial marriage, explores its protagonist's rationality rather than her sensibility. Nevertheless, several sentimental novels do offer a sustained engagement with slavery. The problem for cultural historians of anti-slavery is deciding whether these novels actually challenge slavery as it existed in British colonies or whether what Sypher called their 'sentimental economy' in fact perpetuates slavery at the same time as calling for its amelioration.[11]

Sarah Scott's *The History of Sir George Ellison* (1766) is a case in point. The book presents a fictional biography of a benevolent man of feeling who is able to solve almost any problem presented to him by the liberal application of tears and cash. The problem is that his cash comes from the sale of goods produced by enslaved people and, in two early chapters of the book, he 'inherits' a large plantation with 'a numerous race of slaves' when he marries a wealthy widow in Jamaica. Shocked by the cruelty shown to the plantation's enslaved labourers, he proposes a more humane system of management, which leads to some testy discussions with his wife. Through these, the reader is confronted with arguments about the humanity and policy of plantation slavery. Critics have been divided over the relationship between those arguments and the emerging discourse of anti-slavery. Some, like Markman Ellis, maintain that the novel 'argued for the mitigation of the conditions of slavery, but not its abolition'.[12] Others, like myself, suggest that the book 'promotes an antislavery view which confines itself to what, in 1766, might have been possible to achieve'.[13] What is striking is the way in which Scott focuses attention on the emotional state of the enslavers as much as, if not more than, the enslaved. In a much-discussed passage, for example, Ellison boasts to his wife of the gratitude shown to him by enslaved people on the plantation when they hear that a threatened punishment for drunkenness is to be set aside:

> Had you, my dear, been present when they threw themselves at my feet, embraced my knees, and lifting up their streaming eyes to heaven, prayed with inexpressible fervency to their supposed Gods to shower down their choicest blessings on me, you would have wept with me; and have owned a delight which nothing in this world can afford, but the relieving our fellow creatures from misery.[14]

The sentimental tone of this passage is unmistakable, but so are the colonial attitudes. Ellison fosters what he interprets as gratitude only because it reflects the arbitrary power he wields over the enslaved people on his plantation. That their gratitude is expressed through invocations to what he calls 'their supposed Gods' reflects his attitude of contempt, or at best patronizing dismissal, towards the complex cultures of those he holds in bondage. Several critics have noted that the sentimental moment hides deeper and nastier forces at work. 'Ellison's vision of an affective economy', argues George Boulukos, 'obscures the suffering and inequality necessary to his system.'[15] Although his approach appears humane, his benevolence can only take place because of the alternatives available to him – flogging, torture and selling slaves to less 'humane' planters. It also offers planters a model whereby they can persuade themselves that they are doing good while they are, objectively speaking, participating in a system of violent exploitation. Ellison's 'delight' as his victims throw themselves at his feet, weeping and praising him, is in this analysis as complicit with the plantation slavery system as it is distasteful and distressing. Overall, the novel is unrealistic and self-indulgent in its sentimental representation of Ellison and the enslaved people on his plantation. By offering the possibility of a reformed plantation, it may even have helped perpetuate the system it appeared to critique. On the other hand, however, in 1766 very few people in the metropolis were talking about slavery at all, let alone about either its amelioration or its abolition. *The History of Sir George Ellison* may not have had convincing solutions to the problem of slavery, but it may have played a part in putting Britain's plantations and the enslaved people who worked on them into the realm of public debate.

A decade later, the arch-sentimentalist himself, Henry Mackenzie, author of *The Man of Feeling* (1771), contributed his own discussion of plantation slavery. *Julia de Roubigné* (1777) contrasts the fake man of feeling Montauban with Savillon, a man with supposed genuine sensibility. The eponymous Julia loves the latter but is married to, and ultimately murdered by, the former. This plot is interrupted by a long section in which Savillon attempts to run a reformed plantation in the French Caribbean colony of Martinique. While there is not the gratuitous sentimentalism of *The Man of Feeling*, or even of *The History of Sir George Ellison*, the novel proposes a sentimental economy which several critics, including Boulukos, Ellis, Sypher and myself, have found problematic or even chilling. The central passage shows how Savillon creates an efficient and orderly plantation in Martinique without direct recourse to the threat of violence. As with Ellison in Jamaica, the indirect threat of violence in fact subsists, but Savillon promotes ties of gratitude and personal loyalty, and offers enslaved people the fiction that they are free since they may choose to work out of gratitude to him rather than being forced to work out of fear. In a notorious passage, he explains how

> I have had the satisfaction of observing those men, under the feeling of good treatment, and the idea of liberty, do more than almost double their number subject to the whip of an overseer. I am under no apprehension of desertion or mutiny; they work with the willingness of freedom, yet are mine with more than the obligation of slavery.

Savillon's psychological manipulation produces a state of internalized subjection that recalls Blake's 'mind-forg'd manacles'. Unlike Blake's Londoners, however, Savillon's men remain actual and not figurative slaves, and while the economic benefit to them (none) is unchanged, their productivity and value to their owner are increased by 'almost double'. If the means of this transformation is the sympathetic bond of the man of feeling, the anti-slavery credentials of the sentimental novel are considerably weakened. Sensibility can be directly employed as a tool of oppression, even with its ameliorative gloss, and the man of feeling becomes just another agent of colonial exploitation. Like Scott before him, Mackenzie may have aided the emerging abolition movement by bringing slavery further into public discourse, and indeed in one part of the novel the narrator claims that he has 'often been tempted to doubt whether there is not an error in the whole plan of negro servitude'. On balance, however, with its psychological manipulation and wholehearted enthusiasm for increasing plantation productivity, it is ultimately difficult to characterize *Julia de Roubigné* as anything other than an apology for plantation slavery.[16]

If Scott and Mackenzie are hard to present unambiguously as anti-slavery authors, Thomas Day, by contrast, is undoubtedly a pioneer of abolitionism. His most important intervention was an extended poem, *The Dying Negro* (1773), in which, with his co-author John Bicknell, he drew attention to the plight of enslaved people in England's capital city. It went through several editions, and was followed up in 1784 with an anti-slavery pamphlet prompted by the end of the American Revolution.[17] Day's contribution to the history of the novel is highly significant, although often overlooked. In the multi-volume *History of Sandford and Merton* (1783–9) he presented a moral tale that has a good claim to be the first purpose-written children's novel in English. Strongly influenced by Jean-Jacques

Rousseau's theories of education as propounded in *Émile, ou De l'éducation* (1762), the book offered a series of short stories bound together by an anti-slavery frame narrative. It charts the transformation of Tommy Merton from a spoilt brat, waited on hand and foot by slaves on his father's Jamaican plantation, to a genuine young man of feeling back home in England, fully capable of shedding 'a tear of real virtue and gratitude'. Along the way, Tommy and his friend Harry Sandford befriend an 'honest negro', originally from the Gambia, who arrived in England as a free man after a period of enslavement in Argentina. He teaches the boys many valuable lessons, giving forcible pronouncements on the equality of different races, backed up with anecdotes from a life in Gambia that veer between the primitivist and the sentimental. These have a profound impact on Tommy:

> His heart expanded in the same proportion that his knowledge improved. He reflected, with shame and contempt, upon the ridiculous prejudices he had once entertained; he learned to consider all men as his brethren and equals; and the foolish distinctions which pride had formerly suggested were gradually obliterated from his mind. Such a change in his sentiments rendered him more mild, more obliging, more engaging than ever; he became the delight of all the family; and Harry, although he had always loved him, now knew no limits to his affection.[18]

Day strongly associates egalitarianism with an expanded heart, implying that true and unaffected sensibility must at once challenge prejudice, prompt social justice and invoke delight in others. This version of sensibility is radically different from that advocated by Henry Mackenzie in *Julia de Roubigné* in which sentiment is used to strengthen rather than weaken the bonds of slavery, and yet, like the novels of amelioration, *Sandford and Merton* also shies away from declaring a full-blooded commitment to ending slavery. Unlike the earlier novels, however, it was unambiguously critical of slavery and enormously more influential. *Sandford and Merton* continued to be republished and read as a standard children's novel throughout the nineteenth century and even into the twentieth. From the 1780s onwards, therefore, exposure to anti-slavery sentiment expressed in a novel of sensibility became part of the shared childhood experience of generations of British and colonial children.

Shandean Anti-slavery Writing

The most notable contribution to anti-slavery discourse in the sentimental novel was what we might call 'Shandean anti-slavery writing', prompted by Laurence Sterne in the 1760s and 1770s. This was significant as much for its digressiveness and intertextuality as for its role in changing public opinion. Sterne's own part, and the part played by his reader Ignatius Sancho, has been much discussed and needs only a brief recapitulation here, despite its importance to the debate over the role of the novel of sensibility in generating anti-slavery sentiment. Sterne and Sancho were not, however, the only authors to produce Shandean anti-slavery writing. This chapter concludes by looking at the wider ramifications of Sterne's engagement with matters of slavery, following an outline of the Sterne–Sancho exchange.

Shandean anti-slavery began in 1760 with a fleeting reference to slavery in Sterne's sermon on Job's 'Account of the Shortness and Troubles of Life' in which he called it 'a bitter draught'.[19] Although it is not entirely clear what kind of slavery Sterne had in mind, six years later the sermon was picked up by Ignatius Sancho, an African butler in the Duke of Montagu's household. Sancho wrote to Sterne in what would become a famous piece of fan mail, albeit one with a serious political purpose. 'I am one of those that the vulgar and illiberal call "negurs"', he began, reminding both Sterne and us that the word 'nigger' has always been offensive, despite some who would have us believe that it was a neutral everyday noun until comparatively recently. Sancho lamented that

> Of all my favorite authors, not one has drawn a tear in favour of my miserable black brethren – excepting yourself, and the humane author of Sir George Ellison. – I think you will forgive me; – I am sure you will applaud me for beseeching you to give one half hour's attention to slavery, as it is at this day practised in our West Indies. – That subject, handled in your striking manner, would ease the yoke (perhaps) of many – but if only of one – Gracious God! – what a feast to a benevolent heart![20]

Sterne did as he was asked. He replied in a celebrated and much published letter to tell Sancho that 'There is a strange coincidence, Sancho, in the little events (as well as in the great ones) of this world: for I had been writing a tender tale of the sorrows of a friendless poor negro-girl.'[21] Whether or not Sancho's letter was the actual prompt, the passage appeared in the final instalment of *Tristram Shandy* in 1767. Uncle Toby and Corporal Trim enter a shop in which they encounter 'a poor negro girl, with a bunch of white feathers slightly tied to the end of a long cane, flapping away flies – not killing them'. Uncle Toby calls this 'a pretty picture' because 'she had suffered persecution . . . and had learnt mercy'. Trim wonders 'if a negro has a soul'. Toby is sure that 'God would not leave him without one'. Finally, Toby muses that it is 'the fortune of war which has put the whip into our hands now – where it may be hereafter, heaven knows! – but be it where it will, the brave, Trim! will not use it unkindly.' As a sentimental parable invoking sympathy for the oppressed, this may well have generated discussion in a decade of slowly increasing anti-slavery sentiment – but it hardly qualifies as radical abolitionism.[22]

In 1768, Sterne offered an extended metaphor about a talking starling in *A Sentimental Journey*. He hears a caged British bird in France calling 'I can't get out', which leads him to quote from and paraphrase his own sermon on Job's troubles: 'Slavery! said I – still thou art a bitter draught.' As in the sermon, it is not entirely clear what form of slavery Sterne is excoriating. There is no reference to Africa or the Caribbean. Instead, he offers a vignette about a prisoner in a dungeon, presumably the Bastille, since the bird's sorrowful call interrupts a meditation on that prison. Problematically, if we are to claim Sterne as an abolitionist, the starling never gets out of its cage. Instead, Sterne, or rather his alter ego Mr Yorick buys the bird for a bottle of Burgundy and brings it back to England where he soon sells it to Lord A:

> In a week Lord A gave him to Lord B – Lord B made a present of him to Lord C – and Lord C's gentleman sold him to Lord D's for a shilling – Lord D gave him to Lord E – and so on – half round the alphabet – From that rank he pass'd into the lower house, and pass'd the hands of as many commoners.[23]

The bird thus remains chattel and is widely traded. This may be a neatly ironic commentary on the depth to which the British establishment are implicated in slave trading or it may merely be a case of Sterne the author failing to take the issue of chattel slavery seriously. If it is a satire on British slave trading, however, it again hardly qualifies as explicit abolitionism – even less so, one feels, than the story of the friendless poor negro-girl. It is difficult to be convinced, even if Sancho was, that Sterne had the abolition of the slave trade close to his heart.

Sancho's correspondence was posthumously collected and published in 1782 as *Letters of the Late Ignatius Sancho, an African*. The letters are distinctly Shandean in style with their love of whimsy, digression and typographical oddity. Unlike Sterne, however, Sancho firmly asserts an identity as a family man who celebrated and sustained genuine personal friendships. Despite Sancho's African origins, only a small number of his letters deal with matters of race or slavery, but the book was explicitly aligned with the emerging anti-slavery movement by his editor Frances Crew, who stated that 'Her motives for laying them before the publick were, the desire of shewing that an untutored African may possess abilities equal to an European.'[24] I have discussed Sancho's *Letters* at length in various places.[25] While they are unambiguously important contributions to the discourses of both sentiment and anti-slavery, in this chapter I conclude by looking at two less well-known examples of Shandean anti-slavery writing to suggest that, whatever the shortcomings of Sterne's personal commitment to anti-slavery, the Shandean mode remained attractive to novelistic participants in the abolition debate into the 1790s.

The first of these is Susanna Rowson's three-volume novel *The Inquisitor, or, Invisible Rambler*, which appeared in 1788, explicitly, if paradoxically, imitating 'the style of the inimitable Sterne'. The novel has scarcely any plot. Its hero, a sort of Addisonian spectator, is granted a magic invisibility ring which allows him to circulate undetected in social and personal circles otherwise closed to him. This ancient thought-experiment allows the philosopher to ask whether people would remain virtuous when the fear of detection is removed. Most authors, from Plato to H. G. Wells, have concluded that no one could acquire invisibility and remain honest and just. Not so the hero of a sentimental novel. The eponymous Inquisitor uses the power of invisibility to go about righting wrongs, usually by applying large quantities of cash. The second volume commences with a discussion of slavery in which Rowson deploys one of the most successful sentimental arguments against slavery: the notion of the equality of feeling. Does 'the man who with unmerciful hand scourges his slave', she asks, 'remember that the person he is chastising is endowed with the same sense of feeling as himself, and is as sensible of pain, hunger, thirst, cold, aye, and all the social blessings of life?' This argument lay at the root of most sentimental appeals to the humanity of readers, not just those concerning slavery, and while it has obvious affinities with Enlightenment moral sense philosophy, its call to action invokes the far older principle that we should do to others as we would want them to do to us. Since we all feel the same we should all be treated the same, the argument goes, and since we all feel the same we all know instinctively how to treat others. This argument is paramount for Rowson, and even uttering the word itself unleashes an assault on the sensibility of the reader (or writer) of feeling:

> Slave! said I, rising as I spoke, while the sanguine tide that plays about my heart rushed unbidden to my cheeks –
>
> Why did I blush, why did I tremble, as I pronounced the word slave? – It was because I was ashamed of the appellation – It is a word that should never be used between man and man – The negro on the burning sands of Africa was born as free as him who draws his first breath in Britain – and shall a Christian, a man whose mind is enlightened by education and religion, for a little sordid pelf, sell the freedom of this poor negro, only because he differs from him in complection[?]

The Inquisitor's embarrassment leads him into a reverie in which he conjures up an imaginary African, 'a man born to a good inheritance; and surrounded with all the comforts, all the blessings, he desired – but he was a negro'. He imagines this man's life, home and family, and how he was betrayed into slavery, transported to Barbados and sold. 'Alas! poor man', he apostrophizes, 'tears and entreaties are vain; you are in the hands of the sons of Mammon.' The slave's misery grows worse until

> He is weary of life – he offers up a prayer for his still dear companion, for his children, his hapless enslaved child – He dies – and is thrown into the grave without a prayer to consecrate the ground, without one tear of affection or regret being shed upon his bier.
>
> Had not that poor Negro a soul?[26]

The parallel with the 'negro-girl' passage in *Tristram Shandy* is obvious. The rhetorical technique is familiar too. This is a sentimental parable, presented in the context of a novel which continuously blends emotion with social and political argument, and which outlines an individual story of misery to act synecdochically for a wider social evil. The moral – that Africans are human beings endowed with souls – is made explicit at the end and readers, who would have been well aware of the then current national debate about the slave trade, are implicitly invited to take action. The book's language may seem overblown today, but it was certainly consistent with other Shandean anti-slavery writing. No doubt it found its audience at the time even if it is unlikely, alone, to have turned many supporters of the slave trade into abolitionists.

Susanna Rowson became a celebrated author, particularly in her adopted United States, after publication of her seduction novel *Charlotte Temple* in 1791. By contrast, the author of *Memoirs and Opinions of Mr Blenfield*, which appeared in 1790, remains unknown. The title-page announces that it was written by the author of *Tales of Sympathy*. This sounds like a plausible title for the 1780s, but I have not been able to find any record of its existence, nor have I been able to trace any book, 'by the same author', called *Tales Entertaining and Pathetic Inscribed to the Heart*, despite *Memoirs and Opinions of Mr Blenfield* containing an advertisement and a complete review of that volume, extravagantly praising it. Tellingly, neither the advertisement nor the review mentions either a publisher or a bookseller, and the review is extracted from an unknown journal. These parallel volumes appear to be an elaborate joke, or the construction of whimsical Shandean identity. As readers, we should probably be guided by the final words of the first volume, which announce the reasons for Mr Blenfield's sentimental journey to Switzerland as 'A mystery not worth fathoming'.[27] Apparently, few readers attempted to fathom the book. The complete verdict of the *Critical Review* said no more than that 'This Shandeyan performance aims at wit, humour, pathos, and eccentricity. Though more connected than the Life and Opinions of Tristram, it is inferior in every other respect; and we must confess that we have felt little mirth, little interest, and little instruction in perusing it.'[28]

The novel does have some interest for scholars of anti-slavery since it contains a figure called Shirna Cambo, an African man of sensibility, unambiguously modelled on Ignatius Sancho. Cambo, who appears for about ten pages in the first volume, is born on a slave ship, his mother dies, his father commits suicide, and he is brought to England as a child and presented as a gift to an 'opulent friend' of the slave trader. This is essentially a rewrite of the childhood biography of Ignatius Sancho that had been written by Joseph Jekyll to preface Sancho's *Letters*. Whether or not Jekyll's biography was entirely accurate remains an open question, but clearly the author of *Mr Blenfield* was inspired by it.[29] What is perhaps more interesting is Cambo's character, which either reflects the author's personal acquaintance with Sancho or, more likely, his reading of Sancho's character through the letters inflected by his understanding of the Shandean persona. Cambo, the author says, 'yielded to no master but virtue and himself' and became an 'industrious and respectable member of society'. He was a man of sensibility who 'for every decent merriment had a smile, for every sorrow had a tear'. Like Sancho, Cambo is a family man:

> He was the indulgent father of four children, when I was first introduced to him; his philanthropy and integrity were the examples and admiration of his neighbourhood; sensibility was a distinguished feature of his character; his imagination was pure, but unlimited; his conceptions nervous; and his conversation animated and engaging.

If he had a fault, says the author, it was simply that 'his sentiments, however, were sometimes mingled with an asperity, which I afterwards discovered arose from, perhaps, a too zealous principle in the cause of virtue'. Ignatius Sancho was almost certainly a more conscious and more active anti-slavery advocate than appears from a surface reading of the letters, and the portrait of Cambo, if it agrees with the historical Sancho, would corroborate that view. Cambo is shown to speak out actively against slavery: 'It was in *his* conversation', says the book's author, 'that I first learned the disgrace, the indelible shame of my country' – by which he means the slave trade.[30] In this vignette, Cambo appears to represent both an archetype of the Shandean sentimental hero as it was reimagined in derivative fiction, as well as a central figure of British literary abolitionism: the sentimental hero who has both suffered enslavement and can sympathetically communicate the pain of his enslavement and his anger at it, in the most affable, agreeable and urbane way possible.

Cambo returns to the topic of slavery several chapters later, in a ten-page defence of sensibility in which he quotes Edmund Burke's 'ingenious work of the Sublime and Beautiful', discusses the favourite biblical text of both sentimentalists and abolitionists, the Parable of the Good Samaritan, and asks 'will Sterne's Lefevre ever lose its estimation? Do not men quarrel in support of the author's fame?' The portrait is entirely consistent with what we know of the historical Sancho and, even if it was not drawn directly from life, it suggests either that he had an enduring public reputation for voicing anti-slavery sentiment, or that an author writing ten years after his death thought he ought to have had. Like the historical Sancho, the underlying philosophy is sentimental. 'What fills our theatres?' he asks:

> 'What stretches out the hand to relieve distress, or rescue danger? Surely it is sensibility; and without it we should not know for what we are born. Teach this doctrine among your women', added he to me; 'you will do a service to the cause of humanity, for which they will esteem you, and every transplanted African will pour forth all his sighs and tears in your behalf'.

Cambo is a little-known literary figure, but represents the culmination of Sterne's influence on the British abolition movement. A few chapters later, the narrator reports his death. Like Sancho, 'he was of a gross habit', which is to say that he was overweight, and suffered from 'a fluctuating rheumatic gout, which rendered him impatient'. His death turns out to be 'a harbinger to awaken our fortitude' and leads into a second misfortune: 'it is so in the common things of life, wherein Mr Sterne has justly said, there is a great coincidence'.[31] Cambo's death in the novel seemingly serves merely to cheaply round out a maxim of Sterne's from his correspondence with Sancho, but his presence in the novel is an act of solidarity with the abolitionist movement at its peak in 1790. It is also the end point of a quarter-century of Shandean, Sanchovian, whimsical, sentimental, but ultimately perfectly serious and politically engaged anti-slavery writing.

In conclusion, the novel of sentiment, in particular the Shandean novel, played a discernible role in bringing discussion of slavery and the slave trade into the public sphere, even though its contribution was often more notable for its political than its aesthetic merits. Some authors, such as Sarah Scott and Henry Mackenzie, either inadvertently or deliberately gave succour to slaveholders by arguing for reform of plantations rather than the abolition of slavery. Later authors, more explicitly aligned with the abolition movement, found it irresistible to place a piece of sentimental prose damning slavery somewhere in their novel regardless of how incongruously it sat with the rest of their text. Some of these works, like those of Laurence Sterne or Thomas Day, remained popular for many years after slavery had been abolished entirely in the British colonies. Most sank almost without leaving a trace. Whether any of them actually changed any minds on their own is an open question, but there can be no doubt that many sentimental novelists contributed directly – and feelingly – to public debate over the problem of slavery.

Notes

1. Wylie Sypher, *Guinea's Captive Kings: British Anti-Slavery Literature of the XVIIIth Century* (Chapel Hill: University of North Carolina Press, 1942), 266, 1–2.
2. David Brion Davis, *The Problem of Slavery in the Age of Revolution, 1770–1823* (Ithaca: Cornell University Press, 1975), 42, 82, 45.
3. Markman Ellis, *The Politics of Sensibility: Race, Gender and Commerce in the Sentimental Novel* (Cambridge University Press, 1996), 3–4.
4. Marcus Wood, *Slavery, Empathy, and Pornography* (Oxford University Press, 2002), 18.
5. George Boulukos, *The Grateful Slave: the Emergence of Race in Eighteenth-Century British and American Culture* (Cambridge University Press, 2008), 8.
6. Lynn Festa, *Sentimental Figures of Empire in Eighteenth-Century Britain and France* (Baltimore: Johns Hopkins University Press, 2006), 2.
7. Brycchan Carey, *British Abolitionism and the Rhetoric of Sensibility: Writing, Sentiment, and Slavery, 1760–1807* (Basingstoke: Palgrave Macmillan, 2005), 40.
8. Srividhya Swaminathan, *Debating the Slave Trade: Rhetoric of British National Identity, 1759–1815* (Farnham: Ashgate, 2009), 4.

9. Stephen Ahern, *Affect and Abolition in the Anglo-Atlantic, 1770–1830* (Farnham: Ashgate, 2013), 2.
10. Sypher, *Guinea's Captive Kings*, 272–303.
11. Ibid., 270.
12. Ellis, *Politics of Sensibility*, 87.
13. Carey, *British Abolitionism*, 52.
14. Sarah Scott, *The History of Sir George Ellison* (1766), ed. Betty Rizzo (Lexington: University Press of Kentucky, 1996), 11. For an extended discussion, see Carey, *British Abolitionism*, 50–7.
15. Boulukos, *Grateful Slave*, 130.
16. Henry Mackenzie, *Julia de Roubigné, A Tale, in a Series of Letters*, 2 vols. (London: W. Strahan and T. Cadell, 1777), II: 40, 41. For an extended discussion, see Carey, *British Abolitionism*, 63–7, although I have now revised my opinion given there that 'Mackenzie presents the clearest example of antislavery rhetoric to be found in a novel of the 1770s' (67).
17. [John Bicknell and] Thomas Day, *The Dying Negro, A Poetical Epistle, Supposed to be written by a Black (Who lately shot himself on board a vessel in the river Thames;) to his intended Wife* (London: W. Flexney, 1773); Thomas Day, *Fragment of an original letter on the slavery of the negroes; written in the year 1776* (London: John Stockdale, 1784). For discussion, see Carey, *British Abolitionism*, 75–84.
18. Thomas Day, *The History of Sandford and Merton, A Work Intended for the Use of Children* (1783–9), 8th edition, 3 vols. (London: John Stockdale, 1798), III: 308, 297–8.
19. Laurence Sterne, 'Sermon X: Job's Account of the Shortness and Troubles of Life, Considered', in *The Sermons of Laurence Sterne* (1760), ed. Melvyn New (Gainesville: University Press of Florida, 1996), 91–102.
20. Ignatius Sancho, *Letters of the Late Ignatius Sancho, An African* (1782), ed. Vincent Carretta (Peterborough, ON: Broadview Press, 2015), 128.
21. The entire Sancho–Sterne correspondence is reproduced by Carretta in Sancho, *Letters*, 331–6.
22. Laurence Sterne, *The Life and Opinions of Tristram Shandy, Gentleman* (1759–67), ed. Melvyn New and Joan New, 2 vols. (Gainesville: University Presses of Florida, 1978), II: 747–8. For discussion, see Carey, *British Abolitionism*, 57–63; Ellis, *Politics of Sensibility*, 67–71.
23. Laurence Sterne, *A Sentimental Journey through France and Italy* (1768), ed. Melvyn New and W. G. Day (Gainesville: University Press of Florida, 2002), 94–100. For discussion, see Ellis, *Politics of Sensibility*, 71–9; Festa, *Sentimental Figures*, 85–6.
24. Sancho, *Letters*, 47. For discussion, see Brycchan Carey, '"The hellish means of Killing and Kidnapping": Ignatius Sancho and the Campaign against the "abominable traffic for slaves"', in *Discourses of Slavery and Abolition: Britain and its Colonies, 1760–1838*, ed. Brycchan Carey, Markman Ellis and Sara Salih (Basingstoke: Palgrave Macmillan, 2004), 81–95.

25. For a complete annotated bibliography of works mentioning Ignatius Sancho, see Brycchan Carey, *Ignatius Sancho: a Bibliography*, online at www.brycchancarey.com/sancho/.
26. Susanna Rowson, *The Inquisitor, or, Invisible Rambler*, 3 vols. (London: G. G. J. and J. Robinson, 1788), I: xi; II: 2–8.
27. *Memoirs and Opinions of Mr Blenfield. By the author of Tales of Sympathy*, 2 vols. (London: W. Lane, 1790), I: 244.
28. *Critical Review*, 69 (May 1790), 592.
29. Sancho, *Letters*, 49–52. For discussion, see Brycchan Carey, '"The extraordinary Negro": Ignatius Sancho, Joseph Jekyll, and the Problem of Biography', *British Journal for Eighteenth-Century Studies* 26 (2003): 1–13.
30. *Blenfield*, II: 48, 51. For discussion of Sancho's abolitionism, see Carey, 'Hellish Means'.
31. *Blenfield*, II: 151–2, 208.

CHAPTER 9

Sentiment and the Gothic: Failures of Emotion in the Novels of Mrs Radcliffe and the Minerva Press

Hannah Doherty Hudson

Is the gothic novel sentimental? We may not think so at first; for many readers, the gothic is more likely to be associated with skeletons and screams of horror than the sympathetic and morally improving tears of the sentimental novel. The novels of Ann Radcliffe, however, do find their way into scholarly discussions of sentimentality with some regularity,[1] and, as Diane Long Hoeveler's description of 'the gothic formula . . . : part sentimental virtue in distress, part novel of manners, part melodramatic confrontation between good and evil' suggests, Radcliffe's are certainly not the only gothic works to incorporate sentimental themes.[2] What I propose here, however, is that while gothic novels are inarguably and deliberately sentimental in certain aspects of their content, they are, in many ways, anti-sentimental in effect. Early popular gothic novels incorporate the tears, persecuted innocents and heightened sensibility of their sentimental predecessors, but in so doing effectively undermine the moral promise of the sentimental novel. The admirable qualities often associated with sentimental benevolence are thrown into doubt by the inexorable grinding of the gothic plot gears: in these pages, compassion can no longer be translated into action, and sentiment is rarely usefully manifested in tears. Reading Ann Radcliffe's *Mysteries of Udolpho* alongside a selection of other gothic novels of the early 1790s, by such authors as Anna Maria Mackenzie, Richard Warner and Eliza Parsons, I argue that the extremities of emotion experienced by gothic heroes and heroines co-opt and refigure older sentimental models, ultimately suggesting something rather *horrifying* – as a gothic heroine might say – about the sentimental genre itself.

The 1790s Gothic Novel

While the gothic novel arguably began in English in the 1760s, with the publication of Walpole's *Castle of Otranto* (1764), followed by Clara Reeve's *Old English Baron* (1778) the following decade, the fashion didn't reach its height until the 1790s, when Ann Radcliffe's early novels brought the genre into prominence.[3] The year 1790 was also when the London publisher William Lane began publishing popular fiction under the Minerva imprint. With 217 novels in just its first decade,[4] the Minerva Press transformed the literary landscape during the very years when the gothic genre began to seem ubiquitous to literary observers.[5] This confluence explains, to some degree, the strong (though not entirely accurate) association of the Minerva Press with the gothic novel in general.[6]

By 1794 the gothic fad was in full flower with the publication of Radcliffe's massive, and massively popular, *Mysteries of Udolpho*, which famously sold for £500, had a first print run of more than 1,300 copies and had reached a third edition by the following year.[7] Dozens of other gothic novels also hit the shelves during the first half of this decade, many from the Minerva's in-house printing presses,[8] and it is this moment in the gothic's history, after it was unquestionably established, but before the massively successful and divisive gothic hits of 1796 and 1797 (especially Radcliffe's *The Italian*, Lewis's *The Monk* and Roche's *Children of the Abbey*), that I explore in this chapter, reading *Udolpho* alongside six popular gothic novels published by the Minerva Press. While novels like *The Danish Massacre* (1791),[9] *The Castle of Wolfenbach* (1793) and *The Haunted Castle* (1794)[10] received little of the critical praise (to say nothing of the financial rewards) of the record-breaking *Udolpho*, they, with their peers *The Necromancer* (1794),[11] *Count Roderic's Castle* (1794)[12] *and Netley Abbey* (1795),[13] appear to have been widely read and in some cases were positively reviewed.[14] While many studies of the gothic focus on Radcliffe's novels alone or compare them with an undifferentiated mass of 'Minerva gothics', there is much to gain from reading these novels alongside each other and on relatively equal terms.[15] It allows us to see, for one thing, that despite their diverse plots and themes, each shows, in different ways, the fundamental distrust of sentiment I see as central to the gothic project.

The novels I discuss in this chapter cover a broad range of settings and gothic tropes. While Radcliffe's *Mysteries of Udolpho* is set in sixteenth-century France and Italy, the others cluster in various Western European locales and span nearly a thousand years in time.

Count Roderic's Castle is set in a vaguely early modern Lombardy; *The Danish Massacre* takes place in Anglo-Saxon England, during the unhappy reign of Ethelred; *The Haunted Castle* takes place in thirteenth-century France, during the conflict between Philip of France and King John of England; *The Necromancer* is set mainly in eighteenth-century Germany. The events of *The Castle of Wolfenbach* unfold in locales from Bath to Tunis, in a seemingly modern setting, and *Netley Abbey*'s in late thirteenth-century England, with early excursions to Sicily and Palestine while one character is on crusade. While all feature scenes of terror, with hints – or more – of the supernatural, novels like *Count Roderic's Castle* and *Castle Wolfenbach* share Radcliffe's approach of providing a rational (if not always plausible) explanation for the terrifying events characters encounter. *The Haunted Castle* and *Netley Abbey*, in contrast, unabashedly allow spectres and visions to move the plot along, and *The Necromancer*'s characters alternate between genuine belief in the supernatural and accusations of 'disordered fancy', or outright fraud (*N*, 88). *The Danish Massacre* (as its title perhaps suggests) primarily depicts grim events, such as the on-page murder of children, so shocking as to need little supernatural adjuvant to horrify a reader. All of the novels feature old and mysterious buildings somewhere in the plot; all deal with scenes of abduction or imprisonment; all use disguise or uncertain identity as a plotline; beyond these similarities, however, and the overarching theme of extreme moments of terror, the specifics of their stories vary considerably.

Returning to our sentimental theme, one further thread connects these works: an emphasis on their protagonists as men (or women) of feeling. Their distant dates and locales often serve to highlight the advanced sensibilities of their heroes and heroines: the baron de Villars is said to have 'formed the most finished character of the 13th century', noted for 'candor . . . sweetness of manners, and . . . benevolence of heart' (*NA*, 1–3), while the narrator claims that the twelfth-century Pierre du Pin's 'virtues distinguished, and raised him above the mass of mankind; pointing him out as one possessed of piety and benevolence – one, who only saw the sufferings of the rest of men, to hold out the hand of relief so far as his power permitted' (*HC*, 1: 2). Though raised in a 'heathenish' age when 'mercy, gentleness, and humanity were banished [from] the land' (*DM*, 1: 17, 4–5), King Ethelred's daughter Elfrida manages to be a good Christian herself, and if she sees someone suffer, 'her benevolence suggest[s] the probability of removing . . . the sorrow which, by the magnetic power of sympathy, had transferred its effects' (*DM*, I: 47). And Emily St Aubert is in possession of naturally 'uncommon delicacy of mind, warm affections, and ready benevolence' (*MU*, 5).

Yet, however admirably sentimental the heroes and heroines, sentiment often proves a fragile and illusory basis for interpersonal relationships as the gothic plots of these novels unfold. Emily's father fears that her highly developed sensibilities will be injurious to her happiness, which certainly proves true for her and many of the other protagonists of these novels. But even the calmly restrained emotions and practical virtue espoused by St Aubert prove hard to put into practice. He exhorts his daughter to believe 'that one act of beneficence, one act of real usefulness, is worth all the abstract sentiment in the world' (*MU*, 80), while the Countess Wolfenbach instructs her young protégée Matilda that 'the truly beneficent mind looks upon every child of sorrow as their relation' (*CW*, 116). Yet (as we shall see) these models of sympathy prove not only impracticable, but misleading and even oppressive to Matilda, Emily and other protagonists. Not only 'gothic times' but the gothic genre itself, as I will suggest, prove inimical to the idea of a laudable and useful sentimentality.

Sentiment and Selfishness

To examine the failings of the sentimental mode in these novels, I want to begin with a close look at a series of moments that will be familiar to any reader of sentimental novels: characters in tears. A classic marker of the sentimental novel is the extreme tearfulness of its protagonists; as we will see, lachrymosity is just as characteristic of gothic novels. Indeed, whereas the characters in Mackenzie's *The Man of Feeling* air their feelings in forty-seven tearful interludes (according to the convenient 'Index to Tearfulness' included in the 1886 edition of the novel),[16] Radcliffe's *Mysteries of Udolpho* features weeping characters literally hundreds of times.[17] And this is by no means an aberration; the much shorter *Castle of Wolfenbach* contains approximately ninety mentions of tears or weeping. This works out to one on virtually every other page of my 203-page edition – surely a prime example of what Claudia L. Johnson has called the 'egregious affectivity' of the 1790s sentimental/gothic novel.[18] Indeed, it would more than fill the allotted pages of this chapter merely to list the tearful moments found in the novels I analyse. Characters cry wild bursts of tears; silent single tears; happy tears and tears of despair; their tears fall on each other and on to the pages they are writing. Men and women alike cry; characters cry in anticipation of future evils and in remembrance of evils already done them.

When the unfortunate Danish hostage Athela inadvertently foils her husband's attempt to rescue her by calling for help (she is unable to recognize him due to his disguise), she shows her grief by '[c]lasping my fingers, and weeping'; as she later recollects, he too lets his emotions flow in liquid form: 'a tear dropped from his eye upon my cheek' (*DM*, I: 178–9). After escaping from her imprisonment by Sir Hildebrand, the murderer of her father, the young heroine of *Netley Abbey* tells her rescuers of the villain's actions, and 'A torrent of tears fell from Agnes on this retrospect of her distresses' (*NA*, II: 70). The similarly beleaguered Matilda of *Castle Wolfenbach* weeps before any misfortunes have actually befallen her: upon overhearing her guardian discussing his scurrilous plans for her, 'I threw myself on the ground, and preserved myself from fainting by a copious flood of tears' (*CW*, 14).

Tears in these novels are the product of a wide range of situations. Near the end of *The Haunted Castle*, the hero Ignatius's future father-in-law, De Lacé, 'raise[s] and embrace[s] [Ignatius and his beloved, Adelais], whilst tears of joy ran from his eyes' (*HC*, II: 138). While De Lacé cries from joy at the reunion of two young people lately revealed to be his own lost daughter and nephew, in the very next line, the villain who tore the family apart in the first place by jealously murdering Ignatius's father is also described as tearful: 'Hendred was so affected, that he wept aloud' (*HC*, II: 138). Emily of *Udolpho* cries when remembering a book her beloved father had read to her before his death – 'she looked at the page, wept, and looked again' (*MU*, 95) – as well as when her suitor Valancourt turns out not to be dead after all: 'Did you indeed honour me with a thought – a tear?' he demands rapturously; 'O heavens! you weep – you weep now!' (*MU*, 625). In *The Necromancer* a character identified only as 'the Austrian' cries in rage at being deceived by the Necromancer, Volkert: 'The tears ran down his cheeks, as he pronounced these words, spoken in the most violent passion' (*N*, 105). If we conclude anything about the gothic from examining the outward physical markers of emotion that, scholars have argued, characterize both the sentimental novel and the gothic novel, it is that gothic characters feel strongly, frequently, and in ways that are transparent to both fellow characters and engaged readers.[19] And in this sense, it may seem that gothic novels, if different in plot details, do align with the emotional priorities of many sentimental novels.

All of these tears, however, have something in common, something so obvious as perhaps to be easily overlooked: they are essentially selfish. While the sentimental novel's emotional excesses are, at least theoretically, outward-turning, inspired by the suffering of others and channelled towards the alleviation of that suffering, the gothic novel's excesses turn inward, focusing on the self. Even as the drops, floods and torrents of tears that drench the pages of the novels demonstrate the ability of their protagonists to feel strongly, to be moved deeply, the *reasons* for the tears often illustrate that the character's manifest sympathies are primarily for him- or herself. The sentimental man or woman of feeling's tears are (or should be) inspired by compassion, in other words – but the tears of a gothic heroine like Emily St Aubert are more often brought on by her own suffering. When Eleanor (the daughter of the exemplary de Villars, and the other heroine of *Netley Abbey*) cries, it is in personal anguish: 'She burst into a violent flood of tears, and exclaimed, "Never, never, my honoured parent can I consent to be sir Hildebrand's wife"' (*NA*, 1: 172–3). *Castle Wolfenbach*'s hapless Matilda marks her despair at having escaped her lecherous guardian only to find herself alone and helpless: what, she demands, ought she to do, '(... shedding a torrent of tears) no friend to advise me, no certainty of a place to receive me'? (*CW*, 28). The heroine's fear, her exhaustion, her anxiety and sadness find vent in tears: while the gothic protagonist's strong feelings are certainly understandable under the circumstances, they are rarely in response to, or anticipating aid of, anyone but herself. Thus we begin to see the twofold breakdown of the unwritten contract of moral sentiments: on the one hand, the tears that might mark sympathetic benevolence are merely used to express suffering; on the other, the responsive sympathies that should be stirred in others by those tears often fail to materialize.[20]

Sentiment's Feeble Virtues

This is not to say that outward-turning sensibility doesn't exist in these novels. As we have seen, the authors take pains to point out that their characters are generous, benevolent and not inherently selfish; while in context these assertions often come across as ironic or simply tragic, there certainly are scenes in all of these works in which we see characters experiencing sympathetic emotions and the urge to benevolent action. However, the very notion of sentiment *as* tied to benevolence, as admirable, as appropriate, is questioned at every turn in these novels, such that even the most generous, best-intentioned character is often unable to turn her or his emotion to any productive end. John Mullan has argued that 'Benevolent remedying of misfortune is invariably the activity of the sentimental protagonist.'[21] But what, the gothic novel compels us to ask, becomes of the sentimental protagonists who are prevented from remedying any misfortunes, through circumstances that make it impossible to help anyone, even – or especially – themselves?

In the most familiar gothic plots, the bar to the protagonist's benevolent activity is overt and external: he or she cannot act because of abduction, coercion or imprisonment. Indeed, these moments where the protagonist wishes she could help but cannot are often occasions for (still more) tears, as when Matilda cries over her inability to provide for her servant, who has accompanied her on her flight: '"what is to be the fate of poor Albert, who has left all to follow me!" Overcome with sorrow, she wept aloud' (*CW*, 7). *The Danish Massacre* too provides numerous examples of this problem: the Danish hostage Athela hopes to aid her children and her husband, but is entirely unable to do so; the evil machinations of her captor, the Duke of Mercia, both prevent her from action and repeatedly foil the attempts of the other female protagonist, King Ethelred's daughter Elfrida, to assist her. Considering examples like these allows us to see how even when gothic tears are not self-centred, they *are* often markers of helplessness and disempowerment.

The Danish Massacre's ironic emphasis on the futility of benevolent feelings and sympathetic attachments suggests that this correlation is not an accident, but a result of the inherent weakness of sentimental motivations. Despite the narrator's praises of Elfrida's caring heart and Christian virtue, the plot features characters who explicitly lament sentiment's shortcomings, its tendency to be overwhelmed by selfish motivations and, most of all, its lack of real power to accomplish change in the face of misfortune or evil. Discussing her own bad romantic choices, Athela reflects,

> 'Alas, Elfrida, when one boundless passion occupies our soul, how feeble are the operations of the more exalted virtues! how firmly do we shut our eyes to reason, justice, humanity, prudence, friendship. A sigh, perhaps a tear, may mark the inefficacious emotions of a heart strongly attached by objects of sympathy; but that is all.' (*DM*, 1: 97)

Her condemnation of the dangers of 'boundless passion' echoes those of countless other heroines led astray by an excess of sensibility, but her description of 'inefficacious emotions' is painfully reminiscent of the unacknowledged tears and sighs of her fellow gothic sufferers. Later in the novel, Athela bemoans the 'horror of ineffectual tears and lamentations, without a possibility of present redress' (*DM*, 1: 181). The emotions she feels and expresses through her tears are characterized in practical terms as 'ineffectual' – as, indeed, they clearly are. Her pitiless captor is more powerful than she; left 'without a possibility of present redress', her only recourse is retreat into 'insensibility' – the potential for a *future* righting of wrongs (in the afterlife?) is plainly insufficient comfort (*DM*, I: 181).

Other novels continue this theme, underscoring the obvious: feelings (or tears), on their own, don't accomplish much. Phrases like 'unavailing tears' (*NA*, II: 8), or 'in spite of their tears and supplications' (*CRC*, 67), repeated scores of times, emphasize the futility of these expressions of emotion: they're no good to anyone else, and often don't even accomplish the desired results – relief, aid, respite – for the sufferer. The feebleness and ineffectuality of emotions are not described only as results of circumstance; they also derive from the unstable and contradictory nature of emotions themselves. At best gothic emotions are represented as an unreliable basis for decision-making, and at worst they're literally paralysing, disabling the helpful action that they could hypothetically inspire. The princess Elfrida's good intentions are derailed by fear at the appearance of the villain Mercia – 'Elfrida had listened with gentle pity: but that pity was changed to terror' as he enters (*DM*, I: 54) – and her helpful actions are just as easily thrown off course.

Admirable, potentially productive emotions, particularly pity and compassion, are often described as oddly mixed with others by the improbable events of gothic plots. When Isabel of *Count Roderic's Castle* discovers that the terrifying bloody spectre before her is actually her lover Rhinaldo in disguise, her emotions are described as dramatically fluctuating: 'Her doubts, however, at length subsided, and pity, at the ghastly appearance of Rhinaldo, took place. She asked him, with a mixture of affection, compassion, and horror, the cause of his present appearance' (*CRC*, 54). These potent admixtures of feeling can be confusing to the reader (horror and affection, in particular, seem unlikely bedfellows), but they're no less so to the characters who experience them. Lieutenant B– of *The Necromancer*, who narrates a large part of the story by letter, 'thrill[s] with horror and pity' when encountering Volkert (the titular Necromancer) in a dungeon and, frozen, 'stand[s] before him like a statue' (*N*, 140). When *Netley Abbey*'s hero, de Villars, is saved from poison by his page Bertram (actually his future wife, Isabel, in disguise), the narrator tells us that 'A variety of emotions tore the heart of de Villars. Admiration, love, gratitude, terror, and grief took possession of his soul, and nearly deprived him of reason' (*NA*, I: 63). Indeed, reason is often described as impaired by the wild tumult of gothic emotions, and the characters' communications are likewise short-circuited by them; when de Villars's son Edward saves the imprisoned Agnes Warren from Sir Hildebrand, she is unable to explain her situation: 'Mingled emotions agitated the mind of the lady, and disabled her from replying' (*NA*, II: 58).

As these examples may suggest, the damaging effects of strong emotion are nowhere more evident than when the gothic hero or heroine turns them on herself. *The Danish Massacre*'s Athela turns her emotions inward in a shockingly physical way: upon discovering her husband locked in a dungeon, she recounts, 'I shrieked ... clasped the bars, – struck my face against them with a violence that forced the blood in torrents from my nose' (*DM*, I: 200–1). A bereaved mother in *The Necromancer* similarly harms herself with the violence of her feelings: 'Having thus given vent to her grief, she tore her hair in wild agony, beating her breast, and the tears of sorrow trickled down her cheeks – she appeared a grisly ghastly figure' (*N*, 60).

Sentiment and the Power of Pity

As we have seen, both heroes and villains in *The Mysteries of Udolpho* and the other novels I discuss here show a range of emotions; as in the sentimental novel, however, compassion – often expressed in the gothic novel as pity – is the emotion that most sharply demarcates the praiseworthy from the reprehensible. In Radcliffe's novel, the scheming Madame Cheron and Montoni repeatedly prove themselves incapable – or perhaps merely unwilling – to feel this most sympathetic emotion. When Emily pleads with Madame Cheron, the latter is unmoved: 'her aunt, neither softened to pity, or awakened to remorse, became enraged, that her will should be opposed' (*MU*, 145). Similarly, Valancourt's requests to Montoni fail to move him: 'he was peremptory in his refusal, and was neither softened to pity by the agony which Valancourt's letters pourtrayed, or awakened to a repentance of his own injustice' (*MU*, 148–9). When Emily's uncle, M. Quesnel, another of the novel's cruel authority figures, learns that Emily is serious in her refusal of the marriage to Count Morano that he has planned for her, we are told that 'he was *incapable of feeling pity* for whatever sufferings of his niece might stand in the way of his ambition' (*MU*, 214, emphasis added). In this, *Udolpho*'s scheming characters resemble many other gothic villains. When Isabel pleads with the evil Rhodolpho to spare her virtue ('for pity's sake spare me', she cries), Rhodolpho merely rebuffs her 'in a tone of cruel and bitter raillery' (*CRC*, 102); similarly, the violent French soldiers who attempt to abduct Ignatius's future beloved, Adelais, are described as 'hurrying her over the rough ground, without pity or compassion' (*HC*, I: 30). And if bad characters do feel a drop of pity, they hide it as best they can: 'Emily ... made a last, though almost hopeless, effort to interest the compassion of Madame Montoni, who, if she did feel any degree of pity, or remorse, successfully concealed it' (*MU*, 220).

Other characters are marked in these works by their inability to bear the emotional excesses of others: in the *Necromancer*, Lieutenant B– declares, 'It is a terrible awful sight to see a *man* weep. I turned my eye away from that affecting scene, not being able to behold it any longer' (*N*, 105). And in the *Danish Massacre*, the worthless monarch Ethelred, having just sat by while his second-in-command Mercia murdered two children in front of him, orders the removal of the grieving mother from his sight: 'Bear her off ... I cannot look upon her grief' (*DM*, II: 230). In other words, even some characters who do feel compassion fight against it, seeking to end their own discomfort rather than alleviate the pain they are witnessing. Indeed, pity of the sort that involves sympathizing with the misery of others is portrayed in *The Necromancer* as quite literally something to flee. When Lieutenant B– returns to a small village where he has previously stayed, he encounters a scene that, in a sentimental novel, would likely inspire a project of assistance and recuperation: 'the inhabitants came running towards us covered with rags, and exhibiting pale woe-worn countenances. I never beheld such a horrid picture of wretchedness and misery; – they wrung their hands, crying for alms, and wept bitterly' (*N*, 79). He does give them money, but when he realizes it is his own over-curious meddling with the supernatural (he has visited a nearby haunted castle) that has apparently led to the destruction of their village, the mingling of guilt with his initial pity is too much to bear:

> Unwilling to behold any longer the marks of sorrow and distress so deeply imprinted on the faces around me, and stung to the heart by the tormenting thought to have partly contributed, by my idle curiosity, to provoke the lurking tempest of woe that had thus cruelly crushed the earthly happiness of the wretched villagers, I hastily inquired for the next village, they shewed us the way, and we bade them farewell with a bleeding heart, riding away in full speed. (*N*, 80)

His desire to 'escape the hideous spectre of self reproach' (*N*, 80) means that the narrative of repentance and sentimental reform we might expect to follow does not materialize: instead, his companion soon persuades him the suffering of the villagers was the work of fate. His memory of the villagers' misery is so thoroughly dispelled by this argument that within 'half an hour's ride' the two have determined to resume the very same quest that led to such disaster the first time (*N*, 81). Refusing or avoiding an unwanted or inconvenient emotional response is, quite clearly, one way gothic characters demonstrate power over other characters.

There is another side to this coin. Those admirable protagonists, including Emily St Aubert, Elfrida and Matilda, who (we are told again and again) *are* capable of feeling pity for others, tend to feel it even when other characters don't actively solicit it. Despite how terribly Madame Montoni treats her niece, late in *The Mysteries of Udolpho* we are told that Emily's 'gentle heart was touched by her [aunt's] distress, and, in the pity thus awakened, she forgot the injurious treatment she had received from her' (*MU*, 277). Emily's spurned suitor Morano is shocked to find the same attitude of forgiveness turned on him, declaring: 'It is from you, Emily, that I have deserved punishment, yet I receive only pity!' (*MU*, 267). As with many sentimental heroines, the impatient reader may occasionally find Emily's nature a shade too forgiving for her own good – as Barbara Benedict notes in this volume (see Chapter 4), sentimental protagonists are often foolish as well as admirable.[22] Terry Castle memorably expresses a related view of the gothic heroine: 'Fear and stupidity in fact *define* gothic femininity; to be female and a character in a gothic tale is to find oneself becoming mortally *dumb and afraid*'.[23]

We find ample evidence for these assertions in the naïvely unsuspicious and forgiving behaviours of gothic characters from Agnes to Count Roderic himself. But in these acts of forgiveness we can also see another way that the gothic distorts – or, more cynically, simply elucidates – sentimental relationships. A power dynamic inevitably structures sympathy and the practice of benevolence; the gothic novel tends to reveal it. Rather than using sentiment to gloss over the social and economic hierarchies implied by one character's pity or aid of another, gothic novels highlight these imbalances. Refusing pity to someone who is pleading for it is obviously an assertion of power; it is in this sense that the frequent 'ineffectual' tears I have noted are expressions of powerlessness. But even when someone *does* experience pity, and does try to relieve the suffering they see, the gothic novel reveals that benevolence is always about power, and never without price.

We can begin to see this in Madame Montoni's less-than-appreciative response to her niece's forgiving nature; when she senses that Emily is viewing her with 'solicitude', the narrator tells us that she 'was vexed to perceive [it, as she] seemed to feel the pity of her niece to be an insult to her pride' (*MU*, 253) Put another way, although Montoni exerts power over Emily with his pitiless treatment of her, Emily's ability to *feel* pity is also a kind of power. Madame Montoni experiences her pity as 'an insult' because to be pitied implies weakness; a short while later, when she does attempt to elicit Emily's sympathies, she wishes to dictate the terms on which they can be felt, but Emily is steadfast. Emily's feelings for her aunt on this occasion, 'a mingled emotion of pity and contempt' (*MU*, 283), exemplify the conflicting and inhibiting emotions experienced by other gothic protagonists, but also suggest the assertion of superiority that is seemingly inherent in the exercise of pity. It isn't altogether surprising, then, that although Emily often bemoans the lack of pity she encounters, when she receives it from the wrong quarter she likes it little more than her aunt.

When her servant Annette comments sympathetically on Emily's mistreatment by Madame Montoni, Emily cuts her off abruptly: 'I thank you for your pity, Annette', says Emily, interrupting her, 'but my aunt was unhappy then, and that disturbed her temper perhaps, or I think – I am sure – You may take away, Annette, I have done' (*MU*, 286). While Emily's resistance to Annette's sympathy ostensibly stems from her belief that it is unseemly to discuss her relatives critically with a servant, her rather ungrateful 'thanks' to Annette for her pity also, I would argue, derives from Emily's awareness of this power dynamic. Emily readily pities people, but she doesn't like to be pitied herself, and most certainly not by someone lower in the power hierarchy than she, as her peremptory direction to Annette, a firm reminder of their respective roles as mistress and servant, makes plain.

Annette, of course, has little power to help Emily, no matter how much she may sympathize with her. But the problematic nature of gothic pity becomes clearer when, as occasionally happens, we do encounter characters who have the power both to pity and to act. One example is the kindly Marquis and Marchioness in *Castle of Wolfenbach*, who take Matilda in and defend her (to a point) from the depredations of gossip and the foul pursuits of her guardian, Weimar. But their assistance comes at a cost. Matilda feels deeply, painfully obligated to them for their help; her gratitude – often expressed in tears – is couched in words that suggest there is no such thing as true disinterestedness in the gothic novel. Matilda describes herself as 'An unhappy orphan . . . a dependent on the bounty of friends' (*CW*, 41), and while her aristocratic guardians urge her to 'let the words favour and obligation be blotted from your vocabulary', this does not prove to be possible (*CW*, 42). Instead, her gratitude drives her future behaviour – she is 'overwhelmed with grateful emotions', constantly remembers that she has 'a thousand obligations to this noble family', and 'her grateful heart impel[s] her to return them by every attention in her power' (*CW*, 41–2).

The language of obligation, of submission, of acquisition, of merit, of gratitude-as-debt permeates *Wolfenbach*'s discussion of emotion, emphasizing the transactional nature of relationships even – or especially – among friends. This becomes painfully clear when Weimar catches up with Matilda and uses strikingly identical language to force her to comply with his desires. Though Weimar, like the Marchioness, 'disclaim[s] the name of obligation; you owe me no gratitude but for my affection' (*CW*, 76), he repeatedly uses this very obligation to exert pressure on Matilda. Asking 'is there no gratitude, no affection due to the man who has supported you from childhood[?]' (*CW*, 68), he persuades her that she 'owe[s] unbounded obligations to a man she had for some time past looked on with detestation' (*CW*, 70). This brings on a crisis of emotion and self-abnegation: 'I have no right to refuse, nor any way of discharging the obligations I owe you for the care of my early life, but by the sacrifice of the maturer part of it', she declares (*CW*, 76).

The novel's constant use of words and phrases such as 'account', 'weight of obligations', 'beyond all possibility of return' and 'indebted', coupled with the descriptions of Matilda's 'grateful heart overflowing with tears' (*CW*, 83–4), suggests the power differential inherent in even benevolent emotional exchanges in the gothic novel. While Matilda's tears of gratitude are theoretically a happy reaction to an appropriately kind response to her painful situation, they – like the hopeless tears of the unpitied prisoner – acknowledge a disempowered position, a favour sought or an obligation incurred. Emily St Aubert's discomfort with the pity of her maid, then, reflects an acknowledgement of the same power dynamics of pity that permeate virtually every emotional exchange in the gothic novel: to ask for pity and not receive it marks a character's powerlessness (and is often acknowledged by tears); so too, to receive pity is to highlight the relative power of the pitier over the pitied. And that power is reinforced, and problematized for the character and reader, by the implication of selfish pleasure gained from even the most unselfish act: when the Countess urges Matilda to put aside the 'oppressive notion of having received [a favour]', she argues that 'when beauty and virtue suffer . . . they receive a superior gratification that have the power of relieving sorrows, than the received can in accepting the favours' (*CW*, 116). Thus pity is described as both something one *earns* or *is owed* (by being beautiful and virtuous, not necessarily traits under the protagonist's control) and something that grants 'superior gratification' to the one whose 'favours' aid the sufferer.

Gothic Machinery

Perhaps the most noticeable thing about gothic novels of this period is the distinctive and replicable 'gothic machinery' about which so many critics complained. What I'd like to suggest here is that thinking about these noticeably reproducible elements of the gothic novel – the castles, the chains, the ghosts, the groans; or, to put this another way, the elements without which, in sufficient proportion, the gothic novel would cease to be gothic – also gives us a way to think about the fundamental problem with the translation of the sentimental into a gothic setting. Gothic machinery is machinery in a narrative sense (the supernatural apparatus that keeps the plot going), but also, perhaps, in the mechanistic sense: it is a combination of elements that *does* something, that produces a predictable effect from a certain grouping of components. And what does gothic machinery produce? The gothic machine churns out emotions – terror or horror, certainly, but also those sentimental standbys, sadness, joy, longing and regret. The failure of the sentimental mode, then, may be an inevitable side effect of the gothic's generic parameters; specifically, that inexorable 'machinery' that forces its suffering heroes and heroines from terror to terror.

Horace Walpole famously wrote in the preface to the second edition of the *Castle of Otranto* that his gothic experiment was designed to make his characters 'think, speak and act, as it might be supposed mere men and women would do in extraordinary positions'.[24] This claim has particularly interesting ramifications for the sentimental components of gothic novels. Whereas the sentimental novel depends on the idea that its protagonists are unusual in their experiences of feeling, the very structure of the gothic novel casts doubt on this assumption. In a 1775 essay on sentiment, the author argues that 'sentiment in all its latitude is a privilege of a favored few; of those exalted and refined spirits alone, who seem composed of purer materials than other mortals, whose exquisite sensations yield to ten thousand impressions, equally unknown and incomprehensible to the vulgar, of whatever condition'.[25] What the formulaic gothic novel manufactures, on the other hand, is essentially *rote* emotions, emotions that are produced through a predictable and deliberate series of events and narrative tropes. In other words, the very fact that *any ordinary person* thrown into the extraordinary circumstances that fill gothic novels would unavoidably experience strong emotions implies from the start that those emotions are not an indicator of special sensibility or unusual compassion.

And this is the very premise of the gothic emotion machine: many characters are portrayed as calm and reasonable at first, but the stakes get higher and higher, and the events more and more dramatic, until the desired emotional effects (e.g. terror, horror, tears, insensibility) are achieved, as every reader knows they ultimately will be. Thus the gothic protagonist's tears never really register as a sign of refined delicacy or special sensibility; indeed, it would be remarkable if anyone were *un*moved after seeing what Matilda, Emily, Athela or Agnes sees. In this way, the gothic novel renders emotion suspect: if it is predictable, replicable, manipulatable, mechanical, then it is surely not a mark of special discernment or well-developed morality, and is perhaps not even reliably indicative of a comforting fellow-feeling among human beings. Gothic sentiment, then, is often ineffective; it is neither egalitarian nor disinterested; most distressingly, it is not an indicator of inherent sensitivity or benevolence and thus (as numerous contemporary critics feared, albeit for slightly different reasons) is unlikely to produce useful goodness on the part of either the character or the reader. Even when the novels end happily, as they often do, the doubt planted in the reader's mind by sentiment's numerous failings remains, shadowing the text.

John Mullan suggests that 'If the novel developed as a genre that made significant the distinctive fate of a particular individual, then sentimentalism was the attempt to rescue that individual from isolation and selfishness.'[26] We might then follow this to say: if 'sentimentalism was the attempt to rescue [the] individual from isolation and selfishness', then the gothic was the reminder that individuals are always fundamentally alone in their emotional experiences; even the most benevolent motivations manifest themselves within a hierarchical matrix of power and invariably turn back towards the self. While we may not find many ruined castles, moaning ghosts or dank dungeons in the sentimental novel, we certainly do, as the other chapters in this volume amply demonstrate, encounter plenty of self-satisfied benefactors, intolerable debts of gratitude, ineffectual tears, overly naïve protagonists and selfish motivations. Perhaps, then, the question we should be asking is not 'is the gothic sentimental?' but rather, 'is the sentimental gothic?' As the works of Mackenzie, Parsons, Radcliffe and many other novelists suggest, the answer may well be – may always have been – 'yes'.

Notes

1. See, e.g., Barbara M. Benedict, *Framing Feeling: Sentiment and Style in English Prose Fiction, 1745–1800* (New York: AMS Press, 1994), 172–95; Claudia L. Johnson, *Equivocal Beings: Politics, Gender, and Sentimentality in the 1790s* (University of Chicago Press, 1995), 73–137. Stephen Ahern argues, in *Affected Sensibilities* (New York: AMS Press, 2007), 29, that 'the amatory, sentimental, and Gothic forms are all sensibility narratives'.
2. Eliza Parsons, *The Castle of Wolfenbach: a German Story*, ed. Diane Long Hoeveler (Chicago: Valancourt Books, 2006), x (cited parenthetically as *CW*). See also Hoeveler's discussion of the 'sentimental/Gothic heroine' (102) in 'The Heroine, the Abbey, and Popular Romantic Textuality', in *Radcliffe, Romanticism and the Gothic*, ed. Dale Townshend and Angela Wright (Cambridge University Press, 2014), 100–16. Other scholars who discuss emotion or sentiment within the gothic novel include Coral Ann Howells, *Love, Mystery, and Misery: Feeling in Gothic Fiction* (London: Athlone Press, 1978) and Kate Ferguson Ellis, *The Contested Castle* (Urbana: University of Illinois Press, 1989), esp. 28–9, 68–70. I am indebted to Howells's readings of the highly melodramatic, externalized and subjective states of gothic feeling.
3. For recent scholarship on Radcliffe, see the essays in *Ann Radcliffe, Romanticism and the Gothic*; chapters 1, 3 and 12, in particular, deal with her early reception and influence on the gothic genre.
4. See James Raven, 'Historical Introduction: the Novel Comes of Age', in *The English Novel, 1770–1829: a Bibliographical Survey of Prose Fiction Published in the British Isles*, ed. Peter Garside, James Raven and Rainer Schöwerling, 2 vols. (Oxford University Press, 2000), ii: 72–3. The 217 figure includes a few works published in 1790 under Lane's name alone. Historical and bibliographical information about the Minerva Press's novels (including authorial attributions) in this chapter are drawn from *The English Novel*; their data in turn draws on the research of Dorothy Blakey, *The Minerva Press* (London: Bibliographical Society at Oxford, 1939) and Deborah McLeod, 'The Minerva Press' (PhD dissertation,University of Alberta, 1997). For more recent work on the Minerva Press's novels, see especially Elizabeth Neiman, 'A New Perspective on the Minerva Press's "Derivative" Novels: Authorizing Borrowed Material', *European Romantic Review* 26 (2015): 633–58.
5. On the perceived ubiquity of the gothic-as-commodity, see, for instance, E. J. Clery, *The Rise of Supernatural Fiction*, 1762–1800 (Cambridge University Press, 1995), esp. chapters 6–7 and 9.
6. On the close association of the Minerva Press and the popular (and critically maligned) gothic, see Clery, *The Rise of Supernatural Fiction*, esp. 135–8; Michael Gamer, *Romanticism and the Gothic* (Cambridge University Press, 2000), 66–7. It is important to note, however, that the Minerva Press published in many other genres, and even many 'gothic' works might more

accurately be described as generic hybrids (ibid., 4; McLeod, 'The Minerva Press', 60).

7. William St Clair, *The Reading Nation in the Romantic Period* (Cambridge University Press, 2004), 631–2. References to *The Mysteries of Udolpho* in this chapter are taken from the edition by Bonamy Dobrée (Oxford World's Classics, 1980) and cited in the text as *MU.*
8. Raven, 'Historical Introduction', 79.
9. Anna Maria Mackenzie, *The Danish Massacre: An Historic Fact*, 2 vols. (London: The Minerva Press, 1791); originally published anonymously. Cited hereafter in the text as *DM.*
10. George Walker, *The Haunted Castle: A Norman Romance*, 2 vols. (London: The Minerva Press, 1794); originally published anonymously. Cited hereafter as *HC.*
11. Carl Friedrich Kahlert, trans. 'Peter Teuthold', *The Necromancer, or, The Tale of the Black Forest: Founded on Facts*, ed. Jeffrey Cass (Chicago: Valancourt Books 2007); originally published as a translation of the work of 'Lawrence Flammenberg'; Cass identifies the real translator as Peter Will (x). Cited hereafter as *N.*
12. Anon., *Count Roderic's Castle: Or, Gothic Times, A Tale*, ed. J. Jenkins, with a new introduction by Hannah Doherty Hudson (Chicago: Valancourt Books, 2017). Cited hereafter as *CRC.*
13. Richard, Warner, *Netley Abbey: A Gothic Story*, 2 vols. (London: The Minerva Press, 1795). Cited hereafter as *NA* This novel was initially published anonymously in Southampton; as Raven notes, it was then 'shamelessly reissued' within the year under the Minerva imprint (1: 74). Thus it may not be, strictly speaking, a 'Minerva Press' novel, but given the prominence of Lane and his library, it seems safe to assume that many readers would have encountered it as such in its own day.
14. Two works on this list, *The Necromancer* and *Castle Wolfenbach*, are probably best known for their mention as 'horrid novels' in *Northanger Abbey.* In terms of reception, *Count Roderic's Castle*, for instance, was described by the *Monthly Review* as 'conceived with originality and elegantly written' (*The Monthly Review* 16, [April 1795], 467); all of the novels but the *Haunted Castle* had second editions in London, Dublin or North America within a year or two of their publications.
15. We can see this tendency even in works like James Watt's *Contesting the Gothic* (Cambridge University Press, 1999). Watt (like Gamer and Clery) gives far more attention to the Minerva Press novel than do many gothic scholars, providing a fascinating account of the press's role in popular literary culture. My own work is indebted to his argument that Minerva Press novels 'generated anxiety primarily because of their quantity, their self-proclaimed commodity status, and – ultimately – their popularity' (70). Still, the structure of the book clearly (if unsurprisingly) prioritizes Radcliffe, devoting one chapter to her (six) novels and another to 'German literature, the Minerva Press, Matthew Lewis' – dozens, if not hundreds, of novels in all. On the

dangers of viewing all popular gothic novelists as mere adherents to a Radcliffean formula, see Yael Shapira, 'Beyond the Radcliffe Formula: Isabella Kelly and the Gothic Troubles of the Married Heroine', *Women's Writing* (published online November 2015): 1–19, DOI: 10.1080/09699082.2015.1110289.

16. Henry Mackenzie, *The Man of Feeling* (London: Cassell and Co., 1886), vi–vii.
17. These counts are approximate and based on word searches for key terms such as 'weep' and 'tear', filtered to exclude homonyms or non-relevant occurrences. Though they shouldn't be taken as exact (it can be difficult, for instance, to distinguish one prolonged episode of crying from multiple short ones), these figures do give a useful sense of just how common tearfulness is in the 1790s gothic novel.
18. Johnson, *Equivocal Beings*, 1.
19. Maureen Harkin, for instance, notes in her introduction to Mackenzie's *Man of Feeling* (Peterborough, ON: Broadview Press, 2005) that 'Sentimental novels ... privilege the visible, somatic expression of ... sympathy'; Howells argues similarly that gothic novelists 'tend to concentrate on external details of emotional display' (*Love, Mystery, and Misery*, 15).
20. I don't mean to suggest that sentiment always works perfectly (unselfishly, usefully) in sentimental novels either; as numerous scholars have shown, many of the 'failures' of emotion I outline here can also be found in earlier sentimental novels. However, I do think the extremity of circumstances and replicability of certain aspects of plot in the gothic novel undermines sentimental morality in a particularly explicit and striking way.
21. John Mullan, 'Sentimental Novels', in *The Cambridge Companion to the Eighteenth-Century Novel*, ed. John Richetti (Cambridge University Press, 1996), 244.
22. Benedict, Chapter 4, 69–70 above.
23. Terry Castle, *Boss Ladies, Watch Out!* (New York: Routledge, 2002), xv.
24. Horace Walpole, *The Castle of Otranto: a Gothic Story*, ed. Nick Groom (Oxford World's Classics, 2014), 9.
25. Quoted in Mullan, 'Sentimental Novels', 247.
26. Ibid., 248.

CHAPTER 10

The Sentimental Novel in America: The History of Emily Montague, Charlotte Temple, The Power of Sympathy, The Coquette

Joseph F. Bartolomeo

In the title of this chapter, the most freighted word is the preposition: a common North American setting should not obscure the varying audiences for these novels, and their divergent representations of the nature and significance of sensibility in America. Both Frances Brooke's *Emily Montague*, often referred to as the first Canadian novel, and Susanna Rowson's *Charlotte Temple*, the best-selling novel in America prior to *Uncle Tom's Cabin*, were originally published in London for British readers, and both emphasize sentimental longing to return home. In *Emily Montague* this desire derives in part from confining sensibility almost exclusively to British characters and decrying its absence in Canadians, while in *Charlotte Temple* the profound isolation of the sentimental heroine is magnified by what amounts to exile in America. The popularity of Rowson's novel in America is related both to readers' residual yearning for a lost homeland and 'family' and to the author's invitation – problematic in its execution but eagerly embraced – to pity and mourn the heroine. The two novels, directed explicitly to readers in the new American republic, offer complex and often contradictory messages about the importance of feeling, its relationship to reason, and its connection to communities of class and gender. William Hill Brown's *The Power of Sympathy* undercuts its stated moral purpose by representing sympathy as both dangerous and admirable, and conveys an equivocal verdict on the levelling of class distinctions that is enabled by sympathy. The title character of Hannah Webster Foster's *The Coquette* is repeatedly admonished to prefer reason over fancy, but this advice is compromised by male suitors often ruled by emotion and 'rational' female mentors who become decidedly unsympathetic. Ostensibly about courtship and seduction, the novel more effectively interrogates sentimental friendship, which proves impossible to sustain.

Informed by Frances Brooke's experience as the spouse of a military chaplain in Quebec, *Emily Montague* (1769) represents many attractive aspects of the new British colony, particularly its sublime landscape. These advantages cannot compensate, however, for what the British characters whose epistolary exchanges constitute the text regard as a conspicuous lack of sensibility among its Native and French inhabitants. Edward Rivers, the principal male character, describes the Indians as 'strangers to the softer passions, love being with them on the same footing as amongst their fellow-tenants of the woods',[1] and while Arabella Fermor initially admires the relative freedom of Native women, she comes to regard them as slaves for submitting to arranged marriages. Although Rivers adds that he has been told that 'though insensible to love, they are not without affections' (37), readers see no evidence of this. Among French Canadians, the men are virtually invisible, but the women are routinely criticized for lacking the sensibility of their English counterparts: Rivers calls them 'gay, coquet, and sprightly; more gallant than sensible' (13), and Arabella believes that 'delicacy, softness, sensibility, tenderness, are attractions to which they are strangers' (189). Yet the only non-British character of any importance, Madame Des Roches, a wealthy widow attracted to Rivers, confounds the stereotype. Both Emily and Arabella come to recognize in her a 'trembling sensibility' (219, 306), and Emily's initial uncertainty about whether she is 'either the most artful, or most noble of women' (197) is resolved decisively in favour of the latter view. Arabella's description of her final encounter with Madame Des Roches includes a rare admission that 'when the heart is really touched, the feelings of all nations have a pretty near resemblance' (306), only to retreat to a self-serving assessment of her as the exception that proves the rule, which does seem to be her primary function in the novel. She never fully joins the circle of sentimental British characters, remains behind in Canada after they return home, and – most significantly in an epistolary novel – is never given the opportunity to speak or write for herself.[2]

In the letters written by the British characters, the word *tenderness*, which Johnson's *Dictionary* defines as 'susceptibility of the softer passions' and 'kind attention; anxiety for the good of another', appears more than 150 times, nearly always in reference to one of the central characters or their correspondents, marking them as exemplars of sensibility. Emily, prone to tears, emotional angst and self-sacrifice, is the most obvious and uncomplicated sentimental character, and is recognized as such by her lover and by her closest friend. Right after he observes that ''tis sensibility alone which can inspire love', Rivers refers to her as 'the tender, the sensible

Emily Montague' (41). The more arch Arabella repeatedly warns Emily about the dangers of excessive emotion, in contrast to her more rational and assertive approach. In her formulation, Emily 'loves like a foolish woman, I like a sensible man' (198), with the latter adjective used here in its more modern sense. Yet Arabella abandons her self-professed coquetry and control upon meeting Captain Fitzgerald, her eventual husband, and she refers to herself as 'absurd as even the gentle love-sick Emily' (252). The prior vocal critic of arranged marriages may retain her vivacious epistolary style, but without knowing it she marries the man her father had intended for her and settles into domesticity. Rivers considers himself 'delicate' (201) in his love, and sensibility as his 'fault' (27), while Arabella admires his 'tenderness of soul, and almost female sensibility' (277), echoing the language of Rivers's sister, Lucy – the recipient of most of the letters from Canada – who speaks of his 'almost feminine sensibility' (133). The word *almost* has unusual force, however, in a text that takes pains to maintain gendered distinctions. Both Rivers himself and his brother-in-law, John Temple, attribute a 'manly' tenderness to him (207, 293), and Arabella calls him 'almost the only one of his sex' she knows 'who has the tenderness of woman with the spirit and firmness of man' (198). Brooke thus participates in what G. J. Barker-Benfield has read as a concerted effort to address uneasiness about the effeminacy of men of feeling by combining sensibility with the 'masculine' qualities of strength and reason.[3] These gendered differences are initially subsumed under a larger sentimental communion that the characters enjoy with each other, and with their absent English correspondents, but not with the Canadian other, making a return 'home' desirable and inevitable.

Questions of national character aside, the intimacy of this circle of friends and lovers raises disquieting questions about their sentimental attachments. Upon first meeting Emily, Rivers compares her to his sister as he explains his attraction to the latter: 'You know, Lucy, you have often told me I should certainly have been in love with you if I had not been your brother: this resemblance is a proof you were right' (22). For her part, Lucy insists that Temple can please her only insofar as he resembles Rivers: ''tis rather hard upon me, I think, that the only man I perfectly approve, and whose disposition is formed to make me happy, should be my brother' (133). When Emily finally meets Lucy, the resemblance between her and Rivers prompts both 'a tenderness for her, which is inconceivable' (289) and repeated glances at Lucy with an 'attention' that causes Emily to blush. Although Rivers may view the pleasure he takes in his sister as 'without the least mixture of desire' (21), the pseudo-incestuous connections have provoked discomfort.[4] Emily and Rivers turn out to be related distantly enough to rule out literal incest, but this revelation only reinforces the extent to which their circle remains closed to outsiders. Likewise, Emily's effusions about seeing in Rivers's 'amiable countenance a sensibility similar to my own' (247) and their souls having 'the most perfect resemblance' (319) unconsciously suggest a degree of narcissism behind their relationship.[5] Seeing oneself in another may lead to empathy and benevolent actions, as Adam Smith theorizes and countless sentimental novels illustrate, but it also opens the sentimentalist to charges of self-absorption. In *Emily Montague*, the inextricable connection of sensibility with romantic attraction troubles both.

The ending of the novel would seem to occlude these concerns by celebrating the reunions, marriages and homosocial bonds that are made possible by the return of the major characters to England, but it also firmly establishes more conventional hierarchal relationships between the sexes than were possible or preferred in Canada. The abiding friendship between Emily and Arabella is complemented by a burgeoning one – and extensive correspondence – between Rivers and Fitzgerald, who see themselves as sharing strong marriages based on a 'trembling delicacy of sentiment' (344) and 'a real sympathy' (346) absent in men like Temple, whose 'affection is mere passion' (344) – a reason why Rivers once had hoped to match Fitzgerald with his sister. At the same time, Rivers rejects 'male friendships' like this for women since he desires 'to engross all Emily's *kind propensities*' to himself, and 'should grudge the least share in her heart, or . . . in her *friendship*, to an archangel' (379). The erstwhile advocate for equality in marriage, who 'wished the word OBEY expunged from the marriage ceremony' (205), comes to embrace a more self-centred conception: 'I would engross, I would employ, I would absorb, every faculty of that lovely mind' (331). Emily is eager to oblige, given her view of Rivers as 'a god' (190) or as 'the most angelic of mankind' (192), with 'the noblest mind that ever animated a human form' (214–15). Rivers's eventual preference for 'the more mild and regular charms' of England over 'the savage luxuriance of America' (300) corresponds neatly with his unresolved marital and financial prospects in Canada giving way in England – via the sudden appearance of Emily's wealthy nabob father and the revelation that he had planned to promote their match – to financial security and a marriage more patriarchal than Rivers might claim or even think.[6] Conversely, Arabella's comparative freedom and teasing courtship in Canada ends in a traditional sentimental union, in which her ongoing wit must substitute for any genuinely transgressive behaviour. Joe Snader has persuasively read the characters' Canadian sojourn as a form of imperial tourism and masquerade, in which British characters are improved 'through contact with an alien environment, alien customs, and alien peoples'.[7] Contact, but never immersion: they remain separate from the other, largely because of a shared and exclusionary sensibility, and eventually return to the place where, however changed, they can find fulfilment in the familiar.

Rather than ending with the foundation of a sentimental family circle, *Charlotte Temple* (1791) begins with one, which serves to emphasize the poignancy of its rupture. Mr Temple, possessed of modest means but also 'a heart open to every generous feeling of humanity, and a hand ready to dispense to those who wanted part of the blessings he enjoyed himself',[8] exercises both by coming to the rescue of the poverty-stricken Mr Eldridge and his daughter, Lucy. In the course of recounting the family's victimization, Eldridge apologizes for losing his composure, calling himself both unmanned and 'a mere infant', but Temple assuages his doubts about his masculinity by assuring him that 'the truly brave soul is tremblingly alive to' feeling and Eldridge readily agrees, recalling the 'exquisite delights' caused by his 'keen sensations', his 'quick sense of happiness or misery' (13). A fellow man of feeling makes for a fitting object of compassion and charity, but Temple's decision to mortgage part of his estate also results from the 'exquisite transport' he anticipates in seeing 'the expressive eyes of Lucy beaming at once with pleasure for her father's deliverance, and gratitude for her deliverer' (16). His benevolence is thus not entirely disinterested, as the narrator underscores by her reluctance to 'enquire too minutely into the cause' (17) that motivates him.[9] Attraction and marriage to Lucy come at the cost of his mercenary father's favour, a small price for a man of 'no ambitious notions' (19), and 'the happy trio' retire to a country cottage and years of 'uninterrupted felicity' (20), magnified by the birth of Charlotte.

Outside the cocoon of the family, sensibility is conspicuously absent, and a protagonist who has never known anything else is defenceless against shrewd and egocentric antagonists. Charlotte's '[i]ntriguing' (20) and immoral teacher, Mlle La Rue, and her 'dissipated, thoughtless, and capricious' (29) paramour, Belcour, behave strictly and consistently in their own self-interest, which for a time includes encouraging Montraville's pursuit of Charlotte. Rowson's narrator distinguishes Montraville from these obvious villains, noting his generosity, liberal opinions and good nature – all characteristics of the sentimental hero – but adds that he was 'eager and impetuous in the pursuit of a favorite object' (29). A younger son like Mr Temple, he by contrast accedes to his father's admonitions against marrying a woman of insufficient fortune, and drifts aimlessly into a seduction of Charlotte. When determining whether or not to accompany him to America, Charlotte weighs romantic feelings against love and duty towards her family, and a tender letter from her mother persuades her to refuse Montraville. Her resolution falters on their meeting, however, and from the point of her half-willing flight she largely remains a passive victim. Before leaving England, Charlotte's sole attempt at regaining some agency by writing to her parents, begging their pardon and seeking a reunion is easily thwarted by Montraville's 'wisely' (42) tearing the letter to pieces and throwing them into the sea, his worldly wisdom depriving her of any sentimental attachment.

Charlotte's arrival in New York only heightens her confinement and victimization. Montraville places her in a house away from the city, allowing him to pursue 'business and pleasure' (50), eventually to fall in love with the heiress Julia Franklin, and all-too-easily to believe Belcour's false imputations against Charlotte. She is isolated not only geographically but socially, since she is identified as a mistress and therefore excluded from polite society. Mrs Beauchamp, the sole neighbour who responds to Charlotte's plight with 'the pellucid drop of humanity stealing down her cheek' (57), overcomes prejudice to befriend her and – in striking contrast to Montraville – arranges for her to write to her parents, informing them of her pregnancy and begging their forgiveness. Charlotte's loss of this rare 'consoling friendship' (62) when Mrs Beauchamp accompanies her husband to a new posting is followed by unrelieved cruel treatment by Belcour, her landlady and her supposed friend La Rue, now the wealthy and ostensibly respectable Mrs Crayton. The only other character to show her any compassion is John, Mrs Crayton's poor servant, who provides her shelter and thus demonstrates that empathy and benevolence, however rare in Charlotte's experience of America, can cross class lines.

John's 'poor little hovel' (82) becomes the setting in which Charlotte gives birth to her daughter, Lucy, and in which she dies, but also appropriately the site of her reunion with the most sympathetic characters: Mrs Beauchamp, who comes to her aid unaware of her identity after hearing of her plight from the doctor who cared for her, since she cannot imagine being 'deaf to the calls of humanity' (84), and her father, to whom she commits her daughter and from whom she seeks a final blessing. This sentimental tableau, 'dreadful' as it is, thus results in 'a sudden beam of joy' (87) on Charlotte's face as she expires. In the remaining two chapters, one of which is aptly entitled 'Retribution', the characters who mistreated Charlotte suffer in direct proportion to their behaviour. Montraville encounters Charlotte's funeral procession and implores her father to kill him, an inconceivable response from a man like Temple, who instead consigns him to be punished by his own 'reflexions' (88), which result in regular tearful visits to her grave and 'severe fits of melancholy' (89) for the rest of his life. Montraville also takes the direct vengeance he sought on himself by killing Belcour, whose lies had alienated him from Charlotte. Ten years later, when a ruined and repentant La Rue appears on the doorstep of the London lodgings of his family, Mr Temple characteristically takes her in, and even after she identifies herself as the 'viper' who 'turned the poor Charlotte out to perish in the street' (89), he cannot 'behold her in this distress without some emotions of pity' (90). The narrator's final words cast La Rue's suffering and death as a form of poetic justice, but the novel conveys a more affirmative and resonant moral message by ending where it began, with the figure of the benevolent man actuated by 'the impulse of a noble feeling heart' (89).

A principal reason for Charlotte's happiness on her deathbed is the knowledge that her abiding desire to return to England and to escape the profound isolation that she has experienced will be realized by her daughter. After the family reunion has taken place, in a scene 'impossible to do justice to' with words but exhibiting feelings readily accessible to '[e]very heart of sensibility', Mrs Temple is also comforted by substitution, as she eventually comes 'to almost fancy she again possessed her Charlotte' (89). Lucy has been read as the embodiment of a fantasy of homecoming and reconciliation for American readers anxious about losing their identity, both familial and cultural, as British.[10] Such an audience would be acutely sensitive to the pathos of Charlotte's situation – exiled to and within a faraway country – which may account for the phenomenal success of the novel in America after a tepid initial reception in England. It remained in print for more than half of the nineteenth century and prompted countless readers to follow Montraville's example and visit an actual gravestone inscribed with Charlotte's name in New York's Trinity Churchyard.

While Rowson could not have anticipated this response, she did actively attempt to shape her audience by addressing imagined readers directly and drawing distinctions based upon capacity for feeling. As with much sentimental fiction, the principal implied audience for the novel, according to the Preface, consists of 'the young and thoughtless of the fair sex' (5), whom it might save 'from the errors which ruined poor Charlotte' (5). The phrasing here, which combines blame with pity, introduces the conflict that Marion Rust has identified between Rowson's professed didactic intentions, which require criticism of Charlotte's conduct, and her desire to elicit sympathy for her protagonist.[11] Another telling example occurs after Charlotte has been severed 'from all her connections, and robbed of innocence' (50), when the narrator contrasts the lot of a wife with that of 'the poor girl by thoughtless passion led astray' (51) in a brief description that anticipates Charlotte's fate. She then asks if 'some passing daughter of youthful mirth' might 'exult in her own unblemished fame' upon encountering the fallen woman's grave, only to conclude that if that woman has 'a heart of sensibility' she will forgive the 'errors' of 'the unhappy victim of folly' (51) and consecrate the grave with a tear. Later, the narrator rebukes the 'young volatile reader' who might be bored with 'so much fainting, tears, and distress', first by suggesting that her tale will not please a heart 'rendered impenetrable by unbounded prosperity, or a continuance in vice', and then by requesting that this reader withhold judgement until she has 'perused the whole' (74). Anticipating the criticism that La Rue's worldly success overshadows the warning provided by Charlotte's suffering, she promises a form of poetic justice and attendant feelings of 'compassion' and 'sympathy' for Charlotte and 'horror and contempt' for La Rue, but also observes that 'gay hearts' might be more engaged with 'scenes of pleasure and dissipation' (75) involving the latter. Rowson addresses but mitigates the heroine's errors by weighing them against the potential interpretive errors of smug, ungenerous and judgemental readers.

Young women are not the only targets of the narrator's corrective interventions. After describing Charlotte's initial feeling towards Montraville, she implores a 'sober matron' – who might deign to read the novel before allowing her daughter to do so – not 'to put on a grave face, and throw down the book in a passion and declare 'tis enough to turn the heads of half the girls in England' (22). She avers that her intention is in fact to ridicule young women's attraction to soldiers, and details the negative consequences likely to ensue. Later she addresses the putative 'disapprobation' of a presumed severe reader identified, in Sternean fashion, as 'Madam', claiming that she does not intend to 'extenuate the faults' (51) of fallen women but also reminding this reader of the many 'secret faults . . . hid in the recesses of our hearts' (52) which should encourage pity and compassion. 'Madam' has a male counterpart in a 'Sir' who might incorrectly cavil about Charlotte's ability to support herself, and the narrator also rebukes the 'eye of contempt' cast on Mr Temple's emotional response to Charlotte's elopement by a reader 'presuming on his own philosophic temper', bidding him to 'remember that man was a father' (40). Addresses to readers who vary in age and gender may indicate a desire to create a community of sentiment among them, but the frequency of these addresses, and their insistent and at times hectoring tone, signals not self-assurance but frustration with the difficulty – for both author and reader – of reconciling feeling and judgement.[12]

William Hill Brown's *The Power of Sympathy: Or, The Triumph of Nature* (1789) uses epistolary form to foreground a similar tension around the key word in its title; sympathy – related to and often paired with sensibility – may be powerful and natural, but should it motivate and regulate conduct? The plot would seem to suggest not, as the sympathy that both central characters, Harrington and Harriot, repeatedly identify as the animating force of their romantic relationship derives at least in part from what they are horrified to discover is their biological connection as brother and sister. As Harriot puts it in her farewell letter to Harrington, 'ALLIED by birth, and in mind, and similar in age – and in thought still more intimately connected, the sympathy which bound our souls together, at first sight, is less extraordinary. Shall we any longer wonder at its irresistible impulse?'[13] This discovery prompts what Harriot characterizes as a tormenting conflict between head and heart, and ultimately leads to her death and Harrington's subsequent suicide, thus emphasizing how an unregulated sympathy can victimize those who embrace it, however innocently.

The novel also critiques sympathetic feelings by representing them as rooted in self-indulgence and divorced from generosity and honesty. Harrington's encounter with a slave who pretended to be guilty and chose to be whipped in order to shield her son from punishment – for breaking a glass – evokes his hope that her 'soul be ever disposed to SYMPATHIZE with' her children and her 'brethren and sisters in calamity' (62) and his naïve prediction that sympathy will lead to personal fulfilment: 'then shalt thou feel every circumstance of thy life afford thee satisfaction; and repining and melancholy shall fly from thy bosom – all thy labours will become easy – all thy burdens light, and the yoke of slavery will never gall thy neck' (62). Notably, this letter immediately precedes the one that reveals that Harriot and Harrington are siblings, invokes the power of sympathy primarily to lament it, and sets into motion the destruction of Harrington's own happiness, proving his blithe confidence in sympathy baseless. Harrington's words to the slave are accompanied by 'feelings of exquisite delight' about an imagined end to slavery and a paean to sensibility, which allows us 'to mitigate the wounds of the stranger who falleth in our way' (62), but his assistance extends no further than advice. He uses the occasion to luxuriate in his own feelings, without ameliorating the slave's condition in any meaningful way.[14] Even more egregious is the conduct of Harrington's father. After he has seduced Maria, a woman of lower social standing, and she has given birth to Harriot, his wife's silent suffering and 'eloquent *tears* of *beauty*' (70) lead him to a contrition that involves sacrificing Maria, but then his sympathy for her results in a resolution to 'screen her from penury and malice' and 'to make provision for the child' (71). Once Maria has disappeared and is taken in by his friend Mr Holmes, however, Harrington Sr tells him, 'Your feelings are your reward' (71) and adds, 'I WILL not so far supersede the fruit of your benevolence, as to presume to offer you any other recompense, than my sincere prayers for your happiness' (72). His feelings do not prompt any generous action, and later they prevent him from accepting responsibility by revealing the truth to his son directly. Regarding his silence, he exclaims, 'My heart failed me!' (78) – words true in more senses than he intends or realizes.

The limitations of sympathy and sensibility buttress arguments for subordinating feelings to reason, voiced most emphatically in the text by Harrington's closest friend, Worthy. Worthy recommends combating fears that result from 'too much sensibility' with 'a manly exertion of reason' (96), without which 'Nature – helpless, debilitated Nature – lost to herself, and every social duty, splits upon the rocks of despair and suicide' (97). Harrington expresses gratitude for his friend's 'good advice' but adds that it 'comes too late' (100), in a letter that amounts to his suicide note. His belief that suicide will reunite him with Harriot in a heaven where their love, which he considers 'the most pure, the most holy' (80), will be 'refined' and 'freed from all criminality' (93) is augmented and perhaps superseded by despair at remaining haunted by her image and living in a world that has become 'a dreary desert' (100). This might seem to reflect negatively on Harrington, but Worthy, in spite of his name, has limitations as a mentor and judge. Early on, we learn that a 'secret sympathy" (30) binds Worthy to Myra, Harrington's sister and his eventual wife, rendering him more similar to Harrington than he would admit. He fails to heed Harrington's plea to return home and arrives only after his death – too late, like his advice, which is always couched in general maxims rather than referring to Harrington's heart-rending situation.[15] His delay in returning corresponds to what the reader experiences as a delay in replying to Harrington's increasingly anguished letters, six in a row before Worthy responds with a letter that begins, 'You argue as if your reason were perverted' (94). Finally, Worthy reproduces the epitaph Harrington has written, claiming that 'a profitable moral is deduced from it' (102), but as Elizabeth Dill has aptly observed, it is 'not at all clear'[16] what that moral may be. The 'Monumental Inscription' variously invokes the loaded terms *Nature* and *Sympathy*, warns against the 'fell Seducer's wiles', and ends with imagining two lovers moved 'with mutual pity' (103) towards Harrington and Harriot.

This final image captures what critics have seen as the novel's reproducing within the reader the sympathy represented in the central relationship and thereby idealizing it and generating ambivalence within the reader.[17] Even David Lawrimore's recent reading against the grain that casts the novel as a deliberate attempt to satirize the socially progressive views associated with sentimentalism admits that it failed, primarily because it, 'like all novels, is a polyphonic hodgepodge of characters and voices'.[18] Polyphony is especially pronounced in epistolary fiction, with its absence of a controlling narrative voice, and Brown's paratextual material does little to close this gap. Taken together, the title-page, the dedication to 'the Young Ladies of United Columbia' (5) and the preface emphasize 'the dangerous Consequences of SEDUCTION' and 'the Advantages of FEMALE EDUCATION' (7). Female education does inform a debate about the impact of the novel on women readers and some letters from Mrs Holmes to Myra, but bears little relation to the principal plot or characters. The repeated warnings against and condemnations of seduction in the text gain resonance primarily from the central event of the pre-history of the narrative, the seduction of Maria by Harrington Sr, the consequences of which are indeed, as the dedication puts it, 'fatal' (5). For Harrington, however, sympathy vanquishes seduction, after a wordless encounter in which the 'language of the eyes' moves him to abandon his plan of making Harriot his mistress and to court her 'on a principle the most just, and the most honourable' (14). Inveighing against seduction does little to gloss their relationship, and is undercut in other ways as well. After Mrs Holmes tells Myra (and the reader) the story of her father's original sin, her next letter warns about 'how a woman may be accessary to her own ruin' (73) without ever applying any of her observations to Maria or offering comfort to the woman to whom she had just revealed devastating details about her family. This bloodless moralizing, which resembles Worthy's, compromises her status as a mentor to either her friend or the reader. Worthy himself regards the kidnapping of a minor character, Fidelia, as a seduction, as does her father, giving the term an elasticity that dilutes its didactic force. Such multivalent and compromised moral guidance encourages divergent responses rather than foreclosing them.

The open-ended form of the novel also thwarts an unambiguous ideological thrust. Several critics have characterized *The Power of Sympathy* as a conservative indictment of the mixing of social classes: had Harrington – and before him, his father – never pursued a woman of lower status, the catastrophic events would not have ensued.[19] Yet Harrington's quick transformation from a would-be seducer who is 'not so much of a republican as formally to wed any person' (11) of Harriot's class to an honourable suitor of her hand in marriage is praised by Worthy, who advises him only to obtain his father's consent. Worthy does not dispute Harrington's subsequent remarks against inequality and class distinctions and his stated preference for a 'democratical . . . kind of government' (34), nor does any other correspondent criticize him in this regard. Harrington's conduct also compares favourably, of course, with his father's seduction and abandonment of a woman of lower social status. If Brown meant to advocate for a natural aristocracy, as he did in other writings, his adoption of the epistolary form instead encourages an utterly democratized reading practice, and his central plot foregrounds a sensibility that, however problematic, transcends class distinctions.

In Hannah Webster Foster's *The Coquette* (1797), multiple letter-writers articulate a single admonitory moral with much greater consistency, namely that the heroine, Eliza Wharton – and presumably the novel's women readers – should prefer reason to fancy and let rationality guide and constrain emotions. Early in the novel, Eliza's closest friend, Lucy Freeman, worries that Eliza's 'fancy will mislead' (124) her to choose the rakish and apparently (but not actually) wealthier Major Sanford over the sober clergyman Mr Boyer, and Eliza's reply justifies her concern: 'My reason and judgment entirely coincide with your opinion; but my fancy claims some share in the decision; and I cannot yet tell which will preponderate' (125). A similar dialogue occurs with Eliza's cousin Mrs Richman, who warns her to 'beware of the delusions of fancy' after she admits that her fancy and judgment 'are in scales' and '[w]hich will finally outweigh, time alone can reveal' (145). One could argue that Eliza's initial refusal to commit to either suitor is in fact rational given that she was only recently freed by his death from a long betrothal to a clergyman for whom she 'never felt the passion of love' (107), wishes to enjoy that presumably temporary freedom, and is 'not sufficiently acquainted with either' (145) suitor to make a decision. But after her persistent indecision leads to Boyer's discovery of her 'in close conversation' (169) with Sanford and his immediate decision to leave her, Eliza herself comes to internalize the judgement of her friends: 'I frankly own, that my fancy, and a taste for gaity of life, induced me to cherish the idea of a connection with Major Sanford; while Mr Boyer's real merit has imprinted those sentiments of esteem and love in my heart, which time can never efface' (185). These sentiments prompt her to write to Boyer requesting reconciliation, which he rejects in a letter in which he criticizes her 'artifice and dissimulation', thanks heaven that 'the snare was broken', and implicitly contrasts her with the 'virtuous, the amiable, the accomplished' (188) woman to whom he is now engaged, judgements she does not dispute. Her subsequent seduction by the then-married Sanford leads her to characterize her story 'as a beacon to warn the American fair of the dangerous tendency and destructive consequences' of associating with a rake and 'of risking their reputation by the practice of coquetry and its attendant follies' (233). Other than Sanford, who has self-interested motives, no other character in the novel explicitly challenges the primacy of rationality.[20]

The behaviour of Eliza's suitors, however, is frequently motivated by intense feeling and hints at its liberating potential. Boyer initially resolves to act 'upon just and rational principles' (111) in courting Eliza, characterizes his break with her as the day on which 'reason assumes its empire' (166), and in his last letter to her asserts that his regard 'was not of that passionate kind which ends in death or despair' but was 'governed by reason, and had a nobler object in view, than mere sensual gratification' (188). Yet his self-representation often flies in the face of his emotional responses to Eliza and to the changing status of their relationship. In his second letter, he admits that his hopes of 'promised bliss' have been 'dashed with the bitter ranklings of jealousy and suspicion' (115), and that when he saw Sanford taking Eliza's hand, he 'stood transfixed by the pangs of disappointment' (116). According to Eliza's description, he responds with equal fervour to her initial reluctance to commit to marriage: 'He spoke with emphasis. The tear of sensibility sparkled in his eye. I involuntarily gave him my hand, which he pressed with ardor to his lips. Then rising, he walked to the window to conceal his emotion' (127). After his discovery of Eliza with Sanford, Boyer describes how her 'extreme emotion softened' (169) him and left him unable to speak, a silence that is repeated when he departs from Eliza, who reports that 'his sensibility overcame him' (179). In private, following their confrontation he finds himself 'perfectly unmanned', gives 'free scope to the sensibility of' (169) his heart and takes comfort in 'the effeminate relief of tears' (170). These moments actually humanize Boyer, but he commonly masks and supersedes that humanity in a posture of self-righteous rectitude, in actions that range from refusing to listen to Eliza's explanation of her conduct to casting his harsh rejection letter as advice from 'a friend' to her 'happiness ... reputation ... temporal and eternal welfare' (171). His judgemental rigidity has led readers to regard him as one of two equally unpalatable options for Eliza.[21]

Sanford does Eliza more obviously irreparable harm, but his character offers glimpses of sincere feeling and the (unrealized) potential for sentimental attachment. To be sure, he readily embraces stereotypical attributes of the calculating rake: revenge against Eliza (118) and her friends (180) as his motive; a Protean nature (121); exultation at the conclusion of his 'long and tedious siege' (217); pride in his 'dissimulation and gallantry' (218) and his 'finesse' (233). Eliza, too, bemoans his 'perfidious arts', including 'the consoling power of friendship, ensnaringly offered' (222) at a time when she most needed it – which led her to succumb to him. But his sympathy actually proves more than a façade. After a pivotal encounter with Eliza at a ball, in which he offers what she calls a tenderness 'now particularly soothing' to her 'wounded heart' (204), he writes to his friend Deighton to rejoice in their reconciliation: 'No devotee could have been more sincere in his penitence, than I was in mine. Indeed, Charles, I never knew I had so much sensibility before! Why, I was as much a woman as the very weakest of the sex!' (205) This passage could be interpreted as sarcastic, particularly in light of a reference in the next sentence to absolution for sins yet to be committed, but it does recall earlier moments when he considers becoming a 'convert to sobriety' (148) or proposing marriage (180) – which he resisted doing primarily for pecuniary reasons – rather than losing Eliza.[22] It also anticipates their final encounter, in which he begs her forgiveness, recoils at her prediction of her impending death, and asks to visit her 'not in continuation of our amour, but as a friend, solicitous to know her situation and welfare' (234) – a marked contrast to Boyer's sanctimonious offer of friendship. Her death leaves him bereft and guilt-ridden for sacrificing 'a virtuous woman' in order to secure 'splendor and equipage' (238), and he warns Deighton against following his example. His immediate reaction – 'I am undone' (238) – fittingly mimics the common cry of the fallen woman and exactly replicates Eliza's words once she has received Boyer's final dismissive letter. Sanford possesses a capacity for genuine connection, but tragically compromises it by adhering to worldly imperatives, much as Boyer does by cleaving to rigid moralism.

Eliza's susceptibility to Sanford's tenderness derives, as many critics have observed, from the conspicuous lack of it shown her by other women.[23] Lucy Sumner née Freeman and Mrs Richman proffer their sober advice and pointed criticism from the secure position of the engaged or married woman, which limits its relevance for Eliza. Her reluctance to accede to their wishes and accept Boyer derives partly from her belief that marriage 'is the tomb of friendship' (123). Hence her gloom at Lucy's wedding at the prospect of 'an alienation of affection, by means of her entire devotion to another' (160). In inadvertent support of this view, Mrs Richman professes to retain interest in her friends and pleasure in their company, but admits 'that conjugal and parental love are the main springs' (182) of her life. After she is rejected by Boyer, Eliza wishes she had Lucy near her, to 'have some friend in whom [she] could repose confidence' (190), which results in Lucy's acceding to her request to send the younger Julia Granby. Julia's later prolonged absence, which provides Sanford the opportunity to fill the void, results from Lucy's desire to have Julia spend the summer with her. She does invite Eliza to come to 'your faithful Lucy', claiming, like Mrs Richman, that marriage 'has not alienated, or weakened' (212) her regard, but when Eliza demurs, she – like Worthy in *The Power of Sympathy* – makes no effort to rush to the side of her obviously more vulnerable and less decisive friend and returns only to weep at her graveside. Immediately before and after Eliza's death, it falls to Julia to serve as intermediary between Eliza and her closest, absent friends, conveying first Eliza's request for their forgiveness and later, more problematically, her 'posthumous papers' (237), which enable them to appropriate her story, as Lucy continues to do by composing the epitaph with which the novel ends.[24] Eliza has been interpreted as a proponent either of proto-liberalism, which focuses on the freely chosen fellowship of autonomous individuals, or conversely of 'an inclusive ... feminist "civic republicanism"', which emphasizes a collective homosocial bond.[25] Either way, she is isolated because of the responses, and lack thereof, from other women. Sentimental fellowship is threatened not, as in *Emily Montague*, primarily by possessive men, but by women themselves.

Eliza's isolation, partially self-imposed and partially determined by external circumstances and the conduct of others, aligns her with the major characters from the other novels. Isolation results both from physical distance, as when British emigrants to America are separated from their mother country and their families, and from emotional distance, generated by the lack of sympathy from corrupt or judgemental would-be friends and mentors. Only in *Emily Montague* are characters able to reunite successfully, by means of a fairy-tale ending that elides but does not resolve troubling views of the North American 'other' and of relations between the sexes. Separation, of course, also provides the pretext for the epistolary form, and the three epistolary novels appeal to readers' feelings by implicitly casting them as the unseen recipients of all the correspondence and thereby interesting them in struggles that often derive from and are magnified by the absence of close confidantes. In Rowson's third-person narrative, readers' sensibility is instead encouraged and mediated through an implied and at times literal dialogue with the narrator. All four novels thus shape, indulge and crucially depend upon sentimental readers who are invited – albeit in complex and often vexing ways – to bridge gaps between characters and continents.

Notes

1. Frances Brooke, *The History of Emily Montague*, ed. Mary Jane Edwards (Ottawa: Carleton University Press, 1985), 37. All citations refer to this edition.
2. For the most thorough discussion of the marginalization of Madame Des Roches, see Dermot McCarthy, 'Sisters under the Mink: the Correspondent Fear in *The History of Emily Montague*', *Essays on Canadian Writing* 51–2 (1993–4): 340–57.
3. G. J. Barker-Benfield, *The Culture of Sensibility: Sex and Society in Eighteenth-Century Britain* (University of Chicago Press, 1992), 104–53.
4. Stephen Carl Arch, 'Frances Brooke's "Circle of Friends": the Limits of Epistolarity in *The History of Emily Montague*', *Early American Literature* 39 (2004): 474.
5. McCarthy, 'Sisters under the Mink', 348–9.
6. Robert Merrett, 'The Politics of Romance in *The History of Emily Montague*', *Canadian Literature* 133 (1992): 92–108, observes that the novel's closure 'elides married love, imperial wealth and patriarchal authority' (106).
7. Joe Snader, 'The Masquerade of Colonial Identity in Frances Brooke's *Emily Montague* (1769)', in *The Clothes that Wear Us: Essays on Dressing and Transgressing in Eighteenth-Century Culture*, ed. Jessica Munns and Penny Richards (Newark: University of Delaware Press, 1999), 139.
8. Susanna Rowson, *Charlotte Temple*, ed. Marion L. Rust (New York: W. W. Norton, 2011), 9. All citations refer to this edition.
9. Kristin Boudreau, *Sympathy in American Literature: American Sentiments from Jefferson to the Jameses* (Gainesville: University Press of Florida, 2002), 41–2, discusses Temple's gaining both a wife and a story of suffering in which he, like the reader, can participate sympathetically.
10. Nancy Armstrong, 'Why Daughters Die: the Racial Logic of American Sentimentalism', *Yale Journal of Criticism* 7 (1994): 9–11; Leonard Tennenhouse, 'The Americanization of *Clarissa*', *Yale Journal of Criticism* 11 (1998): 191–2.
11. Marion Rust, *Prodigal Daughters: Susanna Rowson's Early American Women* (Chapel Hill: University of North Carolina Press, 2008), 75.
12. Julia A. Stern, *The Plight of Feeling: Sympathy and Dissent in the Early American Novel* (University of Chicago Press, 1997), sees sorrow at

Charlotte's death as the basis of a cohesive imagined community that figures the American nation (37), but also finds the narrator's interruptions 'increasingly maddening' (43). For Rust, the 'very ostentation of the Rowsonian narrator's comforting asides' may suggest 'profound self-doubt' (*Prodigal Daughters*, 75).

13. William Hill Brown, *The Power of Sympathy* and Hannah Webster Foster, *The Coquette*, intro. Carla Mulford (New York: Penguin, 1996), 87. All citations of these two novels refer to this edition.
14. Stern, *The Plight of Feeling*, 25; David Lawrimore, 'The Novelist as Organic Intellectual: William Hill Brown's *The Power of Sympathy*, Reconsidered', *American Literature* 88 (2016): 713–14.
15. James Chandler, 'Placing *The Power of Sympathy*: Transatlantic Sentiments and the "First American Novel"', in *The Atlantic Enlightenment*, ed. Susan Manning and Francis D. Cogliano (Aldershot: Ashgate, 2008), 137–8. Cf. Stern, *The Plight of Feeling*, 13–14. Lawrimore ('The Novelist as Organic Intellectual', 706–8) offers a more positive assessment of Worthy.
16. Elizabeth Dill, 'That Damned Mob of Scribbling Siblings: the American Romance as Anti-novel in *The Power of Sympathy* and *Pierre*', *American Literature* 80 (2008): 722.
17. Elizabeth Barnes, 'Natural and National Unions: Incest and Sympathy in the Early Republic', in *Incest and the Literary Imagination*, ed. Elizabeth Barnes (Gainesville: University Press of Florida, 2002), 142, 149; Robert D. Arner, 'Sentiment and Sensibility: the Role of Emotion and William Hill Brown's *The Power of Sympathy*', *Studies in American Fiction* 1 (1973): 125; Chandler, 'Placing *The Power of Sympathy*',139.
18. Lawrimore, 'The Novelist as Organic Intellectual', 714.
19. Anne Dalke, 'Original Vice: the Political Implications of Incest in the Early American Novel', *Early American Literature* 23 (1988): 200; Dill, 'That Damned Mob of Scribbling Siblings', 716. Lawrimore, 'The Novelist as Organic Intellectual', regards the novel as a critique of egalitarianism.
20. Thomas J. Joudrey, 'Maintaining Stability: Fancy and Passion in *The Coquette*', *New England Quarterly* 86 (2013): 60–88, offers the most robust and detailed critical assessment of the novel as repudiating fancy and recommending reason. Cf. Boudreau, *Sympathy in American Literature*, 43. Laura H. Korobkin, '"Can Your Volatile Daughter Ever Acquire Your Wisdom?": Luxury and False Ideals in *The Coquette*', *Early American Literature* 41 (2006): 79–107, also views Foster as a conservative writer who consistently 'shows us Eliza's less heroic side', which includes materialism and 'hostility toward . . . adult responsibility' (79).
21. See, for example, Cathy N. Davidson, *Revolution and the Word: the Rise of the Novel in America*, expanded edition (Oxford University Press, 2004), 225.
22. Elizabeth Dill, 'A Mob of Lusty Villagers: Operations of Domestic Desires in Hannah Webster Foster's *The Coquette*', *Eighteenth-Century Fiction* 15 (2003):

255–79, argues that 'Sanford's intentions shift from sexual exploitation to sentimental love' (261–2).

23. Stern, *The Plight of Feeling*, 90, 117; Ivy Schweitzer, 'Foster's *Coquette*: Resurrecting Friendship from the Tomb of Marriage', *Arizona Quarterly* 61 (2005): 1–32; Sharon M. Harris, 'Hannah Webster Foster's *The Coquette*: Critiquing Franklin's America', in *Redefining the Political Novel: American Women Writers, 1797–1901*, ed. Sharon M. Harris (Knoxville: University of Tennessee Press, 1995), 8–10; Gillian Brown, 'Consent, Coquetry, and Consequences', *American Literary History* 9 (1997): 643.
24. Stern, *The Plight of Feeling*, 145; Claire C. Pettingill, 'Sisterhood in a Separate Sphere: Female Friendship in Hannah Webster Foster's *The Coquette* and *The Boarding School*', *Early American Literature* 27 (1992): 199.
25. Stern, *The Plight of Feeling*, 73; Schweitzer, 'Foster's *Coquette*', 9.

CHAPTER 11

Novel Anachronisms: Sophia Lee's The Life of a Lover *and Frances Burney's* The Wanderer

Melissa Sodeman

In the preface to what would be her last published novel, *The Life of a Lover* (1804), Sophia Lee decries the changes that have swept over the novel since she began her literary career. Aware her book will seem out of place among more recent works, she indicates *The Life of a Lover* was written decades ago, even before *The Recess* (1783–5), the work that secured her literary reputation and made her one of the most highly respected novelists of the later eighteenth century. Having kept *The Life of a Lover* to herself over the many years she and her sisters ran a school for young ladies in Bath, Lee presents her novel as a youthful production and a work belonging to a previous era, a time before the French Revolution overturned the political and literary status quo in Britain. Not only was the work composed 'at the early age when imagination takes the lead of reason, and the heart occasionally over-rules both', but its volumes also preserved in their pages a novelistic order that existed before 'The revolutionary system . . . pervaded literature, even in the humblest of its classes – novels!'[1] Seeking to hold on to a fictional mode that existed before the French Revolution called forth 'changes in nations, manners, and principles' (1: viii), she presents her novel as a literary survival. In this chapter, I consider how Lee's suggestive framing of her last and least known work can shed new light on another anomalous fiction, similarly out of joint with its own moment of publication: Frances Burney's *The Wanderer; or, Female Difficulties*, a novel that appeared in 1814 but was gripped by the revolutionary politics of two decades before.

I read *The Life of a Lover* and *The Wanderer* as novel anachronisms, works that resist the smooth flow of literary history to assert the claims of the past. Not only were these novels out of place in the early nineteenth-century literary marketplace, but they evince a self-conscious awareness of their startling violations of literary chronology. As novel anachronisms, *The Life of a Lover* and *The Wanderer* serve as textual repositories for the novel's sentimental past. The novels look back to key moments in the development of sentimental fiction, recalling on the one hand Samuel Richardson's use of epistolary form to affect and to edify his readers, and, on the other, the combustible mixture of politics and sentiment that flared to new life in polemical fictions of the 1790s. Read together, these works indicate their authors' ongoing commitment to the sentimental novel at a moment when it had become passé, archiving in their pages an effort to hold on to the genre for its ability to incorporate what more sedate literary forms tended to leave out – not only the gendered forms of experience Burney called 'female difficulties', but the strange and unruly affects, the ugly feelings, these difficulties inevitably induced. Understood this way, the novel of sentiment is not, for Lee and Burney at least, a retreat from modernity or an evasion of politics, but a genre that, through its ideological contradictions and capacity for untoward feeling, made formally meaningful the paradoxes of female self-assertion.

Both *The Life of a Lover* and *The Wanderer* created a stir when they first appeared. *The Life of a Lover* was the first novel Lee offered the public since *The Recess* had charted new terrain for sentimental fiction by blending historical incident with heart-rending narrative, though in the intervening years she had contributed two narratives to *The Canterbury Tales* (1797–1805), a multi-volume work mostly written by her sister Harriet Lee. Even had it not been two decades since the first volume of *The Recess* had appeared, Lee's literary fame was such that any new work of fiction by her would necessarily, in the words of the *British Critic*, 'excite attention'.[2] *The Wanderer* was even more highly anticipated. The first work of fiction to follow the success of Burney's third novel, *Camilla* (1796), it was eagerly awaited; as an anonymous reviewer put it, 'We can scarcely remember an instance where the public expectation was excited in so high a degree, as by the promise of a new novel from the pen of their old favourite.'[3] Such enthusiasm testified to the formidable literary reputations of both Lee and Burney, by the turn of the nineteenth century well established as two grand dames of the novel.

However highly anticipated, the novels' indifferent critical receptions indicate that *The Life of a Lover* and *The Wanderer* were strangely inaccessible even to their first readers. Not only did reviewers complain the works were 'too prolix' and even 'unnaturally lengthened' – not altogether unwarranted objections, given that *The Life of a Lover* extends to six volumes and *The Wanderer* to five – but they noted the novels seemed mired in the past.[4] According to the *Annual Review*, the epistolary style of *The Life of a Lover* recalled an antiquated Richardsonian approach, while the hero, Lord Westbury, seemed an incongruous amalgam of Richardsonian characters, evincing 'a strange mixture of the Lovelace and the Grandison'.[5] By the same token, the novel's final volumes, describing the married life of the heroine, Cecilia, comprised 'a kind of imitation of Pamela in high life'.[6] Worse, the novel's frank treatment of sexual desire caused reviewers to gripe that the work did not befit a proper lady, let alone a redoubtable headmistress; as the *Monthly Review* put it, 'the libertine turn of thought and conduct of certain personages introduced in the narrative is painted with more force and precision than become the delicacy of a female writer'.[7] It was a view shared by even other novelists, for as Charlotte Smith wrote to a mutual friend, 'where was our friend Sophia's Critic & Corrector? ... Upon my word, I am concerned for her – & for the honor of the novel writing Ladies.'[8]

The Wanderer crashed even more dramatically against the rocks of critical expectation. Though the book initially sold well, blazing through its first edition of 3,000 copies in less than three weeks, a second edition stalled out amid rancorous complaints it was out of tune with the modern age. Set during 'the dire reign of the terrific Robespierre', and begun, as Burney admitted, before the turn of the century, *The Wanderer* reprised revolutionary debates that had long since lapsed.[9] Its interest in the Rights of Woman debates sparked by Mary Wollstonecraft appeared especially dated. According to the *British Critic*, 'The revolutionary spirit, which displays itself in the sentiments and actions of Miss Elinor Joddrel, is, fortunately for a bleeding world, now no longer in existence: few of our female readers can remember the *egalité* mania, which once infested the bosoms of their sex.'[10] Given how eminently forgettable that mania had proved, Burney's recursion to Wollstonecraftian feminism seemed a perverse return of the repressed. John Wilson Croker of the *Quarterly Review* offered the most stunningly misogynistic denunciation of the novel's untimeliness, excoriating it as 'Evelina grown old', the hopelessly out-of-date work of an old woman. For Croker, 'the vivacity, the bloom, the elegance, "the purple light of love" are all vanished; the eyes are there, but they are dim; the cheek, but it is furrowed, the lips, but they are withered'.[11] Conflating the material body of the novel with Burney's own ageing form (she was sixty-two in 1814), Croker condemns the work for its lack of topicality and dated themes.[12]

The Life of a Lover and *The Wanderer* recall past cycles of novelistic taste at what would prove an inopportune moment. By the late 1790s, after all, sentimental fiction had fallen into critical and popular decline.[13] Its repetitive plots and predictable incidents seemed signs of a spent fictional mode, an exhaustion as existential as it was formal. Mary Robinson indicated how bleak things had become when she depicted the heroine of *The Natural Daughter* (1799) shopping around a book manuscript only to learn that sentimental novels like hers would 'only sell for waste paper'.[14] At a moment when novels had become reliable commodities and novelistic demand was being reoriented from old favourites towards new titles, the market-reshaping effects of consistently available new fictions had dire implications for genres that had come to seem dated.[15] These market effects were reinforced as sentimental fiction was abandoned by some of its best-known practitioners. After 1797, Elizabeth Sophia Tomlins stopped publishing works of fiction, and by 1800, Charlotte Smith had turned away from novels to write educational works for children. When Robinson – a devotee of sentimentality even as she inscribed sentimental decline in her works – died in 1800, it marked the end of an era. The next generation of writers – Maria Edgeworth, Amelia Opie, Jane Austen – would write novels that responded powerfully to the sentimental order that had preceded them, but they no longer wrote from the same aesthetic or cultural ground.

Lee and Burney, however, still did. Invoking the novel's sentimental past at a moment when everyone else had moved on, *The Life of a Lover* and *The Wanderer* were jarringly out of place in a literary marketplace that favoured tales, gothic narratives and fictions of moral evangelicalism. They were also late-career acts of literary defiance. Both Lee and Burney leveraged their literary reputations to publish extraordinarily long novels that their publishers, Robinson and Longman, respectively, would hardly have offered to the public without the imprimatur of their names. Lee, at least, seemed to recognize the gamble she was taking, observing coolly that 'As an author cannot be certain of pleasing any human being but himself, he must be weak indeed who loses his own approbation, when that may eventually be the sole reward' (1: x–xi). Lee's equivocation speaks not only to her ambivalence regarding literary fame, but more crucially to her awareness of the hazards of writing as a woman, to the risk to reputation she had experienced first-hand during her literary debut, when she was assailed by critics scandalized by the sexual politics of her play, *The Chapter of Accidents* (1780).

If *The Life of a Lover* and *The Wanderer* risked their authors' hard-won reputations, their publication also demonstrates a sustained commitment to sentimental fiction as a means of revealing what Burney called 'female difficulties'. They do so in part by depicting the precarious existences of working women, whose struggles had been portrayed in earlier works like

Smith's *The Banished Man* (1794) and Robinson's *The Natural Daughter*. Lee's heroine, Cecilia Rivers, leverages her education to find work as a governess and companion, while Burney's Juliet Granville finds employment as a music teacher, performer, companion, governess, haberdasher, seamstress, milliner and shopkeeper. The novels emphasize the mortifications of seeking work, the frequency with which working women, particularly in domestic situations, are exploited or abused, and the financial hardship that results when labour goes unremunerated. In *The Life of a Lover*, Cecilia takes several positions as a governess only to find each untenable. Not only is she prey to the whims of her employers, but she is beset by demands that test her virtue, her delicacy and her health. The most trying situation comes when working for the already-married Lord Westbury, who pressures her to run away to the Continent to live as his mistress, and while he comes to accept her refusal as evidence of her 'exalted mind' (II: 62), she learns she must leave his roof to preserve her independence and self-respect. Subsequent positions are hardly less taxing, for in them she is subject to blackmail, unwanted advances, suspicion, unwarranted scrutiny and baseless accusations. Her health precarious after being turned out of yet another household, she becomes itinerant and is robbed of her few possessions by another traveller. Eventually she makes her way to France as the companion of Lady Killarney, a former mistress of Lord Westbury, only to discover a worse servitude than any she has already endured; she has become 'a slave – *alias* a companion' (III: 55). Believing she has only a short while to live, Cecilia marries a gouty and much older colonel who seems to have taken a kindly interest in her, and while she discovers after their marriage that his intentions were far from pure, their marriage is at least short, for he conveniently dies, leaving her a small independence.

If Lee indicates a fundamental incompatibility between Cecilia's delicacy and her employers' demands, Burney goes further in *The Wanderer*, assailing the conflict between financial necessity and the demands of proper femininity. Juliet is thrust on her own resources when her purse is stolen as she flees France. Initially an incognita who is later known only by an alias, her name and identity remain cloaked in mystery for hundreds of pages as she lives 'without a family she dare claim, without a story she dare tell, without a name she dare avow' (181). Though eventually revealed as the long-lost daughter of an aristocratic English family, she is destitute for much of the novel, taking on one grinding position after another. Despite her varied career, she remains on the edge of indigence, for she discovers that whether she gives music lessons or takes in sewing, people of fashion are little inclined to pay her. Nor is she the only working woman in *The Wanderer*. Juliet's poverty and displacement link her to other *émigrés* who have fled France, including her friend Gabriella, like Juliet 'Sprung from one of the first houses of Europe' (636), and like her forced to toil 'manually, not to degrade it mentally' (637). Gabriella's plight, like Juliet's, results from the French Revolution's cataclysmic jolt to established order, a jolt that has devastated long-standing systems of rank and class and displaced those whose social and economic positions were once secure. If Burney evokes sympathy for women who in a pre-Revolutionary world would not have had to work, it is out of a sense that the French Revolution has upset an ordered world, displacing people and overturning social and political structures that had only seemed immutable. As Burney put it in *Brief Reflections Relative to the Emigrant French Clergy*, a 1793 treatise urging Englishwomen to act charitably on behalf of French clerics, 'events . . . in our neighbour kingdom have convulsed all order'.[16] Her novel examines what the dislocations wrought by revolution mean for women, who find themselves caught between the persistent demands of proper femininity and the urgent need to earn a subsistence. 'How insufficient', Juliet muses, 'is a FEMALE to herself! How utterly dependent upon situation – connexions – circumstance! how nameless, how for ever fresh-springing are her DIFFICULTIES, when she would owe her existence to her exertions!' (275) No matter what she does, Juliet remains 'utterly dependent', her agency blocked. In Burney's analysis, working women are stuck between a legal system that presumes female dependency and an economic system that fails to provide for them, and which even fails to give them a real means of providing for themselves.

Though both novels attend to the limited agency of working women, *The Life of a Lover* also examines what it posits are more fundamental sources of female suffering – women's more delicate frames and their greater capacity for feeling. The novel does not just uphold eighteenth-century medical theories that held that the delicacy of women's nerves gave them greater sensibility; it casts sensibility as an essentially feminine trait. Women's heightened capacity for feeling means they suffer more than men in affairs of the heart, for as Cecilia observes, 'men, indeed, talk of tenderness, but it is women only who feel it' (IV: 101). Women's susceptibility to feeling provides the novel with its animating structure. Through the fourth volume (which ends with Cecilia at long last marrying Lord Westbury), *The Life of a Lover* traces the deleterious effects of the marriage plot on its heroine. Yet the delicacy that makes possible Cecilia's social ascent, elevating her from governess to countess, also makes her unfit for the corruptions of the world, and Lee ultimately gives *The Life of a Lover* two self-consciously Richardsonian endings, sending her heroine to the altar before she is called to the grave. Like *Pamela* and its sequel, *The Life of a Lover* marries its heroine to an erstwhile libertine and devotes hundreds of pages to portraying life after marriage. And like *Clarissa*, it traces the long-drawn-out death of a heroine for whom death offers the only respite from the torment of feeling. Lee's novel, that is, has it both ways, joining aspects of *Pamela* and *Clarissa* to register the ideological contradictions of sentimentality.

While *The Life of a Lover* draws its double plot from *Pamela* and *Clarissa*, Lee parts ways from Richardson in suggesting the depths of women's feeling necessarily eludes male understanding. Physiology poses an insuperable barrier between the sexes, one that cannot be breached by love or even by sympathy, for disparities in feeling are the inevitable consequence of sexual difference. 'Lord Westbury himself cannot guess what I suffered', Cecilia tells one of her female confidantes, 'for even the most affectionate of men wants much of the tenderness of a woman' (VI: 2). Because only women can fathom what lies in the female heart, Cecilia turns for sympathetic understanding to a network of female correspondents, embodying her felt experience in letters that serve to 'awaken' and 'revive' (VI: 2) sensations in their readers. Her letters transmit otherwise ineffable feelings to their recipients, whose sympathetic responses ensure Cecilia's experience lives on. In the affective economy of *The Life of a Lover*, however, the transporting exchange of sympathy exists only between women – a pointedly gendered elaboration of Adam Smith's conception of sympathy as an imaginative capacity to enter into the experience of others.[17]

If Cecilia's story relays the emotional and physiological vulnerability of women, its subplots collectively reinforce the point that suffering is women's default condition. The novel's supporting tales of woe present variations on Cecilia's story, depicting characters like Amelia Fermor (who like Cecilia falls in love with a married man, but is drugged and raped by him) and Diana Selwyn (who is also in love with Lord Westbury, but determines to make a rational match and ends up regretting her choice). Even the quietly contented Amelia Forrester, who enjoys domestic felicity for much of the novel, does not end up living happily ever after, for over time she loses her daughter and her husband. In laying bare myriad varieties of female suffering over six volumes and hundreds of pages, Lee advances a project she describes in her novel's preface as 'indulg[ing] the bias of my own heart in tracing that of woman through almost every tender and silent suffering which is a sad distinction of my sex' (I: vii). Lee's statement cues us to recognize the narrative logic at work in *The Life of a Lover*. By grafting lengthy excursions into varieties of female anguish on to a Richardsonian ur-plot that begins rather like *Pamela* but ends like *Clarissa*, Lee not only indicates it takes a long, long novel to tell the story of women's 'tender and silent suffering'. She also implies, through her effort to rewrite Richardson's novels of female susceptibility, that for sentimental novels to tell the truth of women's lives, they must be written by and for women.

However disabling sensibility appears in *The Life of a Lover*, Lee does not inveigh against it. Rather, she rails against Mary Wollstonecraft and other advocates of revolutionary feminism in her novel's preface as 'a sturdy race of female argumentators' (1: ix) who have rocked the foundations of later eighteenth-century gender ideology by critiquing sensibility as a fashionable affectation. In *A Vindication of the Rights of Woman*, Wollstonecraft had assailed sensibility as a cherished form of weakness that made women dependent on men by limiting the development of their intellect and reason. Sensibility, Wollstonecraft argued, 'naturally relaxes the other powers of the mind, and prevents intellect from attaining that sovereignty which it ought to attain to render a rational creature useful to others'.[18] For Lee, however, sensibility is innate rather than learned, 'a sixth sense' that 'heightens and restricts the other five' (1: 167). And though innate, sensibility requires careful cultivation, for it can either grow unrestrained or wither away without the modulating effect of education. Seen this way, sensibility is intrinsic to femininity, as Lee indicates when she criticizes adherents of the Rights of Woman as short-sighted: 'the delicacy of the sex has often been wholly sacrificed to the assertion of a hardy equality with man, that, even if it assured to us an increase of esteem, would cause an equal deduction of tenderness: a bad exchange for the sex upon the great scale' (1: viii–ix). In blaming the diminishing cultural status of sensibility at the end of the eighteenth century on those who would seek 'a hardy equality with man', Lee represents the decline of sensibility as something of an existential threat to women, portraying the sex as beset by 'sturdy argumentators' whose denial of sensibility and masculine vigour makes them something other than real women. Looked at this way, Lee's antipathy towards revolutionary feminism in the preface to *The Life of a Lover* is not incidental but fundamental to her novelistic effort to preserve sentimental fiction as a genre capable of revealing the depths of female feeling.

The Wanderer makes perhaps even more grandiose claims for its author's narrative ambition. To relay the unprecedented dislocations of the French Revolution and its effects on women, Burney sends her itinerant heroine on an extended search for what Julia Epstein has called 'a way to exist in the world'.[19] It is a journey in which the destination is perpetually out of reach, narrative closure continually deferred. Seeking refuge in Britain after having spent most of her life in France, Juliet makes the perilous voyage across the Channel only to experience her native land as alien territory. 'I feel myself', she cries, 'though in my native country, like a helpless foreigner; unknown, unprotected' (214). Cut off from home and family and deprived even of a sense of national belonging, she wanders across southern England, moving through rather than settling into each of the places she visits. She is continually out of place, and seems shaken loose from time as well, causing one character to speculate, 'You may be a person of another century' (485). Though the novel reveals Juliet's plight as the result of revolutionary upheaval, at another level *The Wanderer* indicates her situation transcends historical explanation, for Juliet's dislocation both results from the collapse of the *ancien régime* and lays bare women's more fundamental dispossession under the law. Her relentless and arbitrary movement breaks from any forward narrative momentum and becomes mired in repetition, since no matter where she goes, she finds more of the same. Even the revelation of her name – an act of nomination that in other novels would set in motion the closural systems of the non-narratable – stops short of curtailing her incessant movement. Instead, this revelation makes little difference, and she is set adrift for another 200 pages. By prolonging Juliet's story, Burney not only extends her indictment of a world that consistently fails women, but also forces on the reader something like Juliet's experience, for to read *The Wanderer* is to experience narratively something like Juliet's numb exhaustion at a world that makes no place for her.

Burney's extended rehearsal of 'female difficulties' draws narratively on the explosive mixture of politics and sentimentality that had typified polemical fictions like Wollstonecraft's *The Wrongs of Woman, or, Maria* (1798), Smith's *Desmond* (1792) and Mary Hays's *The Victim of Prejudice* (1799). *The Wanderer*'s restaging of the Rights of Woman debates makes palpable this novelistic inheritance; Burney uses Juliet's story to protest the cultural, legal and economic codes that fail to protect women even as she caricatures Wollstonecraft's revolutionary feminism through the figure of Elinor Joddrel. Elinor, a hoydenish young woman whose time in France has made her an enthusiastic *democrate*, thrills to revolutionary events as spectacle, confessing:

> The grand effect . . . of beholding so many millions of men, let loose from all ties, divine or human, gave such play to my fancy, such a range to my thoughts, and brought forth such new, unexpected, and untried combinations to my reason, that I frequently felt as if just created, and ushered into the world – not, perhaps, as wise as another Minerva, but equally formed to view and to judge all around me. (156)

Here and elsewhere, Burney indicts Elinor's revolutionary zeal by revealing it as a kind of aesthetic response, that of an impassioned spectator who mistakes geopolitical events for theatrical entertainments. Elinor's theatrical bent plays out as well in her rejection of the social norms governing female behaviour, leading her to pursue Harleigh and, when he fails to return her affections, to collapse dramatically back into the cultural scripts restricting female desire by attempting to end her own life. In such moments, Elinor recapitulates the suicide attempts and passionate love affairs related in William Godwin's memoir of Mary Wollstonecraft, allowing Burney to link her to the same forms of public disgrace that had damaged Wollstonecraft's reputation after 1798.[20] It is a move that would seem to discredit revolutionary feminism, were not Juliet simultaneously revealing its necessity. In the end, Elinor is as much a tragic figure as a Wollstonecraftian caricature, for however much she bristles under 'old rules and forms' (156), she cannot imagine into being new ones and is left to view her own life as already scripted, wondering whether it will play out as 'comedy, tragedy, or farce' (161), 'epithalamium – or a requiem' (162). Yet her exhilaration at the prospect of 'a new road for life when the old one was worn out' (156) forces into view questions about how the French Revolution could be represented aesthetically, questions that preoccupied Burney throughout the novel, for 'the sheer novelty of the French Revolution', as Ronald Paulson reminds us, 'required new forms of representation and even more basically raised the central aesthetic challenge: how to represent the unprecedented'.[21] So despite the way Elinor is forced to recant in the novel, admitting she 'has strayed from the beaten road, only to discover that all others are pathless' (873), the questions she raises about how to represent revolution are precisely Burney's own. Elinor's narrative lays bare the inadequacy of old forms to account for the complexity of the revolutionary moment even as Juliet's story, which retreats into romance as her identity is revealed to long-lost relations and her inheritance restored, plays out a desire for old forms to reassert themselves.

If, as I have argued to this point, Lee and Burney found in earlier works of sentimental fiction crucially important models for *The Life of a Lover* and *The Wanderer*, it was at least in part because for writers of their generation, the representation of female distress was inextricably bound up with sentimental form. It is not just that sentimental novels had long included tableaux of female suffering among their repertory of sentimental effects, or even that sentimental fiction had been crucial to the development of novelistic techniques for disclosing private experience, from Richardson's 'writing to the moment' to Laurence Sterne's use of narrative fragmentation and ellipsis. It is also that sentimental fiction, especially as it was taken up by women writers in the 1780s and 1790s, brought into view aspects of female experience that had been left out of more decorous fictional modes. If sentimental fiction had from its beginnings carved out space for aestheticized displays of female suffering, as the genre became the purview of women, it came to license persistent forms of female complaint and even became a medium for uncomfortable, less-readily-aestheticized forms of affect.

Take, as a telling example of the shifts running through sentimental fiction at the end of the eighteenth century, the novels of Charlotte Smith. In ten novels published between 1788 and 1798, Smith authorized her lived experience by drawing on semi-autobiographical characters who shared her dispossession and alienation. Repeatedly copying out her own story into her novels, Smith brought to sentimental fiction a kind of irritable grousing, a 'bitter and querulous tone of complaint', as Anna Letitia Barbauld put it, that made evident the kinds of affect that could be accommodated by sentimentality.[22] Though women's anguish could take on operatic proportions, leaving them mad or taking them to the grave, their anger tended to be constrained, cut down to the irritation with which Smith's fiction seethes. Described by Sianne Ngai as 'a minor, low-intensity negative affect' and an 'inherently disproportionate feeling', irritation undoes the classic work of sentimental fiction, generating friction instead of sympathetic response, putting the reader off rather than soliciting her tears.[23] Because Smith's fiction was written out of the irritations of her life, it bristled with annoyance and exasperation, with impatience at the perennially straitened finances that gave her no choice but to write another book to support her family. In the preface to *The Banished Man* (1794), she wrote that after completing the novel, she could only look forward to 'a repetition of exertions on my part', a further effort to write amid 'insults' and 'inconveniences'.[24] Worsening matters, writing was itself no small physical irritant for Smith, who was afflicted with an arthritic complaint that made writing difficult in the final years of her life. Irritation marked her fiction at the level of reception as well, for Smith's tendency to emplot her story into her novels tended to annoy some readers, including an anonymous critic for the *Universal Magazine* who saw fit to eulogize Smith by opining that at times her works 'shewed more ill-nature than good sense'.[25]

The palpable irritation that runs back through Smith's fiction merits discussion here because it can orient us to the late-century sentimental novel's incorporation of what Ngai calls 'ugly feelings'. These are feelings that index 'the predicaments posed by a general state of obstructed agency', ambiguous affects Ngai excavates in relation to a later period that are also rife in late-century novels of sentiment.[26] In Smith's novels, and again in Lee's and Burney's late-career fiction, ugly feelings like irritation and envy register the untenability of women's position under the law and under a sentimental regime that converted limits on women's agency into touching set-pieces meant to elicit tears and little else. Contextualized this way, *The Wanderer*'s five volumes may appear a tour de force of novelistic irritation, forcing on the reader the aggravation Juliet is too ladylike to express. (And more broadly, we might now see that if *The Wanderer* feels like a departure for Burney, it is because it is made out of the raw materials of a Charlotte Smith novel.) *The Life of a Lover* has its own negative affect – the envy that is everywhere apparent in the novel, from the early volumes in which Cecilia struggles to rein in her passion for the already-married Lord Westbury to the later volumes when she is plagued by the machinations of a jealous rival. Seeping out, as Ngai reminds us, in situations of lack or inequity and often coded as a specifically female moral deficiency, envy propels Cecilia to ransack Lord Westbury's library and even to steal a miniature portrait of him. The envy that prompts Cecilia to lay illicit claim to Lord Westbury's painted image also drives the grotesquely vindictive Lady Killarney's efforts to divide Cecilia from Lord Westbury. In *The Life of a Lover*, however, the cost of envy is high. By pitting women against one another, envy not only prevents them from recognizing the circumstances that cause them to compete for male favour, but bars them from entering into the novel's female networks of sympathetic understanding. The ugly feelings of Lee's and Burney's late-career novels – the irritation and envy with which they teem – are uncomfortably noncathartic, rebuffing the release of tears we associate with sentimental literature. Conspicuously failing to provide release from the problems of female difficulties, Lee's and Burney's novels call attention to, but do not resolve, the problems of women's suspended agency, problems that had become more pressing at the turn of the nineteenth century as conservative backlash set in and as routes previously opened up by revolutionary feminism appeared closed off.

In incorporating ugly feelings alongside more assimilable forms of affect, *The Life of a Lover* and *The Wanderer* draw out the ideological contradictions of sentimental literature. Like other sentimental novels, Lee's and Burney's works rely for aesthetic effect on the suffering they deplore, and in this way remain structured by – even as they register discomfort with – sentimentality's perpetuation of the status quo. Neither novelist, after all, finds a solution to her heroine's predicament of genteel poverty other than marriage or the recovery of a lost title and inheritance, though *The Life of a Lover* entertains another possibility when Amelia Fermor, who has survived rape, a suicide attempt and disinheritance, proposes founding a sanctuary for 'female orphans, under the age of fifteen, too well born for a life of mere labour, and too destitute for any other mode of subsisting' (VI: 304). Lee's novel imagines for a moment an alternative to its reliance on female suffering, but in its final pages returns to business as usual. By stopping short of calling for broader reforms that would improve women's lives, Lee and Burney abandon legal, economic and social remedies to the problems of women's limited agency, instead embodying in their novels the contradictions of sentimentality. It is a representational strategy that allows us to understand differently their novels' maddeningly contradictory politics, the way in which *The Wanderer*, as Claudia L. Johnson puts it, 'protest[s] the effects of social injustice while making sure that the social structures, customs, and attitudes that produced them remain intact'.[27] The ideological contradictions of *The Life of a Lover* have escaped scrutiny only because there has been so little critical commentary on the work. Johnson's observation that *The Wanderer* proceeds as though 'it were possible to rewrite Wollstonecraft's *The Wrongs of Woman* from within the values of dominant culture' holds for *The Life of a Lover* as well, for both novels decry and ultimately remain committed to the sentimental ideology that upholds women's marginalized status under the law.[28]

While Johnson reads *The Wanderer*'s implication in the compromising protestations of sentimentality as evidence of critical and aesthetic failure, we might also now be able to see Burney's last work of fiction as deliberately preserving what had been left out of more restrained literary forms – the ugly feelings of good girls in impossible situations.[29] Where would such feelings go, after the collapse of sentimental fiction? What other forms or genres would make space for them? At a moment when it was not yet clear whether the problems of female agency could or would be brought into emergent forms of fiction, Lee and Burney held on to sentimental fiction precisely for its ability to represent the ungainly contours of women's feeling. In conserving the novel's sentimental past, they sustained a fictional mode that tended to be more outré and inchoate, more accommodating of female feeling and desire, and more ideologically conflicted than the fiction that succeeded it. In their different ways, that is, Lee and Burney protracted into the early nineteenth century the space opened up by sentimentality, a space of contradiction and also possibility. Their late-career novels, published as sentimentality had gone into abeyance, exist anachronistically in the early nineteenth-century literary marketplace.[30] As novel anachronisms, as works of temporal and aesthetic rupture, of schism and upheaval, *The Life of a Lover* and *The Wanderer* recall a novelistic mode that had become passé, however urgent it once seemed. Preserving unassimilated aspects of the novel's past, they put conspicuously on display sentimentality's broken presence in the early nineteenth century.

Nowhere is this broken presence more evident than when Juliet finds herself at Stonehenge, a moment that serves in *The Wanderer* as a *mise en abyme* of novelistic reflexivity. In the novel, Stonehenge exists anachronistically in the present, standing as a reminder of a past that is both materially present and unknowably distant. The stones appear so old that they seem almost to have originated in nature, making up a 'wild edifice' (765) in which human art has all but receded into its natural surroundings. What remains is mysterious and evocative but finally incomprehensible, for the monument figures the persistence of form long after its ability to relay meaning has been lost. Its presence in the novel introduces an encounter with what Burney had, after her own visit to Stonehenge in 1791, called the 'undisquisitionable'.[31] The monument, after all, rebuffs Juliet's efforts to make sense of it; to the extent she is able to 'pierce' (765) the stones, it is through 'sympathy in what seemed lonely and undone' (765) rather than through the understanding. Resisting rational comprehension, Stonehenge leaves Juliet lost in thought: 'Here . . . was room for "meditation even to madness;" nothing distracted the sight, nothing broke in upon the attention, nor varied the ideas. Thought, uninterrupted and uncontrouled, was master of the mind' (766). As the outer world becomes 'nothing' from the isolated perspective of the monument, Juliet is left to reflect on the evocative remains of an unassimilable past, on the disjunctive condition of anachronism.

The scene at Stonehenge puts *The Wanderer*'s questions about how to represent the broken historical legacies of sentimental fiction and revolutionary feminism into a new and discordant temporal register, making visible the novel's strenuous effort to depict the dilemma of writing after sentimentality's end. Read this way, Stonehenge emerges as a figure of sentimental decline – a figure of such strained grandiosity it could only be hazarded in a novel of sentiment. Yet if Stonehenge stands in *The Wanderer* for the decay of form, and points to Burney's self-conscious awareness that the sentimental mode from which she writes has already been occluded, the laboured grandiloquence of the scene also collapses on itself when Juliet's reflections are interrupted by the elderly Sir Jaspar Harrington, who jokily remarks that she seems entranced by something even older than himself. Juliet's need to manage Sir Jaspar reroutes the novel back to the familiar terrain of female difficulties, but taken together, the self-consciously elevated scene at Stonehenge, and its fall into irritation, demonstrates the range of the sentimental mode recollected in *The Wanderer*. Spanning a dislocated present and an inaccessible past, aestheticized scenes of female distress and ugly feelings, the personal and the political, sentimental fiction enabled writers like Lee and Burney to make formally meaningful the contradictions under which they wrote.

More broadly, however, attending to untimely novels like *The Life of a Lover* and *The Wanderer* allows us to read against the grain of literary history, to trouble our critical and our increasingly data-driven narratives about the rise and fall of various strands of fiction. If we are now in a moment in which big data has become ascendant, a moment in which practices of distant reading continue to transform how we read and understand the novel, works that resist – that *irritate* – the broader histories of the novel now emerging can allow us to recollect what is being left out of those histories. By reading closely works that are strange, aberrant, out-of-place and anachronistic, we may – like Lee and Burney – hazard anachronism, but we also stand to construct a more nuanced understanding of generic emergence and decline – as well as hold on to much of what makes reading matter in the first place.

Notes

1. Sophia Lee, *The Life of a Lover*, 6 vols. (London, 1804), 1: vi, viii. All citations refer to this edition.
2. *British Critic* (September 1804), 317.
3. *British Critic* (April 1814), 374.
4. *Monthly Review* (December 1804), 366; *British Critic* (April 1814), 385.
5. The review makes another connection to Richardson: 'the story is tediously told in letters; and . . . the style, evidently borrowed from Richardson, is often quaint, and never graceful', *Annual Review and History of Literature for 1805* (London, 1806), 654.
6. *Anti-Jacobin Review and Magazine* (June 1806), 137.
7. *Monthly Review* (December 1804), 359–60.

8. Charlotte Smith to Sarah Rose, 4 July 1804, in *The Collected Letters of Charlotte Smith*, ed. Judith Phillips Stanton (Bloomington: Indiana University Press, 2003), 632–3.
9. Frances Burney, *The Wanderer; or, Female Difficulties*, ed. Margaret Anne Doody, Robert L. Mack and Peter Sabor (Oxford University Press, 1991), 11. All citations refer to this edition.
10. *British Critic* (April 1814), 385.
11. Quoted in Margaret Anne Doody's *Frances Burney: the Life in the Works* (New Brunswick, NJ: Rutgers University Press, 1988), 335.
12. For an extended discussion, see Devoney Looser, *Women Writers and Old Age in Great Britain, 1750–1850* (Baltimore: Johns Hopkins University Press, 2008), 31–41.
13. Bibliographic research has shown that after 1800, 'there are scant signs of a revival in fiction of the cult of "sentiment" and "sensibility", which had stood at its height in Britain from the 1770s to the mid-1790s'. See Peter Garside, 'The English Novel in the Romantic Era: Consolidation and Dispersal', in *The English Novel, 1770–1829: a Bibliographical Survey of Prose Fiction Published in the British Isles*, ed. Peter Garside, James Raven and Rainer Schöwerling, 2 vols. (Oxford University Press, 2000), II: 55.
14. Mary Robinson, *The Natural Daughter*, in *A Letter to the Women of England* and *The Natural Daughter*, ed. Sharon M. Setzer (Peterborough, ON: Broadview Press, 2003), 208.
15. See Franco Moretti, *Graphs, Maps, Trees: Abstract Models for Literary History* (London: Verso, 2005), 5.
16. Frances Burney, *Brief Reflections Relative to the Emigrant French Clergy*, in *Considerations on Religion and Public Education by Hannah More and Brief Reflections Relative to the Emigrant French Clergy [Frances Burney]*, intro. Claudia L. Johnson (Los Angeles: William Andrews Memorial Clark Library, 1990), 2.
17. On gender and *The Theory of Moral Sentiments*, see Maureen Harkin, 'Smith's The Theory of Moral Sentiments: Sympathy, Women, and Emulation', *Studies in Eighteenth-Century Culture* 24 (1995): 176.
18. Mary Wollstonecraft, *A Vindication of the Rights of Woman*, ed. Carol H. Poston, 2nd edition (New York: Norton, 1988), 61.
19. Julia Epstein, 'Marginality in Frances Burney's Novels', in *The Cambridge Companion to the Eighteenth-Century Novel*, ed. John Richetti (Cambridge University Press, 1996), 207.
20. William Godwin, *Memoirs of the Author of the Vindication of the Rights of Woman* (London, 1798).
21. Ronald Paulson, *Representations of Revolution (1789–1820)* (New Haven: Yale University Press, 1983), 26.
22. Anna Letitia Barbauld, *Selected Poetry and Prose*, ed. William McCarthy and Elizabeth Kraft (Peterborough, ON: Broadview Press, 2002), 437.
23. Sianne Ngai, *Ugly Feelings* (Cambridge, MA: Harvard University Press, 2005), 174, 175.

24. Charlotte Smith, *The Banished Man* (London, 1794), vi, viii.
25. *Universal Magazine* 7 (March 1807), 260.
26. Ngai, *Ugly Feelings*, 3.
27. Claudia L. Johnson, *Equivocal Beings: Politics, Gender, and Sentimentality in the 1790s: Wollstonecraft, Radcliffe, Burney, Austen* (University of Chicago Press, 1995), 170.
28. Ibid., 171.
29. Ibid., 165.
30. On anachronism, see Srinivas Aravamudan, 'The Return of Anachronism', *MLQ: Modern Language Quarterly* 62 (2001): 331–53; James Chandler, *England in 1819* (University of Chicago Press, 1998).
31. Frances Burney, *The Journals and Letters of Fanny Burney (Madame D'Arblay)*, ed. Edward A. Bloom and Lillian D. Bloom (Oxford: Clarendon Press, 1978), VI: 21–2.

CHAPTER 12

Jane Austen and the Sentimental Novel

Albert J. Rivero

Jane Austen had a complex relation to the sentimental novel, which she both critiqued and embraced. The topic, while not new, remains of central importance in assessing her works. Given renewed scholarly interest in the sentimental novel over the past few decades, the time has come for another look at Austen's place in the sentimental tradition. As is well known, Austen began her writing career by satirizing the conventions of sentimental novels; her last completed novel, *Persuasion* (1818), strikes many sentimental chords. Yet, during her final illness, she was writing *Sanditon*, a novel left unfinished, which, in its anti-sentimentality, recalls her early work. In it, we meet Sir Edward Denham, who 'had read more sentimental novels than agreed with him. His fancy had been early caught by all the impassioned and most exceptionable parts of Richardson's.'[1] A bad reader, Sir Edward has had the sentimental strain injected the wrong way. Austen's anti-sentimental (re)turn in *Sanditon* is instructive. Among other things, it reminds us that, three decades after her initial attack, Austen still feels that the sentimental strain is potent enough to merit further satirical intervention. It is also clear that, while placing some of the blame on Richardson for including 'exceptionable parts' in his works, Austen focuses our attention more specifically on their corrosive hold on Sir Edward's 'fancy' and weak mind.

The dangers of reading sentimental novels lie not in their 'impassioned' content, but in the mental capabilities of their readers, both male and female. Austen reminds us that, while sentimental novels were identified with women, they were also read – and misread – by men. Thus, for Austen, the best kind of sentimental novel would be that which inoculates its readers against its potentially toxic effects by teaching them to read critically, with discriminating minds as well as feeling hearts. Austen developed a narrative technique, free indirect discourse, fusing first- and third-person viewpoints, which allowed her to regulate her readers' responses. Like Laurence Sterne, Austen understood that irony and satire are not inimical to the sentimental but integral to it. All of Austen's six published novels are sentimental and end in marriage – a satisfyingly sentimental payoff for readers then and now. Austen expects her readers to read her novels sentimentally, with feeling and sympathy, but she also encourages them to exercise their judgement, to be moved but not be stupefied by sensibility.

Like Henry Fielding, who began his novelistic career by parodying Samuel Richardson's *Pamela* (1740) in *Shamela* (1741), Austen started hers by satirizing sentimental novels in a series of sketches she wrote as a young girl. Austen drew inspiration not only from such sentimental novels as Eliza Nugent Bromley's *Laura and Augustus* (1784), one of her sources for *Love and Freindship* (1790), but also, as Paula Byrne and Penny Gay have shown, from such plays as Richard Brinsley Sheridan's *The Rivals* (1775), featuring the bookishly romantic Lydia Languish, which staged the delusions of sensibility.[2] Thus the heroine of Austen's *Fredric and Elfrida* (1787?), distressed 'too much for her delicate Constitution' by bad news, 'fainted and was in such a hurry to have a succession of fainting fits, that she had scarcely patience enough to recover from one before she fell into another'.[3] Similarly, in *Love and Freindship*, while typically mangling sentimental novel conventions into bathetic clichés, Laura describes how she and a 'real freind' she has just met, but with whom she has 'exchanged vows of mutual Freindship for the rest of our Lives', reacted to the 'affecting Scene' of the 'meeting' between their husbands, Edward and Augustus, who greet each other like long-lost lovers: '"My Life! my Soul!" (exclaimed the former). "My Adorable Angel!" (replied the latter) as they flew into each other's arms. – It was too pathetic for the feelings of Sophia and myself – We fainted Alternately on a Sofa.'[4] The final line of this ludicrous sentimental scene is borrowed from a stage direction, following an improbable family reunion, in Sheridan's *The Critic* (1781) – '*They faint alternately in each others arms.*'[5] There is no 'sofa' in Sheridan's play, but having Sophia fainting on a sofa is too tempting a zany association of words for the young Austen to resist. Earlier Laura had summed up her qualifications as sentimental heroine: 'A sensibility too tremblingly alive to every affliction of my Freinds, my Acquaintance and particularly to every affliction of my own, was my only fault, if a fault it could be called.'[6]

The influence of Fielding and Sheridan on the juvenilia looks forward to future developments in Austen's narrative techniques. *The Critic* is a rehearsal play, a type of satirical drama derived from Buckingham's *The Rehearsal* (1672), in which the audience in the theatre observes spectators on stage commenting on the absurdities of a play being rehearsed.

Fielding used the rehearsal format to satirize sentimental comedies and tragedies in such plays as *The Author's Farce* (1730) and *The Tragedy of Tragedies* (1731), the latter being one of the plays acted by the Austen family in private theatricals during the 1780s.[7] The rehearsal format was influential on Fielding's narrative framework in his novels, where an apparently omniscient narrator, in dialogue with the reader, comments on the actions of the characters in the story as well as offering observations on such topics as authors, novel writing, the book trade, love and politics. Austen's free indirect discourse blends elements of the rehearsal play with Fielding's authorial presence, but it is a more sophisticated instrument for calibrating and capturing what passes in a reader's mind. In this respect, Austen's narrative technique resembles that of such sentimental authors as Sterne and Mackenzie, who, as Sir Walter Scott observed, write novels which are 'rather the history of effects produced on the human mind by a series of events, than the narratives of those events themselves'.[8]

The excerpts from the juvenilia cited above operate, for the most part, in the burlesque mode. To a certain extent, this is also true of *Northanger Abbey*, published posthumously in December 1817, but, like *Sense and Sensibility* (1811), originating in the 1790s, and – as we are informed in the advertisement fronting the text – finished in 1803. In the opening line, Austen teases the conventions of sentimental novels by introducing her protagonist as a tomboy devoid of even the smallest amount of the required sensibility: 'No one who had ever seen Catherine Morland in her infancy, would have supposed her born to be an heroine.'[9] But, 'from fifteen to seventeen she was in training for a heroine' (*NA*, 7), and, as the first chapter ends, Catherine is ready, like Burney's Evelina, to make her entrance into the world. In the ensuing narrative, and more pointedly in the second volume, Austen parodies such conventions of gothic novels as ruined castles and abbeys, false walls hiding wives long thought dead or mouldering corpses, trap doors, dark and stormy nights presaging unspeakable horrors. More significantly, she exposes the dangers of reading gothic novels unreflectively.

Gothic novels or romances were a species of sentimental novel which achieved their peak popularity between 1796 and 1806.[10] One could argue that Horace Walpole's *The Castle of Otranto* (1764), traditionally regarded as the first gothic novel, parodies the genre it inaugurates and calls for an ironically intellectual reading. Whatever horrors readers encounter are kept under control by the over-the-top presentation, such distancing devices as fragmentary narrative, foreign and historically remote setting, and a preface which, by the second edition, drops the pretence of being by the translator. Although Walpole called *Tristram Shandy* (1759–67) 'a very insipid and tedious performance', he seems to have been influenced by Sterne's narrative pyrotechnics.[11] In their extravagance, gothic tales are always teetering on the brink of parody or self-parody. But, as they grew in popularity, and their authors vamped up the horrors and readers became less sophisticated, they began to be read in a more absorptive fashion. Catherine believes that Ann Radcliffe's novels are true to life and reliable guides for her conduct. Like Arabella, the heroine of Charlotte Lennox's *The Female Quixote* (1752), one of Austen's favourite novels, whose mind is addled by reading voluminous French romances, Catherine sees the world through the distorting lens of the books she avidly consumes. Austen's point is not that all gothic novels are horrid – though, given its scandalous plot, Matthew Gregory Lewis's *The Monk: A Romance* (1796), John Thorpe's favourite, might prove alarming, especially if readers cannot discern whether what they are reading is intended as parody. On the other hand, Radcliffe's *The Mysteries of Udolpho* (1794), Catherine's favourite, which Austen calls 'charming' (*NA*, 205), is entertaining and morally sound. But, when read by impressionable and undereducated young women, gothic novels can have bad consequences, exposing their readers to humiliation and embarrassment, as happens to Catherine – or worse, seduction by designing men. Austen does not dismiss the benefits of reading gothic novels. If nothing else, some gothic novels get right the nightmare of women living in a society which, while ostensibly valuing them, denied them full civic participation by marriage, property and voting laws that ensured that they would remain in an inferior position. Because she has been reading gothic novels and internalizing their aesthetic of suspicion, Catherine reaches her correct assessment of General Tilney's character as patriarchal tyrant.

Marianne, in *Sense and Sensibility*, is not primarily a novel reader, though her initial reaction to Willoughby's 'person and air were equal to what her fancy had ever drawn for the hero of a favourite story'.[12] She is, however, depicted as the quintessential heroine of over-sensibility in sentimental novels, impulsive, romantic, moved to madness by poetry and to high-flown rhetorical effusions by nature. Victims of their own fancy, the heroines of over-sensibility are naïve, unaware of danger and thus vulnerable to seduction and abandonment by predatory men. On his first appearance, Willoughby is described as 'a gentleman carrying a gun, with two pointers playing round him' (*S&S*, 50). He comes upon some unexpected prey in the injured Marianne, who has slipped and fallen while running downhill in the rain. When Willoughby carries 'her into the house with so little previous formality', Marianne sees 'a rapidity of thought which particularly recommended the action to her' (*S&S*, 51). Further familiarity confirms that 'their taste was strikingly alike' (*S&S*, 56). But Marianne fails to see, as Austen emphasizes, that Willoughby is playing a part: 'her favourite authors were brought forward and dwelt upon with so rapturous a delight, that any young man of five and twenty must have been insensible indeed, not to become an immediate convert to the excellence of such works, however disregarded before' (*S&S*, 51).

We later learn that Willoughby has seduced a young woman and abandoned her when she becomes pregnant; he has already been 'insensible indeed', though neither Marianne nor the reader is yet aware of his duplicity. The young woman, Eliza, is the daughter of another Eliza, whose career as a fallen woman her initial lover, Colonel Brandon, details to Elinor. Brandon loses her to the sexual and financial machinations of his father and brother. The emotionally charged interview between Elinor and Colonel Brandon is a standard feature of sentimental novels.[13] Unmasking Willoughby as a rake, Brandon reveals himself as a man of feeling, whose sensibility is evident in his halting narrative and, like Diderot's friend while reading Richardson, in his pacing about the room.[14] Unlike Diderot's friend, Colonel Brandon stifles his tears, a no less effective performance of sensibility, but one that shows that he, like Elinor, can govern his emotions. Both Willoughby and Colonel Brandon are convincing actors of sensibility but, unlike Marianne, they know how to control their performances.

Elinor also knows how to 'govern' her strong feelings. Austen thus sets up what appears to be a simple binary between one sister's sense and the other's sensibility, a common plot device she might have borrowed from such novels as Jane West's *A Gossip's Story* (1796), in which the heroine of sense, Louisa, contrasts with the heroine of sensibility, also named Marianne. While Marianne emotes all over the place, Elinor is constantly refraining from outward displays of excessive sensibility. However, because for most of the novel we are inside Elinor's mind, in the narrator's double-voiced free indirect discourse, we notice that her fancy can sometimes be as self-deceptive as Marianne's. Willoughby is demonstrably attractive, and Marianne is not deluded when she so regards him. On the other hand, Edward is 'not handsome', but Elinor, after perceiving 'the expression of his eyes' and 'the general sweetness of his countenance', thinks him 'really handsome; or, at least almost so' (*S&S*, 23–4). She also endows him with a taste in drawing, literature and nature which seems imaginary and preposterous to Marianne, who also notices that he is 'reserved' (*S&S*, 109).

Of course, Elinor's judgement of Edward's person and aesthetic sensibility may be due to her deeper penetration, her ability to see beyond surface appearances. But her remark that he is 'really handsome; or, at least almost so' suggests that she has her doubts. When she imagines that the lock of hair in Edward's ring might be her own, without recollecting the occasion of its snipping, she reveals herself as much a victim of fancy as her sister, who at least knows when Willoughby cut her hair, with Margaret serving as corroborating witness. Elinor's self-deception regarding Edward, who is allowing Elinor to fall in love with him while being secretly engaged to Lucy Steele – the cause of the 'reserve' Marianne calls out – seems at least equal to Marianne's regarding Willoughby. Elinor might govern her feelings in public, but she cannot always rely on her reason to rule her passion. The delusive power of love disables even the most vigilant of women. A woman is always most at risk from the man with whom she falls in love, a man who best suits her character. Marianne falls for the poetic Willoughby, Elinor for the prosaic Edward. Even if only one of them is truly selfish and the other bumbling but well-meaning, both men inflict intense pain and suffering.

Charlotte Lucas, in *Pride and Prejudice* (1813), has an even firmer grip on her emotions than Elinor, whose grip, we recall, slips when blinded by her 'esteem' – a word she prefers to use, as Marianne points out, to conceal from herself and others her true feelings for Edward. At twenty-seven, in Austen's fiction the sell-by-date of women in the marriage market, Charlotte is aware that she is running out of time and thus acts with clear-eyed calculation. She trenchantly dismisses Elizabeth Bennet's sentimental panegyric on her sister Jane's ability to unite 'with great strength of feeling, a composure of temper and a uniform cheerfulness of manner' to conceal from the public her affection for Bingley. As Charlotte puts it, 'if a woman conceals her affection with the same skill from the object of it, she may lose the opportunity of fixing him'.[15] It is no coincidence that Charlotte's homespun wisdom calls to mind *Northanger Abbey*, when Austen wittily invokes Dr Gregory's advice to his daughters and declares that 'a woman especially, if she have the misfortune of knowing any thing, should conceal it as well as she can'.[16] Charlotte has little patience with the visions of romance that Elizabeth seems to be entertaining. She desperately needs an 'establishment', and, when the 'heavy looking' but financially solid Mr Collins lands in her neighbourhood, she wastes little time in making him aware of her matrimonial designs. As she tells Elizabeth after she agrees to marry him, 'I am not romantic you know. I never was' (*P&P*, 140).

Having exercised her right as 'a rational creature' by turning down Mr Collins's proposal three days earlier, Elizabeth cannot grasp why her friend 'would have sacrificed every better feeling to worldly advantage' (*P&P*, 141). For her, 'Charlotte the wife of Mr Collins, was a most humiliating picture! – And to the pang of a friend disgracing herself and sunk in her esteem, was added the distressing conviction that it was impossible for that friend to be tolerably happy in the lot she had chosen' (*P&P*, 141). As much an 'imaginist' as Emma Woodhouse and at least as equally ill-equipped at matchmaking, Elizabeth projects her lofty romantic expectations on a woman who, unlike herself, will not be rescued from her precarious financial circumstances and given a sentimentally satisfying happy ending by authorial fiat. As it happens, Jane's reserve nearly ruins her chances with Bingley; Mr Collins and Charlotte seem to be 'tolerably happy' in their married state. Charlotte dwells in the 'real' world, though contained in a fiction, where, happy or not, marriage is 'the only honourable provision for well-educated young women of small fortune' and 'their pleasantest preservative from want' (*P&P*, 138). As Austen acidly comments in one of her letters, 'Single Women have a dreadful propensity for being poor – which is one very strong argument in favour of Matrimony.'[17] Elizabeth and Jane, on the other hand, are born to the extraordinary fate of a select number of lucky romantic heroines in sentimental novels, happy marriages to wealthy and sensible men.

Elizabeth's confidence in her reason and powers of observation is what makes her so attractive to readers. We applaud when she rejects the odious Mr Collins but we should also recognize that her self-confidence places her at risk. She deems irrational Charlotte's highly rational choice because she withholds her sympathy. Feeling superior to her friend's quest for 'worldly advantage', she fails to see that Charlotte's situation is nearly her own, as her father's estate is entailed on Mr Collins and her portion will not be sufficient to attract the kind of suitor to which she believes herself entitled. In this respect, Elizabeth seems more deluded than Marianne, who, as a proper sentimental heroine, downplays the significance of money, yet also knows that a handsome 'competence' would be a nice complement to romantic love. Moreover, Marianne is occasionally aware that she is letting her passions overrule her reason, as when she proudly declares that she will not curb her displays of affection for Willoughby.[18] Like Elinor, Elizabeth sees herself as 'a rational creature' but does not fully grasp the fallibility or limits of reason – in Johnson's words, 'How rarely Reason guides the stubborn Choice.'[19]

Eventually Elizabeth will discover that she has mistaken reason for fancy, that she, 'who have prided myself on my discernment', has been 'blind, partial, prejudiced, absurd' (*P&P*, 230). If *Sense and Sensibility* warns against the dangers of over-sensibility, *Pride and Prejudice* illustrates the delusive attractions of reason for sensible young women like Elizabeth. Elizabeth easily believes that she is 'rational' when she thinks others are not. This is a species of quixotism and selfishness for which Elizabeth does not fully pay the price because, having the author on her side, she is permitted to become aware that she has been wrong, and that self-conviction allows the narrative to proceed to perfect felicity for her. Elizabeth is never in real danger of becoming prey to Wickham's seductive powers, as she is more interested in getting good gossip on Darcy than getting entangled in an affair of the heart. That fate is reserved for Lydia who, again by authorial dispensation, also avoids facing the full consequences of her actions. The emotionally satisfying, sentimental happy ending of *Pride and Prejudice* might make readers forget the questioning of such happy endings at the beginning of the novel, when Charlotte Lucas 'fixed' Mr Collins because Darcy and Pemberley were already destined as reward for her romantic friend.

As has often been remarked, Fanny Price, the heroine of *Mansfield Park* (1814), is no Elizabeth Bennet, but, like her, she is rewarded at the end with the man she loves. Yet the ending of the novel, as the author steps forward to speak the epilogue, recalls the self-reflexive ending of *Northanger Abbey*, where 'the tell-tale compression of the pages' before us reminds us that we *are* reading a novel, more specifically a sentimental novel hastening towards 'perfect felicity' for the hero and heroine.[20] Such does not seem to be the case as we finish reading the penultimate chapter of *Mansfield Park*. Edmund despairs after he finally sees Mary Crawford for who she is and believes that he will never love another woman again. The 'tell-tale compression of the pages' once again gives us a clue that the end is near but 'perfect felicity', or felicity of any kind, seems a remote possibility.

How to bring good out of all this evil, a biblical text that has haunted the narrative, seems a tall order even for the most providentially deft of authors. In a move reminiscent of the conclusion of *Lady Susan* (1794?), where a hitherto hidden Richardson-like editor unexpectedly pops in to announce the end of the correspondence we have been reading and to distribute rewards and punishments, the narrator of *Mansfield Park* abruptly reverses narrative trajectory and wrests comedy out of tragicomedy. The first sentence of the concluding chapter – 'Let other pens dwell on guilt and misery' – calls attention to the 'pen' the author holds in her hand, the material implement enacting her powerful agency.[21] Like Fielding's narrator in *Tom Jones* (1749), who teases readers with dire possibilities that Tom may have committed incest with his mother or may hang for murder, Austen claims her undisputed right as god of her own creation. She then peremptorily informs her readers why she is changing course: 'I quit such odious subjects as soon as I can, impatient to restore every body, not greatly in fault themselves, to tolerable comfort, and to have done with all the rest' (*MP*, 533). Claiming impatience with what has happened thus far, the weary but resolute author summarily dismisses the sentimental novel we have just been reading.

Mansfield Park is indeed a sentimental novel, with a morally upright and Christian sentimental heroine – at least until we are awakened from our absorptive reading of a routine sentimental novel scene, featuring a distraught male lover seeking comfort and pity from a sympathetic female interlocutor. We have noted above a version of such a scene in *Sense and Sensibility*, in Colonel Brandon's interview with Elinor; we witness another one near the end of the novel, when Elinor is implored by Willoughby, who thinks Marianne is dying because of him, to listen to his disingenuous tale of self-inflicted woe.[22] After Austen calls us back to full awareness that we are reading a novel, she immediately informs us that 'my Fanny . . . at this very time . . . must have been happy in spite of every thing' (*MP*, 533), a happiness that has nothing to do with her becoming Edmund's wife, the usual definition of 'happiness' in a courtship plot and in Austen's other novels. Fanny 'must have been a happy creature in spite of all that she felt or thought that she felt, for the distress of those around her' (*MP*, 533). She is especially 'happy' because 'Edmund was no longer the dupe of Miss Crawford' but, of course, 'Edmund was very far from happy himself' (*MP*, 533). Fanny, we are told, is 'sorry' for Edmund, 'but it was with a sorrow so founded on satisfaction, so tending to ease, and so much in harmony with every dearest sensation, that there are few who might not have been glad to exchange their greatest gaiety for it' (*MP*, 533).

Austen moves from declaring that Fanny feels – or *thinks* that she feels, an important qualifier – for the sorrows of others to unequivocally stating that, in fact, she is exuberantly happy in her happiness This diagnosis of her condition is punctuated with such words drawn from the sentimental lexicon as 'harmony' and 'sensation'. Fanny's disregard for the sorrow and unhappiness of others seems to disqualify her as a heroine of sensibility, which we have been led to believe she is throughout the previous narrative, until we recall that selfishness is a prime characteristic of such a heroine. Fanny's feelings are understandable. She is not a paragon but a fictional version of a flawed human being, who feels happy when those who have harmed her or made her life miserable get their comeuppance. As Austen confided to her niece Fanny Knight in March 1817, 'pictures of perfection as you know make me sick & wicked'.[23] By disclosing her heroine's selfish feelings, at a time when such disclosure might undermine our regard for her, Austen challenges her readers to make difficult judgements. Moreover, the showy, arbitrary fashion in which Austen brings about the marriage between Fanny and Edmund – 'I purposely abstain from dates on this occasion, that every one may be at liberty to fix their own'(*MP*, 544) – further shakes our confidence in the sentimental happy ending Fanny gets as anything but authorial overkill. It is an ending intended to conform to expectations raised by the type of sentimental novel we think we are still reading, even after the narrator has been prodding us from the beginning of the chapter to read differently. After all, as we have been explicitly told, Fanny was already happy, long before the author bestowed Edmund on her.

The manner in which Austen destabilizes our sentimental expectations at the end of *Mansfield Park* makes us question the basis and validity of our judgements. It is reminiscent of Swift's strategies of reader vexation. In *A Tale of a Tub* (1704), for example, in the Apology added to the 1710 edition, the author, presumably speaking in his own voice, exhorts his readers to accept a fully orthodox reading of the work, a reassurance of authorial intention not entirely consistent with the disorienting narrative techniques of the ensuing pages. For what it is worth, I believe that Swift intends *A Tale of a Tub* as a defence of Anglicanism, just as I believe that Austen intends Fanny Price as an Anglican, possibly Evangelical sentimental heroine with whom we are meant to sympathize. I thus plead guilty to the intentional fallacy because alternative readings – Swift undermining the Anglican Church in which he is seeking preferment; Austen undercutting the Christian virtue of her heroine – make little sense. My reading experience of both works, however, makes me question that I have nailed down authorial intention. Swift's usual method of impersonation of the positions he is attacking complicates interpretation of his works in ways not applicable to Austen's relatively straightforward but still satirically and ironically told novels. But the impulse is the same. Both authors aim to make readers sceptical and self-conscious of the process by which they construe meaning or deduce authorial intention. Sterne plays similar games with his readers, asking them to bring their imaginations into play in the act of interpretation, 'to halve this matter amicably' with him.[24] So does Fielding, especially in *Tom Jones*, where readers are told, with mock deference and helpfulness, that 'tho' we will always lend thee proper Assistance in difficult Places, as we do not, like some others, expect thee to use the Arts of Divination to discover our Meaning, yet we shall not indulge thy Laziness where nothing but thy own Attention is required'.[25]

Like the narrator of *Tom Jones*, the narrator of *Emma* tells us one story while hiding another in plain sight. The 'hidden' story in *Emma* is the sentimental tale of Jane Fairfax's secret engagement to Frank Churchill. Jane Fairfax, a poor young woman who has been educated by well-meaning guardians to become a governess to earn her bread, is the stereotypically beautiful but sickly and pale heroine of sensibility. Like the anti-sentimental Charlotte Lucas in *Pride and Prejudice*, Jane Fairfax understands her financial predicament. Grasping the opportunity given her to change her situation by a chance meeting at a 'watering-place', she enters into a secret engagement with Frank Churchill, 'the favourite of fortune', as Mr Knightley calls him.[26] Frank Churchill, who is neither frank nor originally surnamed Churchill, uses the cover of a flirtation with Emma to hide his engagement, in the process inflicting pain on the woman he presumably loves and embarrassment on the woman he pretends to court. As Mr Knightley observes, Jane Fairfax 'deserves a better fate' than marriage to Frank Churchill (*E*, 464). Having no portion but her personal accomplishments, she makes a choice which, were she in a different kind of novel, might lead to deadly consequences. As it is, her tale of potentially disastrous love offers a more 'realistic' counterpoint to Emma's comic tale of self-inflicted mortification. Jane Fairfax is truer to women's experience in Austen's time than the financially independent titular heroine.

Emma is emphatically not a sentimental heroine in Jane Fairfax's or Fanny Price's manner. Mrs Weston, her former governess, waxes eloquent on Emma's 'bloom of full health', adding 'there is health, not merely in her bloom, but in her air, her head, her glance' (*E*, 39). Mr Knightley, her interlocutor, agrees, noting that Emma is not 'personally vain' but 'her vanity lies another way' (*E*, 40), namely in thinking herself endowed with superior mental powers. In robust health, then, if not in cleverness, Emma is similar to Elizabeth Bennet. Unlike Elizabeth, Emma is rich; as she tells Harriet, she has 'none of the usual inducements of women to marry' (*E*, 90). Instead, she amuses herself with imagining matches for other people, committing blunder after blunder, until, after unwittingly encouraging Harriet yet once more to set her cap on another unsuspecting suitor, 'it darted through her, with the speed of an arrow, that Mr Knightley must marry no one but herself!' (*E*, 444). She bitterly blames herself for Harriet's 'presumption to raise her thoughts to Mr Knightley!'

(*E*, 450). Echoing Elizabeth's heartfelt words of enlightenment, 'Till this moment, I never knew myself',[27] Emma realizes that 'till now that she was threatened with its loss, [she] had never known how much of her happiness depended on being *first* with Mr Knightley, first in interest and affection' (*E*, 452).

The swiftly following revelation of Jane and Frank's secret engagement removes one obstacle to the sentimental happy ending for Emma and Mr Knightley. Another, and more serious obstacle, Emma's decision not to leave her father's house, is partially overcome when Mr Knightley agrees to live at Hartfield, and completely and ludicrously removed when the theft of Mrs Weston's turkeys, coupled with 'pilfering' of 'other poultry-yards in the neighbourhood', convinces Mr Woodhouse to grant his consent (*E*, 528). Although the theft of turkeys might be (to quote the narrator of *Northanger Abbey*) 'a new circumstance in romance',[28] it nonetheless makes the course of true love run smooth at Hartfield, as hero and heroine inexorably advance towards 'the perfect happiness of [their] union' (*E*, 528). While not exactly a cock and bull story like *Tristram Shandy*, which ends with a paradoxical encomium on the Shandy bull, *Emma* closes with a poultry-yard solution that casts ironic light on the sentimental happy ending. On a more ominous note, given what we have witnessed of their troubled courtship, as well as Frank's unsettling comments on Jane's 'most uncommon complexion' (*E*, 522) and Emma's meditation on Frank's frivolous character and inferiority to Mr Knightley, the union of Frank Churchill and Jane Fairfax rings hollow and might serve as a caveat against the duplicitous representations of sentimental novels.

Persuasion offers its readers not one but two sentimental stories, featuring the same lovers, unfolding eight years apart. One ends in sadness, the other in happiness; the second overwrites and corrects the first. In one, the lovers break off their engagement when the nineteen-year-old Anne Elliot yields to persuasion; in the other, their reunion is brought about, after a period of sentimentally inflected uncertainty, by their own agency, as they find each other on 'Union-street' in Bath. Early on we are told that Anne 'had been forced into prudence in her youth, she learned romance as she grew older – the natural sequel of an unnatural beginning'.[29] Even now, upon the return into her neighbourhood of the wealthy and still attractive Captain Wentworth, Anne keeps trying to persuade herself that she does not blame Lady Russell for then persuading her against marrying the rash and impecunious Mr Wentworth, or herself for taking her advice. But she has been suffering the consequences: 'Her attachment and regrets had, for a long time, clouded every enjoyment of youth; and an early loss of bloom and spirits had been their lasting effect' (*P*, 30).

Anne now knows that her 'prudence' was a false idol; she should have acted upon 'her early warm attachment, and a cheerful confidence in futurity, against that over-anxious caution which seems to insult exertion and distrust Providence!' (*P*, 32). Perhaps it is 'romantic' for Anne to believe now that, in acting against her feelings then, she behaved unnaturally, indeed impiously because against providential design. She doubted her faith in her love and thwarted her destiny. Because Anne's thoughts are revealed to us in free indirect discourse, it is uncertain the extent to which the author endorses her opinions. This is an act of discrimination made even more difficult in *Persuasion* than in Austen's other novels by the close sympathetic identification between narrator and protagonist. Because of her suffering, if nothing else, Anne richly deserves a second chance at happiness. Austen manipulates the narrative to reach that end but she also emphasizes the work Anne and Wentworth, but especially Anne, must do to earn their reunion. The sequel, which we are now reading, will prove that, as Mrs Selby tells Harriet Byron in *Sir Charles Grandison* (1753–4), 'love is a natural passion', that 'it is no disgrace for a young woman of virtue to be in love with a worthy man'.[30]

Anne is no longer a young woman when we first meet her. Like Charlotte Lucas, at twenty-seven she has reached a crisis point. Unlike Charlotte, Anne was, and still is, romantic. She also believes that she has already wrecked her chance at happiness. We learn that she possesses 'an elegance of mind and sweetness of character, which must have placed her high with any people of real understanding', but with her own family she was 'nobody', 'only Anne' (*P*, 6). She is valued by Lady Russell, but, as she passes through her limited world, she is mostly perceived as an 'elegant little woman of seven and twenty, with every beauty excepting bloom, and with manners as consciously right as they were invariably gentle' (*P*, 166). In short, she seems to be a passive sentimental heroine, burdened with sorrow over a lost love, racked with the conviction that she will never be loved again. To be sure, we as readers are aware of her rich mental life, of her intelligence and sensibility, but our overall impression of her is still one of wistfulness, of regret. There was a time when Anne Elliot, like Marianne Dashwood, was impulsive and daring, in love with a dashingly handsome and supremely self-confident young man. Anne seemed to be headed towards an uncertain future – had she been a character in a sentimental novel, her fate could have been either perfect felicity or unmitigated disaster. Guided by her love for Anne but also by her 'prejudices on the side of ancestry' (*P*, 12), Lady Russell, fearing a bad ending, wrote her own conclusion to Anne's sentimental love story. It takes two attempts, but eventually the author of *Persuasion* will provide a sentimentally satisfying happy ending for Anne and Wentworth.

As we move towards the happy ending, there are moments when we palpably feel the author's pen at work. One such moment is when Anne's 'bloom and freshness of youth [are] restored by the fine wind which had been blowing on her complexion' (*P*, 112). An unknown admirer is taken with her – he turns out to be Mr William Elliot, 'heir presumptive' to Anne's father – and his admiration is noticed by Captain Wentworth, who gives her 'a glance of brightness, which seemed to say, "That man is struck with you, – and even I, at this moment, see something like Anne Elliot again"' (*P*, 112). The removal, only a few pages later, of Anne's rival for Wentworth's affection, Louisa Musgrove, by a fall and head injury, is another. It is here, in this episode, that we notice, if we have not done so before, that Anne, in spite of her romantic musings, is not a passive sentimental heroine. While Louisa's brother, Charles, Wentworth and his fellow sailors, who presumably have seen worse injuries in battle, are immobilized with panic, Anne gives them 'directions' (*P*, 119) to seek medical help for the stricken Louisa. Wentworth's remark that 'no one [is] so proper, so capable as Anne!' makes Anne pause 'a moment to recover from the emotion of hearing herself so spoken of'; his turning to her as he praises her, 'speaking with a glow, and yet a gentleness, which seemed almost restoring the past', makes her colour 'deeply' (*P*, 123). Like the wind that earlier restored her 'bloom', his regard reanimates her complexion, as the bodies of the former lovers begin to vibrate in sentimental unison and speak eloquently to each other. Noticing her blush, he 'recollected himself and moved away' (*P*, 123).

Wentworth comes back to Anne, to recollect and redeem the past. He writes a heartfelt declaration of renewed love to her while he sits at a table at the fitly named White Hart and overhears Anne's rending declaration to Captain Harville that women love 'longest, when existence or when hope is gone' (*P*, 256). Using a scheme adapted from William Blake, we could argue that *Persuasion* is an 'organized' sentimental novel, in which Anne and Frederick, having been forced out of their innocent love by Lady Russell and fully experiencing the pain and loss of their separation, triumph over bitterness and regret and generously restore themselves to each other. As the narrative concludes, 'the dread of a future war' (*P*, 275) reminds us that sentimental novels are written and read in the real world, a timely intrusion of reality which might well be Austen's most enduring contribution to the sentimental tradition.

Notes

1. Jane Austen, *Later Manuscripts*, ed. Janet Todd and Linda Bree (Cambridge University Press, 2008), 183. I am grateful to Barbara Benedict, Jocelyn Harris, George Justice, Devoney Looser, Lisa Rivero and Howard Weinbrot for comments on earlier drafts of this chapter.
2. Paula Byrne, *Jane Austen and the Theatre* (London: Hambledon Continuum, 2002); Penny Gay, *Jane Austen and the Theatre* (Cambridge University Press, 2002).
3. Jane Austen, *Juvenilia*, ed. Peter Sabor (Cambridge: Cambridge University Press, 2006), 12.
4. Ibid., 113–14.
5. *The Critic*, III, i, l. 3, in *The Dramatic Works of Richard Brinsley Sheridan*, vol. ii, ed. Cecil Price, 2 vols. (Oxford: Clarendon Press, 1973), 541.
6. Austen, *Juvenilia*, 104.
7. Byrne, *Jane Austen and the Theatre*, 12. On Fielding's use of the rehearsal, see my *The Plays of Henry Fielding: a Critical Study of his Dramatic Career* (Charlottesville: University Press of Virginia, 1989).
8. Sir Walter Scott, *Lives of the Novelists*, 2 vols. (Philadelphia, 1825), II: 154.
9. Jane Austen, *Northanger Abbey*, ed. Barbara M. Benedict and Deirdre Le Faye (Cambridge University Press, 2006), 5. Further references to *NA* are to this edition.
10. Peter Garside, James Raven and Rainer Schöwerling, eds., *The English Novel, 1770–1829: a Bibliographical Survey of Prose Fiction Published in the British Isles*, 2 vols. (Oxford University Press, 2000), II: 56.
11. Horace Walpole to Sir William Dalrymple (4 April 1760), in *Horace Walpole's Correspondence with Sir William Dalrymple*, ed. W. S. Lewis, Charles H. Bennett and Andrew G. Hoover (New Haven: Yale University Press, 1951), 66.
12. Jane Austen, *Sense and Sensibility*, ed. Edward Copeland (Cambridge University Press, 2006), 51. Further references to *S&S* are to this edition.
13. For a reading of this scene, see my ' Doubling Eliza: Austen's Remembrance of Richardson (and perhaps Haywood) in *Sense and Sensibility*', in *New Windows on a Woman's World: Essays in Honour of Jocelyn Harris*, ed. Lisa Marr (Dunedin, NZ: University of Otago Press, 2005), 93–103.
14. For a description of this famous scene of sentimental reading, see Introduction to this volume, 1.
15. Jane Austen, *Pride and Prejudice*, ed. Pat Rogers (Cambridge University Press, 2006), 51. Further references to *P&P* are to this edition.
16. *NA*, 112. John Gregory, *A Father's Legacy to his Daughters* (London and Edinburgh, 1774): 'But if you happen to have any learning, keep it

a profound secret, especially from the men, who generally look with a jealous and malignant eye on a woman of great parts, and a cultivated understanding' (31–2).

17. Jane Austen to Fanny Knight (13 March 1817), in *Jane Austen's Letters*, 4th edition, ed. Deirdre Le Faye (Oxford University Press, 2014), 347. On this topic, see Edward Copeland, *Women Writing about Money: Women's Fiction in England, 1790–1820* (Cambridge University Press, 1995); Robert D. Hume, 'Money in Jane Austen', *Review of English Studies* 64 (2013): 289–310. Hume stresses Mr Bennet's culpable failure to provide for his family after his death.
18. *S&S*, 63–4: 'Marianne abhorred all concealment where no real disgrace could attend unreserve; and to aim at the restraint of sentiments which were not in themselves illaudable, appeared to her not merely an unnecessary effort, but a disgraceful subjection of reason to commonplace and mistaken notions.'
19. Samuel Johnson, *The Vanity of Human Wishes* (London, 1749), line 10.
20. *NA*, 259.
21. Jane Austen, *Mansfield Park*, ed. John Wiltshire (Cambridge University Press, 2005), 533. Further references to *MP* are to this edition.
22. *S&S*, 359–76.
23. To Fanny Knight (23–25 March 1817), *Austen's Letters*, 350.
24. Laurence Sterne, *The Life and Opinions of Tristram Shandy, Gentleman*, 2 vols. (York, 1760), II: 68.
25. Henry Fielding, *The History of Tom Jones, A Foundling*, ed. Martin C. Battestin and Fredson Bowers, 2 vols. (Oxford University Press, 1975), II: 614.
26. Jane Austen, *Emma*, ed. Richard Cronin and Dorothy McMillan (Cambridge University Press, 2005), 467. Further references to *E* are to this edition.
27. *P&P*, 230.
28. *NA*, 253.
29. Jane Austen, *Persuasion*, ed. Janet Todd and Antje Blank (Cambridge University Press, 2006), 32. Further references to *P* are to this edition.
30. Samuel Richardson, *The History of Sir Charles Grandison*, ed. Jocelyn Harris (Oxford University Press, 1986), ii: 303.

Select Bibliography

Primary Sources

Addison, Joseph, and Richard Steele, *The Spectator*, ed. G. Gregory Smith, 8 vols. (London: Dent, 1907).

The Analytical Review, or History of Literature, Domestic and Foreign (London, 1788–98).

Anon., *Count Roderic's Castle: Or, Gothic Times, A Tale*, ed. J. Jenkins, with a new introduction by Hannah Doherty Hudson (Chicago: Valancourt Books, 2017).

Review of *Count Roderic's Castle*, in *The Monthly Review* 16 (April 1795): 467.

Aubin, Penelope, *A Collection of Entertaining Histories and Novels, Designed to Promote the Cause of Virtue and Honour. Principally Founded on FACTS, and Interspersed with a Variety of Beautiful and Instructive Incidents. By Mrs. PENELOPE AUBIN. And Now First Collected IN THREE VOLUMES*, 3 vols. (London: D. Midwinter, A Bettesworth and C. Hitch, J. and J. Pemberton, R. Ware, C. Rivington, A. Ward, J. and P. Knapton, T. Longman, R. Hett, S. Austen and J. Wood, 1739).

Austen, Jane, *Emma*, ed. Richard Cronin and Dorothy McMillan (Cambridge University Press, 2005).

Jane Austen's Letters, 4th edition, ed. Deirdre Le Faye (Oxford University Press, 2014).

Juvenilia, ed. Peter Sabor (Cambridge University Press, 2006).

Later Manuscripts, ed. Janet Todd and Linda Bree (Cambridge University Press, 2008).

Mansfield Park, ed. John Wiltshire (Cambridge University Press, 2005).

Northanger Abbey, ed. Barbara M. Benedict and Deirdre Le Faye (Cambridge University Press, 2006).

Persuasion, ed. Janet Todd and Antje Blank (Cambridge University Press, 2006).

Pride and Prejudice, ed. Pat Rogers (Cambridge University Press, 2006).

Sense and Sensibility, ed. Edward Copeland (Cambridge University Press, 2006).

Barbauld, Anna Letitia, *Selected Poetry and Prose*, ed. William McCarthy and Elizabeth Kraft (Peterborough, ON: Broadview Press, 2002).

Beaumont, Marie Leprince de, *The Triumph of Truth; or Memoirs of Mr de La Villette*, trans. Radagunda Roberts (London: T. Cadell, 1775).
[Beckingham, Charles], *Addison's Maxims, Observations, and Reflections* ... (London, 1719/20).
Berkeley, George, *Essay towards a New Theory of Vision* (Dublin, 1709).
Berry, Mary, *Extracts of the Journals and Correspondence of Miss Berry from the Year 1783 to 1852*, ed. Lady Theresa Lewis, 3 vols. (London: Longmans, Green and Co., 1865).
Bicknell, John, and Thomas Day, *The Dying Negro, a Poetical Epistle, Supposed to be Written By a Black (Who Lately Shot Himself on Board a Vessel in the River Thames) To His Intended Wife* (London: W. Flexney, 1773).
Boswell, James, *Life of Johnson*, ed. R. W. Chapman (Oxford University Press, 1998).
Brooke, Frances, *The History of Emily Montague*, ed. Mary Jane Edwards (Ottawa: Carleton University Press, 1985).
Brown, William Hill, *The Power of Sympathy and Hannah Webster Foster, The Coquette*, ed. Carla Mulford (New York: Penguin, 1996).
Burney, Frances, *Brief Reflections Relative to the Emigrant French Clergy*, in *Considerations on Religion and Public Education by Hannah More and Brief Reflections Relative to the Emigrant French Clergy [Frances Burney]*, intro. Claudia L. Johnson (Los Angeles: William Andrews Memorial Clark Library, 1990).
Camilla or A Picture of Youth, ed. Edward A. Bloom and Lillian D. Bloom (Oxford University Press, 2009).
The Journals and Letters of Fanny Burney (Madame D'Arblay), ed. Edward A. Bloom and Lillian D. Bloom (Oxford: Clarendon Press, 1978).
The Wanderer; or, Female Difficulties, ed. Margaret Anne Doody, Robert L. Mack, and Peter Sabor (Oxford University Press, 1991).
Constant, Benjamin, *Adolphe*, trans. Margaret Mauldon, ed. Patrick Coleman (Oxford University Press, 2001).
The Counsels of Wisdom, Or, a Collection of the Maxims of Solomon, 2nd edition (London, 1735).
Day, Thomas, *Fragment of an Original Letter on the Slavery of the Negroes; Written in The Year 1776* (London: John Stockdale, 1784).
The History of Sandford and Merton, A Work Intended for the Use of Children (1783–89), 8th edition, 3 vols. (London: John Stockdale, 1798).
Descartes, René, *Discourse on Method and Meditations on the First Philosophy*, ed. David Weissman (New Haven: Yale University Press, 1996).
Treatise on Light, in *The World and Other Writings*, ed. Stephen Gaukroger (Cambridge University Press, 1998).
Diderot, Denis, 'Eulogy of Richardson', in *The Works of Samuel Richardson*, ed. Edward Mangin, 19 vols. (London, 1811), i: i–xxx.
'Letter on the Blind for the Use of Those Who Can See', in Kate E. Tunstall, *Blindness and Enlightenment: An Essay* (London: Continuum, 2011), 167–228.
La Religieuse, ed. Robert Mauzi (Paris: Folio Classique, Gallimard, 1972).

Edgeworth, Maria, *Patronage*, 4 vols. (London: Printed for J. Johnson and Co., 1814).
Epictetus, *Enchiridion*, in *All the Works of Epictetus That Are Now Extant . . .*, trans. Elizabeth Carter (London, 1758).
Fielding, Henry, *Amelia*, ed. David Blewett (New York: Penguin, 1987).
The History of Tom Jones, a Foundling, ed. Martin C. Battestin and Fredson Bowers, 2 vols. (Oxford University Press, 1975).
Joseph Andrews, ed. Martin C. Battestin (Middletown, CT: Wesleyan University Press, 1967).
Fielding, John, *The Universal Mentor . . .* (London, 1763).
Fielding, Sarah, *The Adventures of David Simple*, ed. Malcolm Kelsall (Oxford University Press, 1987).
'Flammenberg, Lawrence' [Carl Friedrich Kahlert], *The Necromancer, or, The Tale of the Black Forest: Founded on Facts*, trans. 'Peter Teuthold' [Peter Will], ed. Jeffrey Cass (Chicago: Valancourt Books, 2007).
Fuller, Thomas, *Gnomologia* (London, 1732).
Gauger, Nicolas, *Fires improv'd: being a new method of building chimneys, so as to prevent their smoaking: in which A Small Fire, shall warm a Room better than a much Larger made the Common Way. With the manner of altering such Chimneys as are already Built, so that they shall perform the same Effects. Illustrated with Cuts. Written in French, by Monsieur Gauger: made English and improved, by J. T. Desaguliers, M. A. F. R. S. By whom is added, the manner of making coal-fires, as useful this new-way, as the wood-fires propos'd by the French author, Explain'd by an Additional Plate. The whole being suited to the Capacity of the meanest Work-Man* (London: J. Senex, and E. Curll, 1715).
Godwin, William, *Memoirs of the Author of the Vindication of the Rights of Woman* (London, 1798).
Goethe, Johann Wolfgang von et al., *Goethe's Collected Works*, 12 vols. (Princeton University Press, 1994).
The Sorrows of Young Werther, trans. David Constantine (Oxford University Press, 2012).
Graves, Richard, *A Sermon on the Deliverance of the Kingdom of Ireland from the Invasion lately Attempted by the French* (Dublin: W. Watson and Son, 1797).
Gregory, John, *A Father's Legacy to His Daughters* (London and Edinburgh, 1774).
Guthrie, William, *The Friends: A Sentimental History*, 2 vols. (London: T. Waller, 1754).
Haywood, Eliza, *Lasselia; or, the Self-Abandoned. A Novel* (London: D. Browne and S. Chapman, 1724).
Love in Its Variety: Being a Collection of Select Novels; Written in Spanish by Signior Michael Bandello. Made English by Mrs ELIZA HAYWOOD (London, 1727).
Reflections on the Various Effects of Love (1726), in *Fantomina and Other Works*, ed. Alexander Pettit, Margaret Case Croskery, and Anna C. Patchias (Peterborough, ON: Broadview Press, 2004).

Hobbes, Thomas, *Leviathan*, ed. Richard Tuck (Cambridge University Press, 2004).
The Works of Thomas Hobbes, ed. William Molesworth, 16 vols. (London: Bohn, 1839).
Hooke, Robert, *Micrographia* (1665; New York: Dover, 2003).
Hume, David, *A Treatise of Human Nature*, ed. David F. Norton and Mary J. Norton, 2 vols. (Oxford: Clarendon Press, 2007).
Hutchinson, Lucy, *The Works of Lucy Hutchinson*, ed. Reid Barbour and David Norbrook, 2 vols. (Oxford University Press, 2012).
Johnson, Samuel, *A Dictionary of the English Language*, 2 vols. (London, 1755).
The Vanity of Human Wishes (London, 1749).
Laclos, Choderlos de, *Les Liaisons Dangereuses*, trans. Douglas Parmée (Oxford University Press, 1995).
Lee, Sophia, *The Life of a Lover*, 6 vols. (London, 1804).
Lister, Anne, *No Priest But Love: Excerpts from the Diaries of Anne Lister, 1824–1826*, ed. Helena Whitbread (Yeadon, West Yorkshire: Smith Settle, 1992).
Locke, John, *An Essay concerning Human Understanding*, ed. Peter H. Nidditch (Oxford: Clarendon Press, 1979).
Long, Edward, *The Sentimental Exhibition; or, Portraits and Sketches of the Times* (London: Printed for T. Lowndes, 1774).
Mackenzie, Anna Maria, *The Danish Massacre: An Historic Fact*, 2 vols. (London: The Minerva Press, 1791).
Mackenzie, Henry, *Julia de Roubigné, A Tale, in a Series of Letters*, 2 vols. (London: W. Strahan and T. Cadell, 1777).
The Lounger (Edinburgh, 1785–6).
The Man of Feeling (London: Cassell and Co., 1886).
The Man of Feeling, ed. Maureen Harkin (Peterborough, ON: Broadview Press, 2005).
The Works of Henry Mackenzie, ed. Susan Manning, 8 vols. (London: Routledge/Thoemmes Press, 1996).
Manley, Delarivier, *The Selected Works of Delarivier Manley*, ed. Rachel Carnell and Ruth Herman, 5 vols. (London: Pickering and Chatto, 2005).
Marx, Karl, *Capital*, vol. 1, trans. Ben Fowkes (New York: Knopf, 1977).
Memoirs and Opinions of Mr Blenfield. By the Author of Tales of Sympathy, 2 vols. (London: W. Lane, 1790).
Norris, John, *A Collection of Miscellanies: Consisting of Poems, Essays, Discourses, and Letters, Occasionally Written* (Oxford, 1687).
Palmer, Charles, *A Collection of Select Aphorisms and Maxims . . . Extracted from the Most Eminent Authors* (London, 1748).
Parsons, Eliza, *The Castle of Wolfenbach: A German Story*, ed. Diane Long Hoeveler (Chicago: Valancourt Books, 2006).
Penn, William, *Some Fruits of Solitude, in Reflections and Maxims* . . . (London, 1693).
Plato, *Republic*, trans. Robin Waterfield (Oxford University Press, 1993).

Radcliffe, Ann, *The Mysteries of Udolpho*, ed. Bonamy Dobrée (Oxford World's Classics, 1980).

Reeve, Clara, *The Progress of Romance*, 2 vols. (Colchester: W. Keymer, 1785).

The School for Widows (London, 1791).

Riccoboni, Marie Jeanne de Heurles Laboras de Mezières, *Letters from Lord Rivers to Sir Charles Cardigan*, trans. Percival Stockdale (London: T. Becket, 1778).

Richardson, Samuel, *The Apprentice's Vade Mecum* (London, 1734).

Clarissa, Or the History of a Young Lady, ed. Angus Ross (London: Penguin, 1985).

A Collection of the Moral and Instructive Sentiments, Maxims, Cautions, and Reflexions, Contained in the Histories of Pamela, Clarissa, and Sir Charles Grandison (London, 1755).

Correspondence with Aaron Hill and the Hill Family, ed. Christine Gerrard (Cambridge University Press, 2013).

Correspondence with Lady Bradshaigh and Lady Echlin, ed. Peter Sabor, 3 vols. (Cambridge University Press, 2016).

Correspondence with Sarah Wescomb, Frances Grainger and Laetitia Pilkington, ed. John A. Dussinger (Cambridge University Press, 2015).

Early Works, ed. Alexander Pettit (Cambridge University Press, 2011).

The History of Sir Charles Grandison, ed. Jocelyn Harris (Oxford University Press, 1986).

Meditations Collected from the Sacred Books (1750; reprinted New York: Garland, 1976).

Pamela: Or, Virtue Rewarded, ed. Albert J. Rivero (Cambridge University Press, 2011).

Robinson, Mary, *The Natural Daughter*, in *A Letter to the Women of England* and *The Natural Daughter*, ed. Sharon M. Setzer (Peterborough, ON: Broadview Press, 2003).

Rowe, Elizabeth, *Friendship in Death. In Twenty Letters from the Dead to the Living. To Which Are Added, Thoughts on Death. Translated from the Moral Essays of the Messieurs du Port Royal* (London: T. Worrall, 1728).

Rowson, Susanna, *Charlotte Temple*, ed. Marion L. Rust (New York: W. W. Norton, 2011).

The Inquisitor, or, Invisible Rambler, 3 vols. (London: G. G. J. and J. Robinson, 1788).

Rules and Maxims for the Conduct of Human Life (Salisbury, 1745).

Ruskin, John, *Modern Painters*, ed. David Barrie (New York: Knopf, 1987).

Sancho, Ignatius, *Letters of the Late Ignatius Sancho, An African* (1782), ed. Vincent Carretta (Peterborough, ON: Broadview Press, 2015).

Scott, Sarah, *The History of Sir George Ellison* (1766), ed. Betty Rizzo (Lexington: University Press of Kentucky, 1996).

Scott, Walter, *Lives of the Novelists*, 2 vols. (Philadelphia, 1825).

The Sentimental Magazine: Or, General Assemblage of Science, Taste, and Entertainment (London, 1773–7).

Shelley, George, *Sentences Divine, Moral, and Historical* (London, 1712).
Sheridan, Frances, *Conclusion of the Memoirs of Miss Sidney Bidulph*, ed. Nicole Garret and Heidi Hutner (Peterborough, ON: Broadview Press, 2013).
Memoirs of Miss Sidney Bidulph, intro. Sue Townsend (London and New York: Pandora, 1987).
Memoirs of Miss Sidney Bidulph, ed. Patricia Koster and Jean Coates Cleary (Oxford University Press, 1995).
Sheridan, Richard Brinsley, *The Dramatic Works of Richard Brinsley Sheridan*, ed. Cecil Price, 2 vols. (Oxford: Clarendon Press, 1973).
'Short, Bob', *The Sentiments of Experience* ... (London, 1787).
Smith, Adam, *The Theory of Moral Sentiments* (London, 1759).
Smith, Charlotte, *The Banished Man* (London, 1794).
The Collected Letters of Charlotte Smith, ed. Judith Phillips Stanton (Bloomington: Indiana University Press, 2003).
South, Robert, *Maxims, Sayings, and Explications of the Scripture Phrases ... Extracted from the Writings of the Late Reverend and Learned Dr South*, 2nd edition (London, 1719).
Sterne, Laurence, *Letters of Laurence Sterne*, ed. Lewis Perry Curtis (1935; Oxford: Clarendon Press, 1965).
The Life and Opinions of Tristram Shandy, Gentleman, 2 vols. (York, 1760).
The Life and Opinions of Tristram Shandy, Gentleman, ed. Melvyn New and Joan New, 2 vols. (Gainesville: University Presses of Florida, 1978).
A Sentimental Journey through France and Italy, ed. Melvyn New and W. G. Day (Gainesville: University Press of Florida, 2002).
A Sentimental Journey through France and Italy. By Mr Yorick., 2 vols. (London, 1768).
The Sermons of Laurence Sterne (1760), ed. Melvyn New (Gainesville: University Press of Florida, 1996).
Tillotson, John, *The Works*, ed. Ralph Barker, 3 vols. (London, 1752).
Tomlins, Elizabeth Sophia, *The Victim of Fancy*, ed. Daniel Cook (London: Pickering and Chatto, 2009).
Walker, George, *The Haunted Castle: A Norman Romance*, 2 vols. (London: The Minerva Press, 1794).
Walpole, Horace, *The Castle of Otranto: A Gothic Story*, ed. Nick Groom (Oxford World's Classics, 2014).
Horace Walpole's Correspondence with Sir William Dalrymple, ed. W. S. Lewis, Charles H. Bennett and Andrew G. Hoover (New Haven: Yale University Press, 1951).
Warner, Richard, *Netley Abbey: A Gothic Story*, 2 vols. (London: The Minerva Press, 1795).
Watts, Isaac, *Death and Heaven: or the Last Enemy Conquer'd, and Separate Spirits Made Perfect* (London: J. Clark et al., 1722).
Willis, Thomas, *Two Discourses concerning the Soul of Brutes*, trans. Samuel Pordage (London: Dring, 1683).

Wollstonecraft, Mary, *A Vindication of the Rights of Woman*, ed. Carol H. Poston, 2nd edition (New York: Norton, 1988).

Secondary Sources

Ahern, Stephen, *Affect and Abolition in the Anglo-Atlantic, 1770–1830* (Farnham: Ashgate, 2013).
Affected Sensibilities (New York: AMS Press, 2007).
'Nothing More Than Feelings?: Affect Theory Reads the Age of Sensibility', *The Eighteenth Century* 58 (2017): 281–95.
Allan, David, *Commonplace Books and Reading in Georgian England* (Cambridge University Press, 2010).
Aravamudan, Srinivas, 'The Return of Anachronism', *MLQ: Modern Language Quarterly* 62 (2001): 331–53.
Arch, Stephen Carl, 'Frances Brooke's "Circle of Friends": The Limits of Epistolarity in *The History of Emily Montague*', *Early American Literature* 39 (2004): 46–85.
Armstrong, Nancy, 'Why Daughters Die: the Racial Logic of American Sentimentalism', *Yale Journal of Criticism* 7 (1994): 1–24.
Arner, Robert D., 'Sentiment and Sensibility: The Role of Emotion and William Hill Brown's *The Power of Sympathy*', *Studies in American Fiction* 1 (1973): 121–32.
Backscheider, Paula R., *Elizabeth Singer Rowe and the Development of the English Novel* (Baltimore: Johns Hopkins University Press, 2013).
Baines, Paul, and Pat Rogers, *Edmund Curll, Bookseller* (Oxford University Press, 2007).
Ballaster, Ros, *Seductive Forms: Women's Amatory Fiction from 1684 to 1740* (Oxford: Clarendon Press, 1992).
Barker-Benfield, G. J., *The Culture of Sensibility: Sex and Society in Eighteenth-Century Britain* (University of Chicago Press, 1992).
Barnes, Elizabeth, 'Natural and National Unions: Incest and Sympathy in the Early Republic', in *Incest and the Literary Imagination*, ed. Elizabeth Barnes (Gainesville: University Press of Florida, 2002), 138–55.
Barthes, Roland, *Mythologies*, trans. Annette Lavers (New York: Noonday Press/ Farrar, Straus and Giroux, 1991).
Beebee, Thomas O., *Clarissa on the Continent: Translation and Seduction* (University Park: Pennsylvania State University Press, 1990).
Bender, John, 'Novel Knowledge: Judgment, Experience, Experiment', in *This Is Enlightenment*, ed. Clifford Siskin and William Warner (University of Chicago Press, 2010), 284–300.
Benedict, Barbara M., *Framing Feeling: Sentiment and Style in English Prose Fiction, 1745–1800* (New York: AMS Press, 1994).
Bennington, Geoffrey, *Sententiousness and the Novel: Laying Down the Law in Eighteenth Century French Fiction* (Cambridge University Press, 1985).

Black, Scott, 'Henry Fielding and the Progress of Romance', in *The Oxford Handbook of The Eighteenth-Century Novel*, ed. J. A. Downie (Oxford University Press, 2016), 237–51.

Blakey, Dorothy, *The Minerva Press* (London: The Bibliographical Society at Oxford, 1939).

Boudreau, Kristin, *Sympathy in American Literature: American Sentiments from Jefferson to the Jameses* (Gainesville: University Press of Florida, 2002).

Boulukos, George, *The Grateful Slave: The Emergence of Race in Eighteenth-Century British and American Culture* (Cambridge University Press, 2008).

Bowers, Toni, *Force or Fraud: British Seduction Stories and the Problem of Resistance, 1660–1760* (Oxford University Press, 2011).

Braudy, Leo, 'The Form of the Sentimental Novel', *NOVEL: A Forum on Fiction* 7 (1973): 5–13.

Brewer, John, *The Pleasures of the Imagination: English Culture in the Eighteenth Century* (University of Chicago Press, 1997).

Brissenden, R. F., *Virtue in Distress: Studies in the Novel of Sentiment from Richardson to Sade* (London: Macmillan, 1974).

Brown, Gillian, 'Consent, Coquetry, and Consequences', *American Literary History* 9 (1997): 625–52.

Byrne, Paula, *Jane Austen and the Theatre* (London: Hambledon Continuum, 2002).

Call, M. J., *Infertility and the Novels of Sophie Cottin* (Newark: University of Delaware Press, 2002).

Carey, Brycchan, *British Abolitionism and the Rhetoric of Sensibility: Writing, Sentiment, and Slavery, 1760–1807* (Basingstoke: Palgrave Macmillan, 2005).

'"The extraordinary Negro": Ignatius Sancho, Joseph Jekyll, and the Problem of Biography', *British Journal for Eighteenth-Century Studies* 26 (2003): 1–13.

Carey, Brycchan, Markman Ellis and Sara Salih, eds., *Discourses of Slavery and Abolition: Britain and Its Colonies, 1760–1838* (Basingstoke: Palgrave Macmillan, 2004).

Castle, Terry, *Boss Ladies, Watch Out!* (New York: Routledge, 2002).

Clarissa's Ciphers: Meaning and Disruption in Richardson's Clarissa (Ithaca: Cornell University Press, 1982).

Masquerade and Civilization: The Carnivalesque in Eighteenth-Century English Culture and Fiction (Stanford University Press, 1986).

Chaber, Lois, 'Review Essay', *Eighteenth-Century Fiction* 12 (2000): 597–604.

Chandler, James, *An Archaeology of Sympathy: The Sentimental Mode in Literature and Cinema* (University of Chicago Press, 2013).

England in 1819 (University of Chicago Press, 1998).

'Placing *The Power of Sympathy*: Transatlantic Sentiments and the "First American Novel"', in *The Atlantic Enlightenment*, ed. Susan Manning and Francis D. Cogliano (Aldershot: Ashgate, 2008), 131–48.

Cleary, Jean Coates, 'Introduction', in Frances Sheridan, *Memoirs of Miss Sidney Bidulph*, ed. Patricia Koster and Jean Coates Cleary (Oxford University Press, 1995), vii–xxxiii.

Clery, E. J., *The Rise of Supernatural Fiction, 1762–1800* (Cambridge University Press, 1995).
Cohen, Margaret, *The Sentimental Education of the Novel* (Princeton University Press, 1999).
Cohen, Margaret, and Caroline Dever, eds., *The Literary Channel: The International Invention of the Novel* (Princeton University Press, 2002).
Copeland, Edward, *Women Writing about Money: Women's Fiction in England, 1790–1820* (Cambridge University Press, 1995).
Crane, Mary Thomas, *Framing Authority: Self, Sayings, and Society in Sixteenth-Century England* (Princeton University Press, 1993).
Crane, R. S., 'Suggestions toward a Genealogy of the "Man of Feeling"', *ELH* 1 (1934): 205–30.
Csengei, Ildiko, '"I Will Not Weep": Reading through the Tears of Henry Mackenzie's "Man of Feeling"', *Modern Language Review* 103 (October 2008): 952–68.
Dalke, Anne, 'Original Vice: The Political Implications of Incest in the Early American Novel', *Early American Literature* 23 (1988): 188–202.
Davidson, Cathy N., *Revolution and the Word: The Rise of the Novel in America*, expanded edition (Oxford University Press, 2004).
Davis, David Brion, *The Problem of Slavery in the Age of Revolution, 1770–1823* (Ithaca: Cornell University Press, 1975).
Deleuze, Gilles, and Félix Guattari, *A Thousand Plateaus: Capitalism and Schizophrenia* (Minneapolis: University of Minnesota Press, 1987).
Denby, David J., *Sentimental Narrative and the Social Order in France, 1760–1820* (Cambridge University Press, 1994).
Dickie, Simon, *Cruelty and Laughter: Forgotten Comic Literature and the Unsentimental Eighteenth Century* (University of Chicago Press, 2011).
'Novels of the 1750s', in *The Oxford Handbook of The Eighteenth-Century Novel*, ed. J. A. Downie (Oxford University Press, 2016), 252–63.
Dill, Elizabeth, 'A Mob of Lusty Villagers: Operations of Domestic Desires in Hannah Webster Foster's *The Coquette*', *Eighteenth-Century Fiction* 15 (2003): 255–79.
'That Damned Mob of Scribbling Siblings: the American Romance as Anti-Novel in *The Power of Sympathy* and *Pierre*', *American Literature* 80 (2008): 707–38.
Dixon, Thomas, *From Passions to Emotions: The Creation of a Secular Psychological Category* (Cambridge University Press, 2003).
Donovan, Josephine, *Women and the Rise of the Novel, 1405–1726* (Basingstoke: Palgrave Macmillan, 1999).
Doody, Margaret Anne, *Frances Burney: The Life in the Works* (New Brunswick, NJ: Rutgers University Press, 1988).
'Frances Sheridan: Morality and Annihilated Time', in *Fetter'd or Free? British Women Novelists, 1670–1815*, ed. Mary Anne Schofield and Cecilia Macheski (Athens, OH: Ohio University Press, 1986), 324–58.

Dussinger, John A., 'Introduction', in *A Collection of the Moral and Instructive Sentiments* (1755), vol. iii of *Samuel Richardson's Published Commentary on* Clarissa, *1745–1765*, 3 vols. (London: Pickering and Chatto, 1998).
Dwyer, John, *Virtuous Discourse: Sensibility and Community in Late Eighteenth-Century Scotland* (Edinburgh: J. Donald, 1987).
Eagleton, Terry, *The Rape of Clarissa: Writing, Sexuality, and Class Struggle in Samuel Richardson* (Minneapolis: University of Minnesota Press, 1982).
Ekman, Paul, *Emotions Revealed* (New York: Holt, 2003).
Ellis, Frank H., *Sentimental Comedy: Theory and Practice* (Cambridge University Press, 1991).
Ellis, Kate Ferguson, *The Contested Castle* (Urbana: University of Illinois Press, 1989).
Ellis, Markman, *The Politics of Sensibility: Race, Gender and Commerce in the Sentimental Novel* (Cambridge University Press, 1996).
Ellison, Julie, *Cato's Tears and the Making of Anglo-American Emotion* (Chicago University Press, 1999).
Epstein, Julia, 'Marginality in Frances Burney's Novels', in *The Cambridge Companion to the Eighteenth-Century Novel*, ed. John Richetti (Cambridge University Press, 1996), 198–211.
Erämetsä, Erik, *A Study of the Word 'Sentimental' and of Other Linguistic Characteristics of Eighteenth Century Sentimentalism in England* (Helsinki: Helsingin Liikekirjapaino Oy, 1951).
Ferrand, Nathalie, *Traduire et illustrer le roman au XVIIIe siècle* (Oxford: Voltaire Foundation, 2011).
Festa, Lynn, *Sentimental Figures of Empire in Eighteenth-Century Britain and France* (Baltimore: Johns Hopkins University Press, 2006).
Fowler, James, *Richardson and the Philosophes* (Abingdon, Oxford, and New York: Legenda, Modern Humanities Research Association and Maney Publishing, 2014).
Franklin, Caroline, 'The Novel of Sensibility in the 1780s', in *The Oxford History of the Novel in English*, ed. Peter Garside and Karen O'Brien (Oxford University Press, 2015), 164–81.
Freeman, Lisa A., *Character's Theatre: Genre and Identity on the Eighteenth-Century English Stage* (Philadelphia: University of Pennsylvania Press, 2002).
Gamer, Michael, *Romanticism and the Gothic* (Cambridge University Press, 2000).
Garfinkel, Harold, 'Evidence for Locally Produced, Naturally Accountable Phenomena of Order, Logic, Reason, Meaning, Method, etc. In and as of the Essential Quiddity of Immortal Ordinary Society (I of IV): an Announcement of Studies', *Sociological Theory* 6 (1988): 103–09.
Garret, Nicole, 'Introduction', in Frances Sheridan, *Conclusion of the Memoirs of Miss Sidney Bidulph*, ed. Nicole Garret and Heidi Hutner (Peterborough, ON: Broadview Press, 2013), 9–33.
Garside, Peter, James Raven and Rainer Schöwerling, eds., *The English Novel, 1770–1829: A Bibliographical Survey of Prose Fiction Published in the British Isles*, 2 vols. (Oxford University Press, 2000).

Gay, Penny, *Jane Austen and the Theatre* (Cambridge University Press, 2002).

Genovese, Michael, '"A Mixture of Bad in All": the Character of Self-Interest in Sarah Fielding's *David Simple*', *The Age of Johnson* 22 (2012): 207–31.

Gerrard, Christine, *Aaron Hill: The Muses' Projector, 1685–1750* (Oxford University Press, 2003),

Gevirtz, Karen Bloom, *Women, the Novel, and Natural Philosophy, 1660–1727* (Basingstoke: Palgrave Macmillan, 2014).

Giddens, Anthony, *The Consequences of Modernity* (Stanford University Press, 1990).

Modernity and Self-identity: Self and Society in the Late Modern Age (Stanford University Press, 1991).

The Transformation of Intimacy: Sexuality, Love and Eroticism in Modern Societies (Stanford University Press, 1992).

Goldberg, Rita, *Sex and Enlightenment: Women in Richardson and Diderot* (Cambridge University Press, 1984).

Gordon, Scott Paul, 'Disinterested Selves: *Clarissa* and the Tactics of Sentiment', *ELH* 64 (1997): 473–502.

Goring, Paul, *The Rhetoric of Sensibility in Eighteenth-Century Culture* (Cambridge University Press, 2005).

Greene, Donald, 'Latitudinarianism and Sensibility: The Genealogy of the "Man of Feeling" Reconsidered', *Modern Philology* 75 (1977): 159–83.

Grieder, Josephine, *Translations of French Sentimental Prose Fiction in late Eighteenth-Century England: The History of a Literary Vogue* (Durham, NC: Duke University Press, 1975).

Hargreaves-Mawdsley, W. N., *The English Della Cruscans and Their Time, 1783–1828* (The Hague: Martinus Nijhoff, 1967).

Harkin, Maureen, 'Mackenzie's *Man of Feeling*: Embalming Sensibility', *ELH* 61 (1994): 317–40.

'Smith's *The Theory of Moral Sentiments*: Sympathy, Women, and Emulation', *Studies in Eighteenth-Century Culture* 24 (1995): 175–90.

Harris, Roy, *Introduction to Integrational Linguistics* (Kidlington: Pergamon, 1998).

The Linguistics of History (Edinburgh University Press, 2004).

Harris, Sharon M., 'Hannah Webster Foster's *The Coquette*: Critiquing Franklin's America', in *Redefining the Political Novel: American Women Writers, 1797–1901*, ed. Sharon M. Harris (Knoxville: University of Tennessee Press, 1995), 1–22.

Hoeveler, Diane Long, 'The Heroine, the Abbey, and Popular Romantic Textuality', in *Radcliffe, Romanticism and the Gothic*, ed. Dale Townshend and Angela Wright (Cambridge University Press, 2014), 100–16.

Holmes, Geoffrey, and Daniel Szechi, *The Age of Oligarchy: Pre-industrial Britain 1722–1783* (London: Longman, 1993).

Howells, Coral Ann, *Love, Mystery, and Misery: Feeling in Gothic Fiction* (London: Athlone Press, 1978).

Hultquist, Aleksondra, *Equal Ardor: Female Desire, Amatory Fiction, and the Recasting of the Novel, 1680–1760* (Charleston, SC: ProQuest UMI Dissertation Publication, 2011).

Hume, Robert D., 'Money in Jane Austen', *Review of English Studies* 64 (2013): 289–310.

Jaquier, Claire, Florence Lotterie and Catriona Seth, eds., *Destins romanesques de l'émigration* (Paris: Desjonquères, 2007).

Johnson, Claudia L., *Equivocal Beings: Politics, Gender, and Sentimentality in the 1790s: Wollstonecraft, Radcliffe, Burney, Austen* (University of Chicago Press, 1995).

Johnson, Glen, 'Richardson's "Editor" in *Clarissa*', *Journal of Narrative Technique* 10 (1980): 99–114.

Jones, C. B., *Radical Sensibility: Literature and Ideas in the 1790s* (Abingdon: Routledge, 2016).

Joudrey, Thomas J., 'Maintaining Stability: Fancy and Passion in *The Coquette*', *New England Quarterly* 86 (2013): 60–88.

Kaplan, Marjin, 'Marie Jeanne Riccoboni's *Lettres d'Elisabeth Sophie de Vallière*: a Feminist Reading', *Women in French Studies* 13 (2005): 25–36.

Kaplan, Marjin, ed., *Translations and Continuations: Riccoboni and Brooke, Graffigny and Roberts* (London: Pickering and Chatto, 2011).

Kelly, Gary, *Women, Writing, and Revolution, 1790–1827* (Oxford: Clarendon Press, 1993).

Keymer, Thomas, *Richardson's* Clarissa *and the Eighteenth-Century Reader* (Cambridge University Press, 1992).

'Sentimental Fiction: Ethics, Social Critique and Philanthropy', in *The Cambridge History of English Literature, 1660–1780*, ed. John Richetti (Cambridge University Press, 2005), 572–601.

Kim, James, 'Mourning, Melancholia, and Modernity: Sentimental Irony and Downward Mobility in *David Simple*', *Eighteenth-Century Fiction* 22 (2010): 477–502.

Kinkead-Weekes, Mark, '*Clarissa* Restored?', *Review of English Studies* 10 (1959): 156–71.

King, Kathryn, *A Political Biography of Eliza Haywood* (London: Pickering and Chatto, 2012).

Knight, Bill, '*David Simple* and the Ethics of Genre', *Genre* 50 (2017): 267–95.

Korobkin, Laura H., '"Can Your Volatile Daughter Ever Acquire Your Wisdom?": Luxury and False Ideals in *The Coquette*', *Early American Literature* 41 (2006): 79–107.

Koselleck, Reinhart, *The Practice of Conceptual History: Timing History, Spacing Concepts*, trans. Todd Samuel Presner et al. (Stanford University Press, 2002).

Lamb, Jonathan, *The Evolution of Sympathy in the Long Eighteenth Century* (London: Pickering and Chatto, 2009).

Langford, Paul, *A Polite and Commercial People* (Oxford University Press, 1989).

Latimer, Bonnie, *Making Gender, Culture, and the Self in the Fiction of Samuel Richardson* (Farnham: Ashgate, 2013).

Lawrimore, David, 'The Novelist as Organic Intellectual: William Hill Brown's *The Power of Sympathy*, Reconsidered', *American Literature* 88 (2016): 695–721.

Lewis, Ann, *Sensibility, Reading and Illustration: Spectacles and Signs in Graffigny, Marivaux and Rousseau* (Oxford: Legenda, 2009).

Leys, Ruth, *The Ascent of Affect: Genealogy and Critique* (University of Chicago Press, 2017).

'The Turn to Affect: A Critique', *Critical Inquiry* 37 (March 2011): 434–72.

Looser, Devoney, *Women Writers and Old Age in Great Britain, 1750–1850* (Baltimore: Johns Hopkins University Press, 2008).

Lynch, Deidre, *The Economy of Character: Novels, Market Culture, and the Business of Inner Meaning* (University of Chicago Press, 1998).

'Personal Effects and Sentimental Fictions', *Eighteenth-Century Fiction* 12 (2000): 345–68.

McCarthy, Dermot, 'Sisters under the Mink: The Correspondent Fear in *The History of Emily Montague*', *Essays on Canadian Writing* 51–2 (1993–4): 340–57.

McCarthy, William, *Anna Letitia Barbauld: Voice of the Enlightenment* (Baltimore: Johns Hopkins University Press, 2008).

McGann, Jerome, *The Poetics of Sensibility: A Revolution in Literary Style* (Oxford: Clarendon Press, 1996).

McGirr, Elaine, 'Manly Lessons: *Sir Charles Grandison*, The Rake, and The Man of Sentiment', *Studies in the Novel* 39 (2007): 267–283.

McHoul, Alec, *Semiotic Investigations: Towards an Effective Semiotics* (Lincoln, NE: University of Nebraska Press, 2006).

McLeod, Deborah, 'The Minerva Press' (PhD dissertation, University of Alberta, 1997).

McMurran, Mary Helen, *The Spread of Novels: Translation and Prose Fiction in the Eighteenth Century* (Princeton University Press, 2010).

Mander, Jenny, ed., *Remapping the Rise of the European Novel* (Oxford: Voltaire Foundation, 2007).

Mangano, Bryan, 'Ideal Friendship and the Paradoxes of Narration in Sarah Fielding's *David Simple*', *Eighteenth-Century Fiction* 26 (2013–14): 165–88.

Marcus, George E., *The Sentimental Citizen: Emotion in Democratic Politics* (University Park: Pennsylvania State University Press, 2002).

Maslen, Keith, *Samuel Richardson of London, Printer: a Study of his Printing Based on Ornament Use and Business Accounts* (Dunedin, NZ: University of Otago, 2001).

Massumi, Brian, *Parables for the Virtual: Movement, Affect, Sensation* (Durham, NC: Duke University Press, 2002).

Mayo, Robert D., *The English Novel in the Magazines, 1740–1815* (Evanston: Northwestern University Press, 1962).

Merrett, Robert, 'The Politics of Romance in *The History of Emily Montague*', *Canadian Literature* 133 (1992): 92–108.

Moretti, Franco, *Graphs, Maps, Trees: Abstract Models for Literary History* (London: Verso, 2005).

Signs Taken for Wonders: Essays in the Sociology of Literary Forms (London: Verso, 1997).

Morgan, Greg, '"Give me the consideration of being the bondsman": Embarrassment and the Figure of the Bond in the Sentimental Fiction of Samuel Richardson', *Eighteenth-Century Fiction* 28 (2016): 667–90.

Mullan, John, *Sentiment and Sociability: the Language of Feeling in the Eighteenth Century* (Oxford: Clarendon Press, 1988).

'Sentimental Novels', in *The Cambridge Companion to the Eighteenth-Century Novel*, ed. John Richetti (Cambridge University Press, 1996), 236–54.

Nazar, Hina, *Enlightened Sentiments: Judgment and Autonomy in the Age of Sensibility* (New York: Fordham University Press, 2012).

Neiman, Elizabeth, 'A New Perspective on the Minerva Press's "Derivative" Novels: Authorizing Borrowed Material', *European Romantic Review* 26 (2015): 633–58.

Ngai, Sianne, *Ugly Feelings* (Cambridge, MA: Harvard University Press, 2004).

Oliver, Kathleen M., 'Frances Sheridan's Faukland, the Silenced, Emasculated, Ideal Male', *Studies in English Literature, 1500–1900* 43 (2003): 683–700.

Parisot, Eric, 'Suicide Notes and Popular Sensibility in the Eighteenth-Century British Press', *Eighteenth-Century Studies* 47 (2014): 277–91.

Parnell, Tim, 'Sterne's Fiction and the Mid-Century Novel: the "Vast Empire of Biographical Freebooters" and the "crying Volume"', in *The Oxford Handbook of the Eighteenth-Century Novel*, ed. J. A. Downie (Oxford University Press, 2016), 264–81.

Paulson, Ronald, *Representations of Revolution (1789–1820)* (New Haven: Yale University Press, 1983).

Pettella, Tera, 'Devotional Reading and Novel Form: The Case of *David Simple*', *Eighteenth-Century Fiction* 24 (2011–2), 279–99.

Pettingill, Claire C., 'Sisterhood in a Separate Sphere: Female Friendship in Hannah Webster Foster's *The Coquette* and *The Boarding School*', *Early American Literature* 27 (1992): 185–203.

Pinch, Adela, *Strange Fits of Passion: Epistemologies of Emotion, Hume to Austen* (Stanford University Press, 1996).

Plamper, Jan, *The History of Emotions: An Introduction* (Oxford University Press, 2017).

Raven, James, *British Fiction, 1750–1770: A Chronological Checklist of Prose Fiction Printed in Britain and Ireland* (London: Associated University Press, 1987).

Rawson, Claude, *Satire and Sentiment, 1660–1830* (Cambridge University Press, 1994).

Reddy, William, *The Navigation of Feeling: A Framework for the History of Emotions* (Cambridge University Press, 2001).

Richards, I. A., *Practical Criticism: A Study of Literary Judgment* (New York: Harcourt Brace, 2014).

Rivero, Albert J., 'Doubling Eliza: Austen's Remembrance of Richardson (and Perhaps Haywood) in *Sense and Sensibility*', in *New Windows on a Woman's*

World: Essays in Honour of Jocelyn Harris, ed. Lisa Marr (Dunedin, NZ: University of Otago Press, 2005), 93–103.

The Plays of Henry Fielding: A Critical Study of His Dramatic Career (Charlottesville: University Press of Virginia, 1989).

Rivers, Isabel, *Reason, Grace, and Sentiment: A Study of the Language of Religion and Ethics in England, 1660–1780*, 2 vols. (Cambridge University Press, 1991–2000).

Rosenwein, Barbara H., *Generations of Feeling: A History of Emotions, 600–1700* (Cambridge University Press, 2016).

Rule, John, *Albion's People: English Society, 1714–1815* (London: Longman, 1992).

Rust, Marion, *Prodigal Daughters: Susanna Rowson's Early American Women* (Chapel Hill: University of North Carolina Press, 2008).

Sabor, Peter, 'Introduction', in *Letters and Passages Restored from the Original Manuscripts of the History of* Clarissa, vol. 11 of *Samuel Richardson's Published Commentary on* Clarissa, 3 vols. (London: Pickering and Chatto, 1998).

St Clair, William, *The Reading Nation in the Romantic Period* (Cambridge University Press, 2004).

Schweitzer, Ivy, 'Foster's *Coquette*: Resurrecting Friendship from the Tomb of Marriage', *Arizona Quarterly* 61 (2005): 1–32.

Shapira, Yael, 'Beyond the Radcliffe Formula: Isabella Kelly and the Gothic Troubles of the Married Heroine', *Women's Writing* (published online 26 November 2015): 1–19. DOI: 10.1080/09699082.2015.1110289.

Sill, Geoffrey, 'Developments in Sentimental Fiction', in *The Oxford Handbook of the Eighteenth-Century Novel*, ed. J. A. Downie (Oxford University Press, 2016), 426–39.

Siskin, Clifford, *The Work of Writing: Literature and Social Change in Britain, 1700–1830* (Baltimore: Johns Hopkins University Press, 1997).

Skinner, Gillian, *Sensibility and Economics in the Novel, 1740–1800: The Price of a Tear* (London: Macmillan, 1999).

Snader, Joe, 'The Masquerade of Colonial Identity in Frances Brooke's *Emily Montague* (1769)', in *The Clothes That Wear Us: Essays on Dressing and Transgressing in Eighteenth-Century Culture*, ed. Jessica Munns and Penny Richards (Newark: University of Delaware Press, 1999), 119–42.

Sodeman, Melissa, *Sentimental Memorials: Women and the Novel in Literary History* (Stanford University Press, 2015).

Spacks, Patricia Meyer, *Desire and Truth: Functions of Plot in Eighteenth-Century English Novels* (University of Chicago Press, 1990).

Spedding, Patrick, *A Bibliography of Eliza Haywood* (London: Pickering and Chatto, 2004),

Starr, George A., 'Only a Boy: Notes on Sentimental Novels', *Genre* 10 (1977): 501–27.

'Sentimental Novels of the Later Eighteenth Century', in *The Columbia History of the British Novel*, ed. John Richetti (New York: Columbia University Press, 1994), 181–98.

Stern, Julia A., *The Plight of Feeling: Sympathy and Dissent in the Early American Novel* (University of Chicago Press, 1997).

Stewart, Joan Hinde, *Gynographs: French Novels by Women of the Late Eighteenth Century* (Lincoln, NE: University of Nebraska Press, 1993).

Stockhorst, Stefanie, ed., *Cultural Transfer through Translation: The Circulation of Enlightened Thought in Europe by Means of Translation* (Amsterdam: Rodopi, 2010).

Sussman, Charlotte, *Eighteenth-Century English Literature* (Cambridge: Polity Press, 2012).

Suzuki, Mika, 'Sarah Fielding and Reading', in *The Eighteenth-Century Novel*, vol. II, ed. Albert J. Rivero and George Justice (New York: AMS Press, 2002), 91–112.

Swaminathan, Srividhya, *Debating the Slave Trade: Rhetoric of British National Identity, 1759–1815* (Farnham: Ashgate, 2009).

Sypher, Wylie, *Guinea's Captive Kings: British Anti-Slavery Literature of the XVIIIth Century* (Chapel Hill: University of North Carolina Press, 1942).

Tennenhouse, Leonard, 'The Americanization of *Clarissa*', *Yale Journal of Criticism* 11 (1998): 177–96.

Thacker, Eugene, 'Black on Black', in *The Public Domain Review, Selected Essays, Vol.* III, ed. Adam Green (Cambridge: PDR, 2016).

Tierney-Hynes, Rebecca, *Novel Minds: Philosophers and Romance Readers, 1680–1740* (Basingstoke: Palgrave Macmillan, 2012).

Todd, Janet, *Sensibility: An Introduction* (London: Methuen, 1986).

The Sign of Angellica: Women, Writing, and Fiction, 1660–1800 (New York: Columbia University Press, 1989).

Tomkins, Silvan, and Bertram Karon, *Affect, Imagery, Consciousness* (New York: Springer, 1962).

Townshend, Dale, and Angela Wright, eds., *Ann Radcliffe, Romanticism and the Gothic* (Cambridge University Press, 2014).

Traver, John C., 'The Inconclusive Memoirs of Miss Sidney Bidulph: Problems of Poetic Justice, Closure, and Gender', *Eighteenth-Century Fiction* 20 (2007): 35–60.

Van Dijk, Suzan, 'Lire ou broder: Deux occupations féminines dans l'œuvre de Mmes de Graffigny, Riccoboni et de Charrière', in J. Herman and P. Pelckmans, eds., *L'epreuve du lecteur: Livres et lectures dans le roman d'Ancien Régime* (Louvain: Peeters, 1995), 351–60.

Van Sant, Ann Jessie, 'A Dictionary of Morality: Reading for the Sentiment', in *A Collection of the Moral and Instructive Sentiments* (1755), vol. III of *Samuel Richardson's Published Commentary on* Clarissa, *1745–1765*, 3 vols. (London: Pickering and Chatto, 1998), 411–37.

Eighteenth-Century Sensibility and the Novel: The Senses in Social Context (Cambridge University Press, 1993).

Vila, Anne C., *Enlightenment and Pathology: Sensibility in the Literature and Medicine of Eighteenth-Century France* (Baltimore: Johns Hopkins University Press, 1998).

Walmsley, Peter, 'Whigs in Heaven: Elizabeth Rowe's "Friendship in Death"', *Eighteenth-Century Studies* 44 (2011): 315–30.

Warner, William B., *Licensing Entertainment: The Elevation of Novel Reading in Britain, 1684–1750* (Berkeley: University of California Press, 1998).

Reading Clarissa*: The Struggles of Interpretation* (New Haven: Yale University Press, 1979).

Watt, Ian, *The Rise of the Novel* (1957; London: Pimlico, 2000).

Watt, James, Contesting the *Gothic* (Cambridge University Press, 1999).

Welham, Debbie, 'The Political Afterlife of Resentment in Penelope Aubin's *The Life and Amorous Adventures of Lucinda (1721)*', *Women's Writing* 20 (2013): 49–63.

Williams, Kate, 'Women Writers and the Rise of the Novel', in *The History of British Women's Writing, 1690*–1750, ed. Ros Ballaster, vol. IV of *The History of British Women's Writing*, general eds. Jennie Batchelor and Cora Kaplan (Basingstoke: Palgrave Macmillan, 2010), 113–24.

Wilputte, Earla, *Passion and Language in Eighteenth-Century Literature: The Aesthetic Sublime in the Work of Eliza Haywood, Aaron Hill, and Martha Fowke* (New York: Palgrave Macmillan, 2014).

Wimsatt, William K., and Monroe C. Beardsley, *The Verbal Icon: Studies in the Meaning of Poetry* (Lexington: University Press of Kentucky, 1989).

Wood, Marcus, *Slavery, Empathy, and Pornography* (Oxford University Press, 2002).

Zias, Heather, 'Who Can Believe? Sentiment vs. Cynicism in Richardson's *Clarissa*', *Eighteenth-Century Life* 27 (2003): 99–123.

Index